T0323408

How the Radical Right Has Changed Capitalism and Welfare in Europe and the USA

How the Radical Right Has Changed Capitalism and Welfare in Europe and the USA

Philip Rathgeb

OXFORD
UNIVERSITY PRESS

OXFORD
UNIVERSITY PRESS

Great Clarendon Street, Oxford, OX2 6DP,
United Kingdom

Oxford University Press is a department of the University of Oxford.
It furthers the University's objective of excellence in research, scholarship,
and education by publishing worldwide. Oxford is a registered trade mark of
Oxford University Press in the UK and in certain other countries

Published in the United States of America by Oxford University Press
198 Madison Avenue, New York, NY 10016, United States of America

British Library Cataloguing in Publication Data
Data available

Library of Congress Control Number: 2023943793

ISBN 9780192866332

DOI: 10.1093/oso/9780192866332.001.0001

Printed and bound in the UK by
Clays Ltd, Elcograf S.p.A.

Links to third party websites are provided by Oxford in good faith and
for information only. Oxford disclaims any responsibility for the materials
contained in any third party website referenced in this work.

Preface

This book started out of a personal curiosity: How does the radical right affect people's livelihoods when it gets to power? The reason I became interested in this question is that the radical right has increasingly come to represent what political and social scientists call the 'losers of globalization'. As these voters have lower levels of education or skills no longer needed, they have been particularly vulnerable to the socially corrosive effects of de-industrialization and globalized competition during the neoliberal era. These so-called 'losers' would need political power to compensate for their declining economic power. It was an open question how radical right parties would respond to the social needs of their new electoral strongholds amid their more general rise towards a mainstreamed party family.

When starting this research project, I relied on my priors as a political economist by viewing the radical right's policy choices through the analytical lens of the economic left–right divide. In theory, I expected that the radical right would pursue redistributive policies in order to consolidate its electoral support among lower middle-class and working-class voters. There was an emerging body of evidence underpinning this hypothesis based on party manifesto data. In reality, however, this is not what I found when studying the radical right's *policy choices* in government. While some of their policies have been protectionist in orientation, they have overall increased rather than decreased economic inequality. Jan Rovny's 'position-blurring' hypothesis gave me another useful cue to address my puzzle. Accordingly, radical right parties would avoid taking a clear position and end up with a centrist policy impact in order to reconcile the ongoing heterogeneity of its electoral base, including both (right-wing) small shop owners and (left-wing) production workers. The radical right's policies seemed indeed difficult to categorize at first. But what they have had in common is that they produce similar groups of economic winners and losers. It thus became clear to me that the conceptual apparatus of the existing debate—distinguishing between 'left' versus 'right' and 'pro-welfare' versus 'anti-welfare' positions—was too coarse to capture the radical right's distributive impact. In other words, the radical right's socio-economic agenda defied the left–right cleavage on which my thinking had been based.

This led me to search for answers in the literature of party politics, which emphasized the nativist and authoritarian worldview of radical right parties. I therefore started to take seriously the sociocultural ideology of the radical right when analysing their policy choices in power. What if these parties are not only short-term electoral vote-seekers, as conventional models of politics would predict, but instead act as ideologically committed actors with hegemonic long-term ambitions? Indeed, radical right parties usually do not moderate when they get to power; they often radicalize even more as they aim to shift the terms of the debate, with destructive consequences for liberal democracy across the Western world. What started out as a policy-focused analysis of the radical right thus turned into a more general inquiry into the distributive outcomes of today's 'culture war'.

To understand the radical right's policy impact I first had to recognize how its sociocultural ideology informed its socio-economic policy preferences. This has led to the first major contribution of this book: the radical right's core ideology of nativism and authoritarianism has clear distributive implications that favour threatened core workers ('labour market insiders') and male breadwinners, typically at the expense of the unemployed, the poor, immigrants, ethnic minorities, and new social risk groups such as working women and precarious non-standard workers ('labour market outsiders'). In other words, selective protections for the native (male) core workforce go hand in hand with the promotion of a racialized and gendered precariat when the radical right gets to decide who gets what, when, and how in contemporary capitalism. The importance of ideological values (nativism and authoritarianism) in shaping distributive policy preferences (selective status protection) illuminates how deeply intertwined cultural and economic conflicts have become.

The commonalities of the radical right's distributive impact might appear hidden by the varieties of policies the radical right has implemented in government. In some contexts, these parties have opted for trade protectionism or economic nationalism, whereas in other contexts, they have prioritized familialism or welfare chauvinism. To make sense of this variation, I built on the literature of comparative political economy and welfare state research that highlights the enduring capitalist diversity in which domestic political actors find themselves. As countries have different economic vulnerabilities and institutional legacies, they have to rely on diverse policy instruments to achieve similar distributive outcomes. This recognition has informed the second main contribution of this book: the political-economic profile of welfare state contexts and growth models provides the radical right with diverse opportunities and constraints when pursuing their nativist-authoritarian agenda. This insight is important not only to make sense of the remarkable variations through which radical right parties have changed national models of capitalism and welfare; it also holds implications for the viability of liberal democracy as such. One of the broader political implications of this book is that the radical right uses the welfare state to manufacture consent for authoritarianism.

Neoliberalism may have come to an end with the fallout of the global financial crisis, the Covid-19 pandemic, the current cost-of-living crisis, and the looming climate crisis, but the political exhaustion of our dominant economic order is by no means a guarantee for the resurgence of inclusive forms of social solidarity. There are different ways in which a sense of solidarity may be reinvigorated in a world of multiple crises. The radical right's policy of selective status protection represents one of them.

Acknowledgements

It is a pleasure to thank the many colleagues and friends on whom I have relied when researching and writing this book. Institutional support came from the German Research Foundation (DFG) in the form of a research grant, the *Zukunftskolleg* at the University of Konstanz where I held a post-doctoral research position from 2018 until 2020, and my subsequent and current employer, the Social Policy Department at the University of Edinburgh. This book would not have been possible without the opportunity to move my research grant from Germany to the UK. I am grateful to Sarah Mutters and Jennifer Seemann at the DFG for facilitating this process at a time when Brexit caused considerable uncertainty in the academic community. Separate and special thanks go to my colleagues for taking over my teaching and administrative responsibilities in autumn 2022, so that I could spend a research sabbatical at the European University Institute in Florence and write large parts of this book at a most congenial setting. It is difficult to overstate how much I have benefited from the intellectual environment and collegial atmosphere of Social Policy in Edinburgh. I am particularly grateful to Marzia Ballardin, Richard Brodie, Daniel Clegg, Niccolo Durazzi, Jan Eichhorn, Richard Freeman, and Elke Heins for their various types of support since my start in Edinburgh in May 2020.

I had the good fortune to be supported by outstanding mentors throughout this project. At the University of Konstanz, Marius Busemeyer commented on my draft grant proposal and various bits and pieces of this research before it turned into my second book project. I have benefited tremendously from his personal support and the inputs received at his working group during my years in Konstanz. At the University of Edinburgh, Jochen Clasen has accompanied this book since its inception and helped me to familiarize with the University of Edinburgh at a time when the pandemic made it difficult to settle down in a new place and find my way at a new institution. I owe a special debt of gratitude to both Marius and Jochen.

A number of colleagues and friends took time out of their schedule to comment on various parts of this book. My thanks go out to Alexandre Afonso, Dorothee Bohle, Reto Bürgisser, Daniel Clegg, Juliana Chueri, Noam Gidron, Daphne Halikiopoulou, Silja Häusermann, Anton Hemerijck, Josef Hien, Jonathan Hopkin, Alexander Horn, Erik Jones, Jan Karremans, Hanspeter Kriesi, Paulina Lenik, Fabian Mushövel, Larissa Nenning, Pontus

Odmalm, Fred Paxton, Ilze Plavgo, Leonce Röth, Waltraud Schelkle, Arianna Tassinari, Jay Wiggan, and Fabio Wolkenstein. I am particularly grateful to Fabian Mushövel for the many conversations we had about this book project during our time in Florence. I also want to give special thanks to Fabio Wolkenstein for accompanying this book project with intellectual sustenance and stimulation from the very beginning.

The manuscript benefited enormously from a book workshop held at the European University Institute in October 2022, providing me with invaluable feedback from Josef Hien, Hanspeter Kriesi, Fabian Mushövel, Fred Paxton, and Waltraud Schelkle. I also want to acknowledge the numerous helpful comments I received from the 'Social Investment Working Group' at the European University Institute in November 2022, the 'Party Politics and Political Economy' Workshop at the University of Edinburgh in December 2022, and the 'The Right and (In)Equality: Myth and Reality' Workshop at the University of Konstanz in May 2023. Chapter 4 is a reworked and augmented version of an article I published as 'Makers against Takers: The Socio-Economic Ideology and Policy of the Austrian Freedom Party' in *West European Politics* (44 (3): 635–660) and an article co-authored with Martin Gruber-Risak and published as 'Deserving Austrians First: The Impact of the Radical Right on the Austrian Welfare State' in *Comparative Labor Law and Policy Journal* (42 (1): 43–60).

I benefited from outstanding research assistance for this book project. Patricia Rodi and Anna KissPal did a superb job with research assignments relating to specific parts of this book. I extend my special thanks to students in my 'Party Politics and Welfare States in Democratic Capitalism' course at the University of Edinburgh where I developed and tested some of the ideas that informed this book. I am indebted to Dominic Byatt and Jade Dixon at Oxford University Press for believing in this project and for making the editorial process exceptionally smooth and efficient. I also benefited greatly from Indumadhi Srinivasan's outstanding support in the production process. I also want to thank the four anonymous reviewers for their excellent feedback and comments on earlier versions of this book. During my visits to Austria, I benefited from the space and material provided by the superb social science library at the Chamber of Labour in Vienna.

This book project had emerged out of a distance relationship in the midst of lockdowns and travel restrictions, but it came to an end with the formation of a new family in the capital of Scotland. In concluding, I want to give my heartfelt thanks to Anja and Jonas, for being there.

Philip Rathgeb
Edinburgh, July 2023

Contents

1
Introduction

Donald Trump assumed office with an unusual promise for an American president. He would bring 'great prosperity and strength' by protecting the 'forgotten men and women' from foreign competition. Not long before him did the political right and the left agree on a fundamentally different premise. In 2000, Bill Clinton argued to the admiration of his Republican contender, George W. Bush, how '[g]lobalization is not something that we can hold off or turn off. It is the economic equivalent of a force of nature, like wind or water'. Meanwhile, his British counterpart, Tony Blair, explained at the Labour Party Conference how 'in the world of the internet, information technology and TV, there will be globalization. And in trade, the problem is not there's too much of it; on the contrary, there is too little of it'. Of course, there was criticism at the time of the socially and environmentally corrosive effects of 'hyper-globalization' (Rodrik 2011), but these were restricted to left-wing fringe movements outside the political mainstream (e.g. Alter-globalization, Attac). Trump used this void and connected a policy of trade protection with conventional neoliberal reforms and an anti-pluralist agenda that ultimately threatened the viability of America's democracy. In many ways, the GOP's ideological platform under Trump, and the Tea Party movement that helped him to power, resembled those of Europe's radical right parties, connecting (white) nativism with authoritarian law and order credentials (Minkenberg 2011, Mudde 2018). However, Trump's economic and social policies were very different from what we can observe on the other side of the Atlantic. In both Eastern and Western Europe, trade protectionism has been by no means a salient feature.

Viktor Orbán, for example, received praise from the American radical right for establishing an 'illiberal' regime (*New York Times*, 19.10.2021), but his economic nationalism diverged from Trump's trade protectionism. Instead of putting constraints on foreign competition, Orbán renationalized key sectors of the economy and imposed discriminatory taxes on multinational companies in favour of domestic capital. While the Trump administration took issue with the cross-border movement of goods, the

How the Radical Right Has Changed Capitalism and Welfare in Europe and the USA. Philip Rathgeb, Oxford University Press.
© Philip Rathgeb (2024). DOI: 10.1093/oso/9780192866332.003.0001

Orbán cabinet contested the cross-border movement of capital. Orbán's anti-liberal promise has also had deep implications for the welfare state. His protectionist promise not only incorporated the domestic business class, but also valorized the 'productive Magyar family' through an unprecedented expansion of monetary family support. Familialist protection and economic nationalism thus formed important instruments with which the Orbán cabinet and other Eastern European radical right governments responded to the mounting dissatisfaction with the neoliberal paradigm that under-pinned the Washington consensus (1990s) and the EU accession process (2000s).

Unlike in Eastern Europe, economic nationalism has been completely absent from the policy platforms of the radical right in Continental Europe. While often sharing a preference for familialist policies and conservative gen-der relations, Continental European radical right parties like the Austrian Freedom Party (FPÖ) prioritized the defence of mature social insurance rights for labour market insiders while downgrading the social rights of labour market outsiders and other new social risk groups. At the same time, its protectionist promise for the 'hard-working' and thus 'deserving' core workforce implied cuts in the benefit entitlements of non-citizens. The anti-immigration appeal of the radical right implied the 'culturalization' of distributive conflict through welfare chauvinism in this region. Hence, the Continental European radical right used government power primarily to protect the relative social status of core workers at the expense of the pre-carious (racialized) fringes of the workforce. These policies reacted against austerity pressures for previously well-protected workers while consenting to cuts for the rest.

The radical right in Northern Europe has neither opposed the cross-border movement of goods (USA) nor capital (Eastern Europe), but it has rejected the cross-border movement of people on economic as much as on cultural grounds, leading to a comprehensive platform of welfare chauvinism that aimed to create greater social divides between natives and immigrants. The Danish People's Party (DF), for example, connected its selective cuts in the benefit entitlements of natives with the defence of protections for labour mar-ket insiders and improved rights for the elderly. At the same time, it placed little, if any, emphasis on social investment measures on which Scandinavian countries have relied so much in the past. Unlike in Continental Europe, familialism has been conspicuously absent in the policy choices of the DF, which contrasts with the FPÖ's policy impact in power. The DF thus mainly aimed to shore up welfare support for the 'deserving' natives with tightly controlled boundaries of solidarity.

The remarkable variations in the radical right's socio-economic policy impacts across Europe and the USA have gone largely unnoticed in the literature. Rather than restricting themselves to what came to be known as 'culture war' issues such as immigration and gender rights, the radical right has had a deep and lasting impact on national models of capitalism and welfare, involving variations of trade protectionism, economic nationalism, traditional familialism, labour market dualism, and welfare chauvinism. Most observers have, however, seen them merely as agents of immigration control that play little role in capitalist development. In this view, radical right parties are likely to blur their social and economic policies in return for tighter restrictions on immigration (Rovny 2013, Rovny and Polk 2020). An alternative view states that radical right parties have turned into pro-welfare parties that can be located on the socio-economic left of the political spectrum. Seen in this way, radical right parties are likely to pursue a policy of redistributive state intervention, in line with their growing working-class support (Afonso 2015, Eger and Valdez 2015, Ivaldi 2015, Harteveld 2016, Lefkofridi and Michel 2017, Afonso and Rennwald 2018). What both lines of research have in common is that they typically focus on individual attitudes and party manifestoes without studying the actual policy choices of radical right parties in office across different political-economic contexts.

In this book, I will show that across the variations described above, the radical right is neither 'blurry' nor 'left-wing' when it really gets to decide who gets what, when, and how in contemporary capitalism. By studying the socio-economic policy choices of radical right parties in office, we not only capture their impact on people's livelihoods; it also provides insights into how they aim to facilitate democratic backsliding.

Research question and argument in brief

This book examines why radical right parties have had such a diverse impact on social and economic policies when coming to power. In doing so, the main argument is that (1) the sociocultural ideology of radical right parties informs their socio-economic policy *preferences*, but (2) diverse welfare state contexts mediate their socio-economic policy *impact* along the following regime-specific lines. In welfare states with conservative family relations, the radical right has pushed for familialist policies (Continental and Eastern Europe). In welfare states with generous social insurance systems, the radical right has defended the benefit entitlements of labour market insiders with long contribution records while excluding non-citizens from welfare entitlements (Continental and Northern Europe). The nativist mirror image of welfare chauvinism may be economic nationalism in welfare states dependent on foreign direct investment (FDI) (Eastern Europe). In the absence of these welfare state features, trade protection becomes a functional equivalent of social protection (USA).

In this introductory section, I will briefly outline how the sociocultural ideology of the radical right promotes a policy of selective status protection that resonates with the material interests of its electoral strongholds (i.e. policy preferences). Afterwards, I will outline how the diverse welfare state contexts in which radical right parties operate have created different opportunities and constraints in legislating their socio-economic reform agenda (i.e. policy impact). I will draw on party politics scholarship to capture the radical right's policy preferences on the one hand (agency), and build on comparative political economy to explain the radical right's policy impact in power on the other (structure).

Party politics scholarship and research on the far right has produced a great body of knowledge on how radical right parties mobilize their voters through their ideology of nativism and authoritarianism, often combined with populism (Mudde 2007, 2019; Art 2022). However, these studies tend to assume that the radical right's core ideology primarily maps onto the sociocultural dimension, with little implications for the socio-economic dimension. In this book, my *first main contribution* is to theorize and show how nativism and authoritarianism motivates a distinct set of social and economic policy preferences.

First, nativism refers to a combination of xenophobia and nationalism, whereby only (white) native citizens should be part of the national community, thereby excluding foreign-born citizens and ethnic minorities. Radical right parties not only influence sociocultural policies as a way of putting 'natives first'; they also *need* socio-economic policies to establish nativist principles, because by influencing the production and distribution of material resources, they can entrench nativist divisions in capitalist societies. More specifically, radical right parties can realize their nativist ideology through economic measures that reward native citizens while discriminating against non-citizens (leading to pro-natalism and welfare chauvinism) and fostering domestic businesses at the expense of foreign capital (leading to economic nationalism) and foreign trading partners (leading to trade protectionism). As such, nativism implies a xenophobic approach to social policy in response to ethnic diversity, but also a nationalist approach to economic policy in response to enhanced international competition.

Second, authoritarianism refers to a desire for order, conformity, and homogeneity with respect to traditional social norms inherited from the past, including (manual) 'hard work', the authority and deservingness of the elderly, and traditional gender norms and family values. A 'law and order' approach against crime is the most common way we tend to think about authoritarianism. However, the welfare state provides a comprehensive set of policy instruments to reward in-groups displaying conformity with traditional social norms and punish out-groups that are perceived to break with them. Conceived in this way, radical right parties may defend and expand the social insurance rights of labour market insiders and the elderly, as these welfare schemes reward people who have contributed to the national cause through long and uninterrupted employment biographies. Conversely, the unemployed and the poor are considered less 'deserving' of welfare support as they are perceived to show less commitment towards 'hard work' and achievement. In a similar vein, family policy creates opportunities for the radical right to promote traditional gender roles and hierarchies within the household. Specifically, the expansion of child benefit payments and tax breaks helps to incentivize families, and thus women in practice, to assume a greater role as caregivers. By contrast, radical right parties typically oppose social investment in (higher) education and childcare facilities, as these policies promote inclusive social mobility and progressive gender values.

While the radical right shares similar ideologies of nativism and authoritarianism, it also pursues widely different policy choices in government. Drawing on comparative political economy, my *second main contribution* is to explain how welfare state contexts translate the radical right's policy preferences into regime-specific policy impacts in power (Esping-Andersen 1990, Bohle and Greskovits 2012, Thelen 2014, Beramendi et al. 2015, Manow et al. 2018, Hassel and Palier 2021, Baccaro et al. 2022). In other words, I argue that the political-economic profile of welfare states and growth models provides the radical right with diverse opportunities and constraints when pursuing their nativist and authoritarian policy platform.

First, the nativist preference for putting 'natives first' led radical right parties to legislate diverse policies, because their domestic economies have been prone to different contestations of globalization, i.e. the cross-border movement of capital, goods/services, and people. Nativism took the form of welfare chauvinism in generous welfare states with growing immigration rates (Continental and Northern Europe), economic nationalism in FDI-dependent growth models after the fallout of the great financial crisis (Eastern Europe), and trade protectionism in a context of chronic current account deficits (USA). Whereas nativism contested the cross-border movement of foreign people in Western Europe, it responded to the cross-border movement of foreign capital in Eastern Europe and foreign goods in the USA, thereby reflecting the diverse economic vulnerabilities posed by the globalization of diverse varieties of capitalism and welfare (Rodrik 2011, Rodrik 2018, Manow 2018). To be sure, radical right parties oppose immigration across the board, but generous welfare states have been more prone to the 'culturalization' of distributive conflict through welfare chauvinism in the form of selective cuts targeted at non-citizens.

Second, the authoritarian preference for traditional social norms inherited from the past stimulates radical right parties to make diverse policy choices, because welfare states display different institutional legacies and thereby entrench different electoral preference structures on gender relations and welfare deservingness. Authoritarianism took the form of insider protection and labour market dualism in welfare states with mature social insurance systems (Continental and Northern Europe) and familialism in welfare states with conservative legacies and/or conservative attitudes (Continental and Eastern Europe). While the strong entrenchment of a more gender-egalitarian dual career model cuts off political support for a conservative family policy in the Nordic welfare state context, the institutional legacies of the male breadwinner model in Continental Europe and the dominance of conservative gender values in Eastern Europe create opportunities for a familialist approach that valorizes traditional gender relations and hierarchies. In a similar vein, the authoritarian insistence on 'hard work' at the expense of labour market outsiders and new social risk groups is easier to realize in mature welfare states where labour market insiders have traditionally enjoyed privileged access to generous benefit entitlements. Trade protectionism not only responds to discontents caused by globalization; it may also act as a functional equivalent of social protection in favour of the 'hard-working' and thus 'deserving' core workforces in declining manufacturing industries (USA). Taken together, we can see that radical right parties use the diverse social and economic policy instruments available within their welfare state context to pursue their nativist and authoritarian agenda in power. The importance of ideological values (nativism and authoritarianism) in determining distributive policy preferences (selective status protection) highlights how deeply intertwined cultural and economic conflicts have become.

To illustrate and test the arguments outlined above, I will use primarily case studies of Austria (Continental Europe), Denmark (Northern Europe), Hungary (Visegrád region), and the USA to test and illustrate the empirical patterns outlined above. The four primary case studies will be supplemented with secondary case studies to further substantiate (but also to nuance) my main argument: The German AfD and Italian *Lega* (compared to the Austrian FPÖ), the Norwegian FrP and Swedish SD (compared to Danish DF), and the Polish PiS (compared to Hungarian Fidesz). If my argument were correct, we should observe similar policy choices within a particular welfare state context from those radical right parties who assumed office (i.e. *Lega*, FrP, PiS) or the absence of such policy choices when radical right parties did not come to power (i.e. AfD, SD).

Winners and losers of the radical right in power

My analysis of the radical right's impact on capitalism and welfare holds broader insights about the distributive outcomes of political conflict in the twenty-first century. While the policies outlined above diverge from the neoliberal paradigm of the recent past, they nevertheless undermine redistributive state interventions that would reduce economic inequality. In other words, a pro-welfare stance does not necessarily imply support for inequality-reducing policies. The radical right pursues instead a socio-economic agenda of selective status protection that restores horizontal inequalities in terms of gender and ethnicity, without addressing vertical inequalities between the rich and the poor.

The diverse policy impacts outlined above have in common that they use policy instruments available within a particular welfare state context to reaffirm the traditionally privileged position of *threatened* labour market insiders and male breadwinners. Following the literature on labour market dualization (e.g. Rueda 2007, Schwander and Häusermann 2013, Rathgeb 2018), 'labour market insiders' refer to workers with relatively well-protected and permanent full-time employment contracts, whereas precarious labour market attachments exclude 'labour market outsiders' from the employment and social rights enjoyed by insiders. The radical right focuses on those labour market insiders and male breadwinners who have seen their dominance ebbing as their employment and citizenship status provides declining protections against the structural displacements and losses that decades of liberalization have yielded in a context of deindustrialization, globalization, and technological change. Hence, the radical right does not primarily cater to those already 'left behind' by structural shifts in the economy; it responds to the *fear* rather than the *outcome* of decline among the previously well-protected native (male) core workforces (Bornschier and Kriesi 2013,

Häusermann 2020). It thus comes as little surprise that the radical right's policy preferences have typically attracted disproportionately high electoral support from white males with lower levels of formal education over the past roughly four decades (Häusermann et al. 2013, Beramendi et al. 2015, Oesch and Rennwald 2018, Häusermann et al. 2022).

This book thus speaks to recent studies showing how perceived status losses—caused by the disappearance of manufacturing jobs, the concentration of well-paid service jobs in urban centres, and the purported replacement of native workers with immigrant workers—have increased radical right support (Gest 2016, Hochschild 2016, Engler and Weisstanner 2021, Gidron and Hall 2017, Kurer and Palier 2019, Kurer 2020, Kurer and Van Staalduinen 2022). For example, production workers are usually labour market insiders with permanent full-time jobs, but the state's retreat from full employment and industrial policies in a context of deindustrialization threatens their economic prospects, which has made them receptive to the protectionist appeals of the radical right. However, whereas the studies cited above show how status anxieties have *caused* electoral support for the radical right, this book shows the distributive *consequences* of the radical right in power.

While radical right parties primarily cater to threatened labour market insiders and male breadwinners, they typically tighten the screws on the unemployed and the poor while opposing a welfare recalibration and social investment measures that would cover new social risk groups, typically at the expense of (working) women, immigrants, ethnic minorities, and the young. In other words, selective protections for the native (male) core workforce go hand in hand with the promotion of a racialized and gendered precariat. Women face heightened challenges in reconciling work and family life in today's 'crisis of care' (Fraser 2016), the young are more likely to end up in non-standard contracts with less steady and secure income, whereas those with low or obsolete skills often face cycles between low pay and no pay (Bonoli 2007). As these groups have traditionally displayed a higher probability of being labour market outsiders with precarious employment and welfare standards (Schwander and Häusermann 2013), they would benefit precisely from those inclusive welfare state arrangements the radical right opposes (e.g. high-quality education across the life course, public childcare arrangements, universal and generous welfare benefits). Labour market outsiders—i.e. workers in precarious employment/welfare standards and the unemployed—therefore typically abstain from voting or support the radical left, whereas threatened labour market insiders—i.e. workers in permanent full-time employment relationships—constitute the radical right's electoral stronghold (Hopkin 2020). In short, nativism and authoritarianism may reflect ideological convictions in the first place, but they have clear distributive implications by promoting a policy of status protection that is regressive and defensive in nature.

Status protection and democratic backsliding

The radical right's policy of status protection has important implications for the study of democratic backsliding. We know that the radical right and the radical left often share an anti-democratic quality by attacking the liberal-constitutional component of democracy, given that checks and balances systems are supposed to dilute the 'general will of the people' (*volonté générale*) embodied by authoritarian strongmen. In other words, the radical right can be considered a form of democratic illiberalism waged against the undemocratic neoliberalism of the late twentieth and early twenty-first century (Berman 2017, Madariaga 2020). Political science scholarship has provided insightful elite-level accounts on the strategies and techniques political actors employ in processes of democratic backsliding (Levitsky and Ziblatt 2018, Mounk 2018, Waldner and Lust 2018). These studies highlight that the viability of liberal democracy depends on a shared culture of mutual toleration and consent among political adversaries, ensured by party elites ('gatekeepers') responsible to prevent processes of populist norm erosion.

My findings on the radical right's policy of selective status protection point to the hitherto unexplored role of welfare state reform in facilitating democratic backsliding. In the neoliberal era, governments of virtually all partisan complexions felt compelled to prioritize 'responsibility' towards market demands at the expense of 'responsiveness' towards voter demands (Mair 2013). The outcome of the neoliberal consensus was the widespread demobilization of voters at the expense of civil society and class-based organizations. This hollowing out of the popular component of democracy has provided fertile ground for radical right parties to challenge the liberal-constitutional component of democracy as a way of giving voice to 'our own people' at the expense of minority protection. The increased threat of (competitive) authoritarianism after the fallout of the global financial crisis cannot be understood without appreciating how the radical right has downgraded its neoliberal legacies in favour of previously dominant groups of voters whose social status has come under pressure in the post-industrial knowledge economy of the twenty-first century. This way, the radical right could generate the political support necessary to pursue authoritarian rule once in power.

Relationship to the literature

The above sections have already highlighted the main contributions to the literature. As this book enters into a dialogue with broader debates and strands of research, I want to use this section to reflect at a more general level on how my theoretical framework and empirical findings draw on and contribute to diverse sub-fields in political science and political economy.

First, this book engages with the study of *comparative politics* on the changing cleavage structures of political competition in the twenty-first century. There is overwhelming evidence on how a sociocultural cleavage has gained relevance and thereby complemented the classic socio-economic left–right divide. As a result, comparative politics—and indeed political science more broadly—has become accustomed to make a distinction between 'culture' versus 'economy' when studying political conflict (on the far right, see Norris and Inglehart 2019 versus Hopkin 2020). Recent works have begun to theorize at the micro level how the two cleavages intersect in voting behaviour, arguing that economic processes of relative (status) decline activate cultural dispositions in favour of the radical right (see e.g. Burgoon et al. 2019, Carreras et al. 2019, Gidron and Hall 2020, Dehdari 2022, Kurer and Van Staalduinen 2022). At its most basic, the findings of this book take this literature further by showing how, in turn, sociocultural values inform the socio-economic policy preferences of the radical right. However, the broader insight derived from my findings is that the two cleavages increasingly intersect and even merge into a sort of 'culture war capitalism' that renders socio-economic and sociocultural questions interdependent. The radical right is an illustrative example in this regard: as economic redistribution would benefit immigrants and ethnic minorities ('culture'), it refuses to address income inequality ('economy'). In a similar vein, the parties and social movements of the radical left oppose capitalism ('economy') as they deem it an economic system that exploits people of colour (Black Lives Matter) and the environment (Extinction Rebellion) ('culture'). The claims that the state benefits non-deserving groups in society (radical right) or that capitalism promotes racism (radical left) are ultimately economic arguments made on cultural grounds.

In short, one of the book's broader key points is that you cannot separate the culture war from capitalism. The culture war does not crowd out economic conflict, because it has itself a strong distributive component. While the 'economy' versus 'culture' distinction may be useful as a heuristic device, it starts from the flawed assumption that non-economic ends can be pursued *without* economic means, and *vice versa*. In fact, the welfare state as an economic institution has always been embedded in broader cultural projects that define the boundaries of national belonging, moral deserv- ingness, and gender normativity. Margaret Thatcher's famous quote that '[e]conomics are the method, but the object is to change the heart and soul' is an instructive reminder of how economic instruments serve cultural goals. Ultimately, the findings of the present book can thus be understood as an invitation for political scientists (focusing on identity politics and culture war issues) and political economists (focusing on capitalist development and macroeconomics) to engage more closely with each other's work, since socio- cultural and socio-economic policies cannot be separated along disciplinary boundaries.

Second, this book interacts with the study of *party politics*. This literature has shown that the radical right's electoral success lies mainly in the polit- ical activation of race, ethnicity, and authority (Mudde 2019, Art 2022). As should become clear from the introduction, I build on this finding in address- ing the radical right's relationship to capitalism and welfare. Nativism and authoritarianism are not only the ideological key tenets of the contempo- rary radical right, but also explain their electoral appeal among its voters, with important implications for their social and economic policies. How- ever, the literature of party politics also emphasizes the strategic voluntarism with which parties choose policy issues in a two-dimensional policy space (Abou-Chadi and Wagner 2020, De Vries and Hobolt 2020). In this line of research, political challenger parties like the radical right can be considered 'issue entrepreneurs' that struggle for political power by developing policies they find expedient to undermine the dominance of mainstream parties (De Vries and Hobolt 2020).

This book departs from agency-based and voluntarist party politics accounts by showing how welfare state contexts provide political actors with different opportunities and constraints in the pursuit of their political agenda. For example, radical right parties may want to enhance social protections for threatened labour market insiders, but some welfare state contexts pose political and fiscal limits, which directs the radical right's protectionism to other policy areas. In this view, radical right parties do not merely pursue short-term electoral gains by developing policy proposals in an opportunis- tic fashion; they instead have long-term hegemonic policy ambitions that are conditioned by institutional legacies and economic vulnerabilities inherited from previous policy choices (for a similar view, see Bohle et al. 2023). Marx (1852 [2016]) himself perhaps best captures this historical-institutionalist line of thinking in his Eighteenth Brumaire of Louis Bonaparte: 'Men make their own history, but they do not make it as they please; they do not make it under self-selected circumstances, but under circumstances existing already, given and transmitted from the past.'

Third, this book speaks to the literature of *welfare state research*, especially in light of its renewed focus on partisanship and the related 'electoral turn' in the explanation of diverse reform trajectories (e.g. Häusermann et al. 2013; Beramendi et al. 2015). In doing so, it draws on the insight that contemporary welfare state reform is multidimensional and thus involves distinct distributive choices on social protection and social investment, which makes clear why a simple focus on 'more' versus 'less' welfare or redistribution fails to capture policy developments in the twenty-first century. Whereas this literature pays close attention to the role of institutional legacies in shaping voter preferences and partisan room for manoeuvre (i.e. fiscal austerity, state capacity), it is less focused on the role of functional equivalents of social protection, for example trade protection in the case of Trump or the conversion of foreign currency loans in the case of Orbán. This omission may be due to its exclusive focus on Western European countries, but it is also a function of its two-dimensional conceptualization of distributive conflict that distinguishes between social 'consumption' and 'investment', which overlooks social policy by other means than social transfers and services.

Perhaps even more importantly, this book goes beyond the 'electoral turn' by showing how welfare state contexts not only influence voter preferences, but also the political-economic vulnerabilities resulting from globalization. It is clear that the radical right's nativism (and thus anti-globalism) contested different elements of the globalized cross-border movement of people (welfare chauvinism), capital (economic nationalism), and goods (trade protectionism). Understanding this variation in the radical right's policy priorities requires a recognition of how domestic models of capitalism and welfare have been exposed to neoliberal globalization. This insight calls for a focus on how the international dimension has created diverse domestic economic vulnerabilities and thus produced diverse anti-system challenges to the neoliberal order (for a similar approach, see Rodrik 2018, Manow 2018, Hopkin 2020).

Fourth, this book takes inspiration from recent scholarship in *comparative political economy* on the origins and trajectories of different 'growth models' (Baccaro and Pontusson 2016, Hassel and Palier 2021, Baccaro et al. 2022). This research shows how the demise of trade union power and thus wage-led growth ushered in a new era of finance- and export-led growth that produced growing inequality, secular stagnation, and populist contestation. In line with this periodization, this book finds that the trajectories of capitalist development are important to understand how the radical right turned from a neoliberal challenger towards an agenda of selective protectionism. Specifically, I draw on this literature by taking into account the international macroeconomic settings and domestic economic vulnerabilities in which radical right parties operate.

Yet, this book deviates from the growth model literature by emphasizing the radical right's core ideology. The scholarship on growth models assumes that the policies of governing parties follow the structural demand to facilitate capital accumulation. As governments are expected to rely on structural elites in dominant economic sectors to achieve their primary objective of strong economic growth, the radical right's nativism and authoritarianism can only be of situational and subsidiary importance in policymaking. In other words, whereas the growth model literature assumes that the 'culture war' in which the radical right engages is a distraction from the real-world policy choices of macroeconomic management, this book argues the exact opposite: the radical right uses social and economic policies to achieve its sociocultural goals. To be sure, political parties of all complexions are compelled to stimulate economic growth in a capitalist economy. However, the radical right's non-economic objectives are important to understand its economic policy choices, including for example the ambition to re-traditionalize gender relations, create divides between natives and 'producers' versus non-natives and 'parasites', or, indeed, to shore up legitimacy for democratic backsliding. As a result, this book contributes to this literature by demonstrating the intricacies of economic and cultural politics and, more specifically, the role of the radical right in legitimizing or altering prevailing growth models as a way of pursuing non-economic goals.

Outline of the book

This book consists of eight chapters and proceeds as follows. *Chapter 2* provides a historical background and contextualization of the radical right's socio-economic trajectory. As most Western European radical right parties emerged as challenger parties during the 1970s and 1980s, their neoliberal programme had an insurgent quality against the 'political class' of the Keynesian post-war era. In the neoliberal era, however, they downgraded their free market appeals in favour of a nativist-authoritarian platform. Meanwhile, the Eastern European mainstream right detached itself from the neoliberal devices of the Washington Consensus and the EU accession process by undergoing an ideological radicalization that moved them closer to the policy platforms of the Western European radical right. In the USA, by contrast, the Republican Party remained loyal to neoliberal economic policies while falling back on a white nativist platform, with openly racist appeals to attract lower-income whites outside the metropolitan coastal areas. I conclude this chapter with existing hypotheses about what kind of policy impact we should expect from the post-neoliberal radical right entering office from the 2000s, before outlining my own framework in the next chapter.

Chapter 3 presents the book's theoretical framework to identify and explain how radical right parties in Europe and the USA have influenced social and economic policies when in power. First, it argues that the radical right's ideological core—i.e. nativism and authoritarianism—translates into distinct deservingness conceptions that favour (threatened) labour market insiders, male breadwinners, and the elderly. Second, it argues that welfare state contexts shape the ways in which radical right parties articulate and implement their deservingness conceptions in policy terms. It then discusses the book's case selection strategy and provides information on the data sources used to illustrate and test the book's main arguments.

Chapter 4 is the first empirical chapter and shows how the Austrian Freedom Party has aimed to defend and expand the welfare entitlements of labour market insiders (e.g. early retirement) and male breadwinners (e.g. child benefits), in line with Austria's conservative welfare regime that has traditionally privileged the status protection of the male core workforce. The FPÖ is thus a case of how conservative legacies translate an ideological agenda of nativism and authoritarianism into insider-oriented and, more recently, welfare chauvinist social policy choices. Whereas the threatened male core workforce has been the material winner of the FPÖ's social policy impact, the opposite can be said about immigrants and those without steady and secure employment, leading to a policy combination I term *chauvinist and familialist insider protection*. Shadow case studies of Germany (AfD) and Italy (*Lega*) support this claim about the radical right's policy impact in welfare states characterized by conservative welfare legacies.

Chapter 5 demonstrates how the Danish People's Party (DF) has prioritized the benefit entitlements of 'deserving' benefit recipients—i.e. the elderly and labour market insiders—while retrenching the social rights of immigrants at the same time. The Danish DF and Austrian FPÖ have thus had a relatively similar pro-elderly and welfare chauvinist policy impact, but they diverged in the area of family policy. Unlike the FPÖ, the DF has not supported a familialist strategy that would allow (and expect) families, mostly women in practice, to reduce working hours in order to care for children. The institutional legacies of Nordic family policy and the related absence of a 'male breadwinner' model cut off political support for a familialist approach. The DF's policy impact may thus be summarized as *chauvinist insider protection*: cuts in welfare for non-citizens while expanding social security for the elderly and labour market insiders. Shadow case studies of Norway and Sweden buttress the primary case study evidence from Denmark.

Chapter 6 shows how the Orbán cabinet in Hungary has prioritized familialism in welfare state reform alongside economic nationalism in economic policy reform. Unlike in Western Europe, the Fidesz–KDNP government's nativist ideology has not translated into welfare chauvinist legislation due to the absence of high immigration rates and generous welfare benefits for non-citizens, whereas fiscal strains put constraints on the expansion of early retirement arrangements for 'deserving' labour market insiders. It could, however, capitalize on culturally conservative attitudes and recast the 'refugee crisis' in a demographic light, which helped to generate widespread support for a pro-natalist and conservative family policy. Taken together, the Orbán cabinet aimed to restore domestic policymaking autonomy in Hungary's FDI-led capitalism and cater to the one social unit deemed essential for the nationalist cause of resisting demographic decline and upholding traditional gender norms, which is the 'productive Magyar family', defined as white, fertile, hard-working, and heterosexual. The Polish case reveals a similar familialist priority, with different distributive implications, however.

Chapter 7 shows how trade protection acted as a functional equivalent of social protection in the socio-economic agenda of the Trump administration. Although the Republican Party (GOP) gradually radicalized towards a nativist-authoritarian agenda similar to European radical right parties, it diverged in its social and economic policy impact under Trump. Rather than enhancing the social protection of labour market insiders or expanding familialist policies, the Trump administration connected the GOP's traditional reliance on tax cuts and deregulatory reform with a new focus on trade protection and immigration control. Understanding Trump's policy impact requires an understanding of long-standing dynamics within the Republican Party as well as a comparative contextualization of America's hostility to a European-style welfare state. Without strong public support for collective risk protection, the radical right's ambition to protect 'deserving' social groups—typically the male (white) core workforce—may shift its attention to questions of trade rather than welfare.

Chapter 8 provides five broad analytical conclusions derived from the preceding empirical chapters and reflects on their political implications and related avenues of future research in the literatures of comparative politics, party politics, comparative political economy, and welfare state research.

2
The Socio-Economic Transformation of the Radical Right

This chapter provides a historical background and context for the impact of the radical right on capitalism and welfare in power. In ideological terms, the relationship between the radical right and capitalism appears ambiguous at first. On the one hand, the radical right typically invokes national unity to obscure or neutralize class divisions. A case in point is for example Carl Schmitt's rejection of what he called a weak 'total state', which he described as a situation in which various social groups make the state serviceable to their particularistic interests—at the expense of the nation's common cause (Schmitt 1932). In this line of reasoning, the economy needs to be liberated from the rent-seeking behaviour of political actors in order to let the market reward the productive and thus deserving sections in society. Seen in this way, the radical right may be perfectly compatible with a strong state that ensures the free play of market forces in a neoliberal fashion (for similar arguments, see Slobodian 2021, Scheiring 2022). On the other hand, the radical right is hostile to the dynamic and autonomous nature of borderless capital. As large-scale businesses pursue private profits across national borders, they have little regard for national communities. The fascist critique of capitalism was therefore that major industries act too independently of the state and thereby promote individualism, cosmopolitanism, and hedonism among wealthy elites at the expense of ordinary citizens (Payne 1995: 10). Hence, the radical right may be equally compatible with a Polanyian counter-movement against capitalist market expansion on ethno-nationalist grounds (for similar arguments, see Hopkin and Blyth 2019, Hopkin 2020).

In this chapter, I will argue that in order to understand the relationship between the radical right and capitalism, we need to adopt a *historical* perspective that appreciates their dynamic co-evolution in the post-war era. In doing so, I aim to show how the radical right's position on the socio-economic dimension has changed from a neoliberal opposition to the Keynesian class compromise towards a particularistic-authoritarian conception of the welfare state in the wake of the neoliberal era. An important

How the Radical Right Has Changed Capitalism and Welfare in Europe and the USA. Philip Rathgeb, Oxford University Press.
© Philip Rathgeb (2024). DOI: 10.1093/oso/9780192866332.003.0002

reason for the programmatic flexibility of the radical right is that its ideology originated from the sociocultural liberalism–authoritarianism cleavage rather than the socio-economic left–right cleavage. Unlike in the case of centre-left and centre-right parties, the core ideology of radical right parties is less attuned to economic questions of production, distribution, and consumption, which allowed them to use economic policies as political instruments to achieve non-economic ends. This involved neoliberal attacks against the 'party cartel' in a post-war context of Keynesian hegemony (1970s–1980s) or the reaffirmation of socioculturally laden goals of nativism, authority, and deservingness in a context of neoliberal hegemony (1990s–2000s). After outlining the broad contours of this historical development, I will conclude this chapter by discussing existing hypotheses about the policy impact we should expect from radical right parties entering government after the turn of the millennium—which I call the 'pro-welfare view' and the 'position-blurring view'—and contrast them with my own approach.

Neoliberalism against the 'Establishment' (1970s–1980s)

In the 1970s and 1980s, radical right parties celebrated their first electoral breakthroughs in Western Europe by mobilizing neoliberal-authoritarian revolts against the Keynesian post-war regime. What they had in common was the claim that tax cuts, privatization, and an end to tripartite concertation would bring about the disempowerment of a 'corrupt elite' as a precondition to reward the 'common man' for his hard work. The neoliberal anti-establishment orientation of this generation of radical right movements had affinities with Hayek's notion of rent-seeking: high taxes would not serve social policy purposes, but benefit instead a self-serving political elite detached from the populace. In this earlier period, the radical right was indeed populist, because it not only defined the 'pure people' in anti-pluralist terms, but its challenger status also provided it with an insurgent anti-establishment appeal in favour of the 'common man'. It is perhaps no coincidence that with the demise of strong economic growth and the related Keynesian class compromise, we can observe the (re-)emergence of pejorative terms signalling the perception of a growing distance between the political elite and ordinary citizens, including for example *La Casta* in Italian, *Classe Politique* in French, or the *Altparteien* in German.

The most influential account of the radical right's neoliberal credentials in the post-war era comes from the seminal study *The Radical Right in Western Europe* by Kitschelt and McGann (1995). Their key argument is that the radical right's winning formula used to be a combination of (1) sociocultural authoritarianism and (2) socio-economic neoliberalism. These parties therefore rejected immigration and defended traditional gender norms in reaction to the liberal value change following the 'silent revolution' in the wake of the 1968 movement (Inglehart 1990), while resisting income equalization and endorsing economic competition in favour of the 'free market' (Kitschelt and McGann 1995: 73). Although the radical right could not establish itself in the majoritarian election systems of the UK and the USA, the centre-right GOP under Ronald Reagan and the Tories under Margaret Thatcher adopted a similar mix of neoconservative and neoliberal positions (Ignazi 1992).

The *petite bourgeoisie* (small shop owners, farmers, police/prison officers) and blue-collar workers exposed to international competition formed the radical right's electoral key constituencies at that time (Kitschelt and McGann 1995: 19). In economic policy terms, the radical right mobilized this cross-class coalition by pitting the sheltered sectors (civil service, state-run industries) against the exposed sectors (private sector). According to this logic, private sector employees and employers came to face the competitive demands of the capitalist economy, whereas political elites and their affiliated bureaucratic apparatuses remained insulated from such pressures and enjoyed instead special privileges and protections thanks to corrupt deals reached behind closed doors. The radical right aimed to politicize this differential exposure to economic competition by calling for the privatization of state-run industries and the infusion of market mechanisms in the operation of the public sector. In this way, the state would put an end to public sector waste and eventually generate the revenues necessary to reward the truly 'hard-working' citizens of the private sector, encompassing both employers and employees.

The connection between pro-neoliberalism and anti-elitism may appear contradictory at first. After all, the neoliberal revolution itself was a project of economic and intellectual elites (Slobodian 2018). In the case of the radical right, however, political demands for tax cuts and privatizations followed not only electoral considerations; they also rested on a power-strategic calculus. By dismantling coordinated welfare systems, labour market protections, and state-owned industries, their policy demands aimed to weaken the power resources of political elites embedded in these institutional arrangements. Hence, the radical right's version of neoliberalism had an anti-establishment appeal as it emerged at a time when national governments and corporatist interest groups enjoyed relatively high levels of influence in macroeconomic management and welfare state administration. In the words of Betz, the radical right's neoliberalism was only 'secondarily an economic program' and constituted instead 'a political weapon against the established political institutions' (1993: 418). Conceived in this way, economic policy demands had not been designed to reshape models of capitalism and welfare as such, but to facilitate an attack on the political mainstream.

Understanding the populist neoliberalism of this 'second wave' of radical right movements (Van Beyme 1988) requires its historical contextualization in the Keynesian post-war capitalism of the Bretton Woods era. The so-called 'golden age of the welfare state' after the Second World War—a term idealizing broadly shared prosperity while disregarding entrenched divisions in gender and ethnicity—rested on high levels of economic growth that paved the way for the rise of relatively homogeneous middle-class societies with low levels of income inequality. Political parties were rooted in distinct class formations and civil society organizations, which competed on the expansion of public goods, whereas trade unions had the associational and structural power to translate productivity gains into real wage growth (on the rise and fall of the wage-led growth regime, see Baccaro and Howell 2017, Hopkin and Blyth 2019). By implication, national societies of the post-war era rejected the laissez-faire capitalist order that characterized the late nineteenth and early twentieth century leading to the Great Depression and World War (Polanyi 1944 [2001]). A new compromise, often coined 'embedded liberalism' (Ruggie 1982), took its place in order to re-embed the economy within domestic political and social relations, involving regulated cross-border trade in combination with welfare states (Western Europe) and the New Deal (USA). As a result, democratic politics exercised high levels of influence over the operation of capitalism (Hall 2022).

However, in addition to structural contradictions of Keynesian post-war capitalism (Streeck 2009, Harvey 2010), the political Achilles heel of this 'golden age' was its reliance on high levels of taxation to fund a bureaucratic and corporatist mode of welfare state organization. In this context, the Scandinavian Progress Parties initiated their tax revolts in the early 1970s against the social democratic class compromise, which also encompassed the bourgeois parties of the centre-right bloc. In both Denmark and Norway, for example, income tax rates reached their highest and most progressive levels under centre-right governments (1968–1971 in Denmark; 1965–1971 and 1972–1973 in Norway). As Goul Andersen and Bjørklund (1990: 201) show, the Norwegian Progress Party articulated its neoliberal resistance to this political-economic arrangement in populist terms: '[T]he elite, encompassing an alliance between politicians and bureaucrats in the public sector, has usurped power from the market via market interventions. The party's task is to restore the balance of the market by cancelling the regulations. In the 'free market', the sovereign consumer is the king. Deregulation of the market implies dispersal of power from politicians and bureaucrats to the consumers, to the people.' In Denmark, the tax lawyer and founder of the Danish Progress Party, Mogens Glistrup, came to public prominence when he declared in a TV interview in 1971 that he refused to pay taxes in protest against the political establishment and praised tax fraudsters as the 'freedom fighters of our time'.

Although the monetarist response to the inflation crisis of the late 1970s put an end to the Keynesian public policy regime, it did not abandon high levels of progressive taxation (Streeck 2011). Dramatic interest rate hikes caused a decline in inflation, but they also increased unemployment rates and thus public debt levels. Hence, as national governments faced 'permanent austerity' in a context of declining growth rates (Pierson 1996), they had to balance the conflictual demands of fiscal stability on the one hand, and the reduced take-home pay of the middle class, which was caused by the automatic tax increases of bracket creep (Goul Andersen and Bjørklund 1990). While the return of heightened distributive conflicts confronted national governments with hard policy choices, it created opportunities for neoliberal challengers to frame public debt as a result of public sector waste.

In the 1980s, radical right parties with neoliberal policy platforms emerged in Continental Europe against this background of high levels of taxation at a time when high levels of growth seemed increasingly out of reach. In France, the founder of the *Front National* (FN), Jean-Marine Le Pen, praised himself as the 'French Ronald Reagan' and compared the state's tax authorities with the blood lust of the Spanish Inquisition (Afonso and Rennwald 2017). He thus demanded radical tax cuts and the dismantlement of the welfare state in favour of a 'minimal state' only concerned with questions of law and order (army, police, prison system, diplomacy) (ibid.). In Italy, the *Lega Nord* (LN) emerged out of Northern Italian secessionist movements and gained popularity especially in the Lombardy and Veneto in the mid-1980s. The LN mobilized primarily small shop owners against high taxes and corruption among political elites (*partitocrazia*) (Bull and Gilbert 2001; see also Hopkin 2020: Ch. 7). It benefited from the collapse of the Italian party system in the wake of the *Tangentopoli* scandal, in which one third of Members of Parliament was found to be involved in organized corruption. Hence, the *Lega* (renamed in 2018) is today the oldest party in the Italian parliament (Vittori 2018).

Similar to the FN and LN, the Freedom Party of Austria (FPÖ) turned into a populist right party with neoliberal reform demands when Jörg Haider took over the party in 1986. Similar to the Italian situation, the problems in Austria's consensus democracy—clientelism, party patronage, and corruption—created opportunities for the radical right to attack the political establishment on neoliberal grounds. While the LN mobilized against *Roma ladrona* ('Rome, the thief'), the FPÖ called for tax cuts, privatizations of state-run industries, and an end to corporatist elite collusion between the two historical major parties and the social partner organizations. As Ennser-Jedenastik (2019) shows, one fifth of the FPÖ's election manifestoes between 1986 and 1999 criticized party patronage, public sector waste, and corporatist concertation, an unusually high value in comparison to the platforms of the social democratic SPÖ, the Christian democratic ÖVP, and the Green Party. As Afonso's (2013, 2015) work shows, the FPÖ's pro-neoliberalism and anti-elitism resembled the attacks the Swiss People's Party (SVP) and the Dutch Freedom Party (PVV) waged against corporatist elite negotiations between governments and organized interests.

Nativism and authoritarianism in the age of globalization (1990s–2000s)

The socio-structural environment of domestic party competition changed dramatically with the demise of the 'golden age' of the welfare state. In Western Europe and the USA, national governments retreated from their commitment to ensure full employment and faced the corresponding 'return of mass unemployment' (Lindvall 2010) with a supply-side approach of economic adjustment (Hall 1989). In Eastern Europe, the collapse of the Soviet Union and the formation of post-communist nation states confronted newly elected governments with the task of 'making capitalism without capitalists' (Eyal et al. 2002). As capitalist market expansion reached the new peripheries of the former communist bloc while North America and Western Europe searched for new ways to stimulate their domestic economies, the stage was set for what Rodrik (2011) has called the 'hyper-globalization' of capitalism, i.e. the widespread elimination of barriers on the cross-border movement of capital, goods/services, and people. The economic winner of this globalization was the unleashed financial sector and its asset management class, who came to substitute for the demise of wage-led economic growth with ever-new financial instruments and speculations (Braun 2022).

This new context shifted the balance of class power away from organized labour towards employers, managers, and international finance (Baccaro and Howell 2017, Rathgeb 2018). Whereas in the post-war era governments shifted towards greater levels of redistributive state intervention, the opposite happened in the neoliberal era, when capital went into the offensive to reverse the tide of squeezed profits (Glyn 2007), while globalization constrained the domestic policymaking autonomy of governments (Rodrik 2011). The creation of free trade zones—e.g. the EU Single Market and the North American Free Trade Area (NAFTA)—helped governments to insulate themselves from electoral pressure against neoliberal reform, as it implied the delegation of greater powers to 'non-majoritarian institutions' such as the European Commission and the World Trade Organization (Mair 2013).

The neoliberalism-*cum*-globalization revolution from the 1990s had at least two important implications for the radical right. First, trade and capital account liberalization translated into stronger competitive pressures for manufacturing workers in the global North (Milanovic 2016). At the same time, skill-biased technological change fuelled economic uncertainty and a loss in social status among manufacturing workers (Iversen and Cusack 2000). Although one of the radical right's important electoral constituencies saw a decline in its economic fortunes (Häusermann 2020, Kurer 2020), most countries retreated from compensatory redistribution from the mid-1990s (Pontusson and Weisstanner 2018, Hall 2022), thereby spurring far-right voting (Vlandas and Halikiopoulou 2019, Vlandas and Halikiopoulou 2022). Second, globalization implied not only international economic competition, but also an increase in immigration rates, which created opportunities for the radical right to translate socio-economic concerns around jobs and wages into sociocultural grievances against non-citizens and ethnic minorities (Halikiopoulou and Vlandas 2020, Burgoon and Rooduijn 2021 Dehdari 2022). As a result, the radical right developed a nativist focus on putting 'our own people first' while it portrayed immigrants as scapegoats for a decline in security (Berezin 2009). As the neoliberal consensus depoliticized material questions of class and power in favour of TINA arguments ('there is no alternative'), it opened the door for radical right parties to politicize sociocultural questions of immigration and identity. In other words, the stage was set for the so-called 'culture wars' of the twenty-first century when the neoliberal consensus took hold among the political mainstream (Evans and Tilley 2011).

The radical right managed to cater to the 'losers' of neoliberal globalization by responding to their opposition to growing immigration rates, international economic competition, and the declining relevance of the nation state vis-à-vis the EU and other non-majoritarian institutions (Kriesi 1998, Kriesi et al. 2008, Steiner et al. 2023). Recent findings show how these economic, cultural, and political developments interact in shaping a status anxiety among a previously dominant group of production workers that makes them receptive to nativist and authoritarian platforms (Gidron and Hall 2017, Carreras et al. 2019, Kurer 2020, Engler and Weissstanner 2021, Steiner et al. 2023). The 'winners' of globalization, by contrast, benefited from the transition to a more service-based, financialized, and internationally connected 'knowledge economy' thanks to higher levels of formal education, which create job opportunities across national borders and contribute to liberal values on cultural and ethnic diversity. This new context reshaped the traditional class and family basis on which parties had competed for votes in the post-war era, as it drove a wedge between 'old' working-class and middle-class voters in rural and suburban places on the one hand, and the highly educated 'new' middle classes in metropolitan areas on the other (Iversen and Soskice 2019, Ch. 5).

Since the 1990s and 2000s, the radical right could therefore attract growing shares of working-class voters (Oesch 2008, Betz and Meret 2012, Afonso and Rennwald 2018). The ensuing 'proletarization' of the radical right (Betz 1993) was, however, restricted to a male-dominated and sector-specific mobilization of native (white) blue-collar workers, whereas a growing share of working-class voters employed in low-value-added service sectors often abstain from voting or lack the right to vote due to foreign citizenship (Abou-Chadi et al. 2021: 16–19). In other words, while globalization and deindustrialization contributed to a *fear* of economic decline among previously well-protected groups of manufacturing workers, the actual *outcome* of unemployment and precarity is more widespread among female and non-white service workers who are significantly less likely to support the radical right (Häusermann et al. 2013, Beramendi et al. 2015, Häusermann 2020).

In this context, neoliberal demands gradually declined in relevance among radical right parties (De Lange 2007, Betz and Meret 2012, Afonso 2015, Afonso and Rennwald 2018), whereas nativist-authoritarian positions became their defining ideological features (Mudde 2007, 2019; Art 2022). During the 1990s and 2000s, centre-left parties accommodated to globalization by following a middle-class oriented 'Third Way' (Giddens 1999) that would prioritize market-conforming over market-constraining state intervention in the interest of economic competitiveness (Mudge 2018). Przeworski (2019) provides a succinct account of how neoliberalism's policy devices received support from both mainstream left and right parties: "As the right moved to the right, the left moved even farther to the right, and the economic policies of the centre-left and the centre-right became almost indistinguishable. Social democrats embraced liberalisation of capital flows, free trade, fiscal discipline, and labour market flexibility, abstained from counter cyclical policies and from using most industrial policies." In the early 2010s, both centre-left and centre-right parties rolled out to compensate for generous bankers' bailouts with another round of austerity policies at the expense of growing inequality and precarity (Bremer and McDaniel 2020). Acute observers therefore reflected upon the 'strange non-death of neoliberalism' after the great financial crisis (Crouch 2011).

However, the fallout of the financial crisis and the Covid-19 pandemic severely undermined the legitimacy of neoliberalism across the political spectrum. More recently, centre-left parties have rediscovered market-correcting types of state intervention, for example, by politicizing wealth inequality and/or supporting green new deals (Manwaring and Holloway 2022). At the same time, centre-right parties have come to balance between the protectionist demands of small shop owners and the liberal demands of managers and business elites while keeping a keen eye on sustaining the remaining generosity of public pensions in an effort to account for the 'grey power' of ageing societies (Beramendi et al. 2015). Meanwhile, the countries hit hardest by the global financial crisis and the subsequent sovereign debt crisis—the UK and Southern Europe—saw the resurgence of radical left movements aiming to repoliticize the economy against the neoliberal mantra of competitiveness and austerity, typically on behalf of labour market outsiders and younger university graduates excluded from the primary labour market (Hopkin 2020). While their demands seemed radical in the wake of the global financial crisis, they essentially followed traditional social democratic priorities to which identity rights and environmentalism have been added.

In Central and Eastern Europe (CEE), the post-communist transition followed the neoliberal devices of the Washington Consensus (1990s) and the EU single market accession process (2000s), involving measures aimed at fiscal discipline, price liberalization, tax reform, elimination of subsidies, reduction of public investment, liberalization of trade and FDI flows, privatization of state-owned enterprises, and secure property rights. The remarkable degree, scope, and stability of neoliberal reform in the CEE countries rested on a competitive dynamic geared to attract Western foreign direct investment (FDI) and signal credibility among international financial institutions (Appel and Orenstein 2018). Despite this overall trend, the post-communist transition process allowed for significant cross-national variation leading to distinct varieties of post-communist capitalism: radical neoliberalism in the Baltics, embedded neoliberalism in the Visegrád region, and the neocorporatist exception of Slovenia (Bohle and Greskovits 2012). The embedded nature of the Visegrád region's embrace of neoliberal reform stems from the ways in which these countries maintained relatively generous welfare states for the 'losers' of economic modernization as a way of generating political support for the post-communist transition process, typically involving labour shedding mechanisms such as early retirement arrangements (Vanhuysse 2006). In the Baltic countries, by contrast, governments managed to mobilize political support for a radical version of neoliberalism that aimed to decouple their economies from Russia. Hence, the nationalist promise of small state independence created better opportunities for neoliberal reformers in the Baltic countries than in the Mediterranean countries after the Eurozone's sovereign debt crisis (Bohle 2017).

As the global financial crisis exposed the vulnerabilities of Eastern Europe's reliance on Western FDI, mainstream right parties started to outcompete the political left on ethno-nationalist rather than neoliberal grounds (Minkenberg 2013, Greskovits 2020). Tavits and Letki (2009) show that already in the 1990s governments were more likely to cut spending if they were of left rather than right orientation. As left parties aimed to prove their disassociation with the communist past, they opted for a more neoliberal approach that could bet on a stable and loyal electorate, at least until the global financial crisis. By contrast, the Eastern European mainstream right at times converged towards the Western European radical right by promoting similar nativist and authoritarian principles, with the Hungarian Fidesz-KDNP under Orbán and the Polish PiS under the Kaczynskis as the most prominent examples.

In the majoritarian election system of the USA, neoliberalism became contested from within the mainstream right and mainstream left. In response to the Great Recession, the political movements of Occupy Wall Street ('We are the 99 percent') and Bernie Sanders signalled a radical left opposition to the neoliberal era, whereas the GOP gradually turned into a radical right party embracing a white nativist and authoritarian agenda (Gerstle 2022). However, the US Republican Party remains more reliant on wealthy donors and think tanks than European radical right parties, which helps explain why it has retained a pronounced neoliberal approach on taxation and deregulation beyond the global financial crisis and the Covid-19 pandemic (Hacker and Pierson 2020).

Leaving aside important cross-national differences for the moment, it is clear that radical right parties prioritized nativist and authoritarian positions while at the same time retreating from neoliberal reform demands with the onset of globalization (with the exception of the USA) (Mudde 2007, Levitsky and Ziblatt 2018). In this context, Mudde (2019) speaks of the 'mainstreaming' and 'normalization' of the radical right, because anti-immigration and law and order positions once confined to the political fringes turned into the political centre of domestic party competition contexts. Hence, while the radical right features a similar ideological core of nativism and authoritarian, it has become a more diverse and variegated group of parties over time (ibid.).

I follow Mudde (2007) in defining the contemporary radical right as a group of diverse parties that share an ideological core of nativism and authoritarianism, often combined with populism. First, nativism refers to a xenophobic or racist version of nationalism, whereby only (white) native citizens should be part of the national community, thereby excluding foreign-born citizens, ethnic minorities, and people of colour. In Western Europe, nativism typically rejects immigration and multiculturalism, whereas in the low-immigration contexts of Eastern Europe it primarily stimulates an opposition to minority rights (Bustikova 2019). In the racialized context of the USA, by contrast, nativism is typically laden with claims to white supremacy alongside anti-immigration appeals (Belew 2022). Second, authoritarianism refers to a desire for order, conformity, and homogeneity with respect to traditional social norms inherited from the past. As these preferences should be ensured by state force if necessary, this ideology implies a strong law and order approach that punishes those out-groups that are perceived to break with traditional social norms and the authority of the state. Finally, populism refers to an anti-pluralist and anti-elitist ideology that assumes a growing distance between the 'pure people' and the 'corrupt elite', and thereby claims that only the populist leader represents the 'pure people' (Mudde 2004). Seen in this way, populism has an anti-democratic quality by attacking the liberal-constitutional component of democracy, given that 'checks and balance' systems are supposed to dilute the 'general will of the people' (*volonté générale*). In other words, contemporary populism can be considered a form of democratic illiberalism waged against undemocratic liberalism (Berman 2017).

Unlike nativism and authoritarianism, populism alone has less clear-cut distributive implications and can therefore be adopted by both left-wing and right-wing challenger parties (Mudde 2004, Mudde and Kaltwasser 2013, Kriesi 2018). The radical right's initially neoliberal-authoritarian programme had had an insurgent populist quality against the 'political class' in favour of the 'common man' (Kitschelt and McGann 1995). Trump was a more recent challenger candidate that also used a populist campaign against the political mainstream from which he felt excluded. In other words, populism remains a powerful ideological outlook especially for political newcomers in a context of electoral dealignment and political demobilization after decades of TINA politics ('there is no alternative') (Mair 2013, Kriesi 2018), but it does not provide clear economic policy devices from which radical right parties can draw when making distributive choices in government. Put simply, there is no such thing as a populist socio-economic agenda that lends itself to a comprehensive policy platform that would benefit the 'pure people' as a whole. Regardless of partisan complexion, distributive policy choices inevitably create winners and losers structured along class, gender, and race. It would also be difficult to contend that radical right parties generally continue to prioritize a populist neoliberalism that claims to remove power from the 'corrupt elite' through tax cuts across the board. The *policy-relevant* implications of populist anti-elitism are thus restricted to reductions in the welfare entitlements of politicians and public sector elites (Ennser-Jedenastik 2016) or institutional reforms aimed at removing power from established party and interest group representatives in the administration of the welfare state (Rathgeb and Klitgaard 2022). Following Mudde (2007, 2019), I therefore consider nativism and authoritarianism the radical right's most important ideological features that shape their socio-economic policy preferences in the twenty-first century.

The radical right in power since the 2000s: Pro-welfare, blurry, or something else?

What are the social and economic policy implications of the radical right's downgrading of neoliberalism? The literatures of comparative political economy and comparative politics provide two major hypotheses in response to this question. First, it may be argued that radical right parties have turned into pro-welfare parties that have gradually moved to the socio-economic left of the political spectrum (Afonso 2015, Eger and Valdez 2015, Ivaldi 2015, Harteveld 2016, Lefkofridi and Michel 2017, Afonso and Rennwald 2018). As radical right parties have experienced growing electoral support among the 'losers' of globalization, we should expect redistributive state interventions from radical right parties while excluding non-citizens from welfare receipt at the same time.

This 'pro-welfare hypothesis' captures an important point about the changing electoral composition of radical right parties. Indeed, there is little reason to assume that neoliberalism forms an enduring part of the radical right's 'winning formula' (Kitschelt and McGann 1995) in light of growing support among voters with lower levels of education in an age of deindustrialization, globalization, and permanent austerity. For example, Afonso and Rennwald (2018: 173) claim, '[a] more pro-welfare position has emerged as the best strategic option for radical right elites to accommodate the preferences of their growing number of working-class supporters'. This approach appears persuasive in explaining why, for example, the working-class-dominated French *Front National* (renamed as *Rassemblement National* in 2018) is more pro-welfare than the agrarian/small shop owner–dominated Swiss People's Party. Beyond the area of social protection, Michel and Lefkofridi (2017: 259) argue that the radical right 'grasped the opportunity to appeal to the working class by moving to the left on socio-economic issues, while remaining on the right on sociocultural issues and especially immigration'. In a similar vein, Eger and Valdez (2015: 118) conclude that the radical right 'can be increasingly characterised as economically left-wing, as contemporary anti-immigrant parties do not take a weak-state stance on taxation, redistribution, or government intervention in the economy'.

However, radical right parties attract their voters through a nativist-authoritarian platform on the sociocultural dimension rather than a left-wing platform on the socio-economic dimension. Recent findings in comparative political economy suggest that even the radical right's electoral base of production workers does not necessarily want economic redistribution as such, but rather *status protection* for themselves. Hence, these voters feel attracted to ethno-nationalist instead of class-based conceptions of solidarity, which cuts off a left-wing approach on the socio-economic dimension. As Beramendi et al. (2015) and Häusermann and Kriesi (2015) show, production workers typically favour insider-oriented welfare entitlements that benefit workers with long contribution records, but not a redistributive welfare state as such. To understand the radical right's policy preferences, it is important to conceptualize contemporary welfare politics in multidimensional terms. Busemeyer et al. (2022) show that radical right voters support the pension entitlements of labour market insiders, but they also demand welfare cuts for immigrants, the unemployed, and the poor while opposing a progressive welfare recalibration that would cover the new social risks of non-standard workers, typically at the expense of women, the young, and the low-skilled. In other words, we can expect that the radical right's changing electoral support base may well motivate a retreat from neoliberal positions, but their (working-class) voters want a more particularistic welfare state that benefits themselves more exclusively, which contradicts the pro-welfare view's proposition of a left-wing turn towards redistributive state intervention.

Second, many observers have seen radical right parties as agents of immigration control that place little emphasis on social and economic policies. In this view, we should expect them to engage in a strategy of 'position-blurring' on the socio-economic dimension in return for concessions on the sociocultural dimension (Rovny 2013, Rovny and Polk 2020). This 'position-blurring hypothesis' starts from the observation that the radical right unites its voters on sociocultural issues, including anti-immigration appeals and support for law and order. On the socio-economic dimension, by contrast, radical right parties 'remain very conscious of the heterogeneous economic interests of their (potential) voters that include (ex-)industrial workers, lower grade white-collar workers, as well as small business owners' (Rovny and Polk 2020: 25). Hence, these parties are expected to emphasize and mobilize voters on the sociocultural issues dimension, while blurring and downplaying their positions on the socio-economic dimension. Conceived in this way, radical right parties should have an incentive to delegate policymaking authority to their (centre-right) coalition partners in economic affairs in order to maximize policy gains in sociocultural domains as much as possible when in office. Indeed, the rejection of immigration and multiculturalism is at the heart of the contemporary radical right, with severe policy implications for the rights of non-citizens (Lutz 2019). The recognition that radical right parties win most of their votes through their anti-immigration appeal is a crucial insight from party politics scholars that should be taken seriously in comparative political economy and welfare state research.

However, the 'position-blurring' view overlooks how the sociocultural ideology of the radical right informs their socio-economic policy preferences. The clearest expression of the radical right's 'culturalizaton' of economic policies is welfare chauvinism. As radical right parties oppose immigration, they also oppose the social rights of non-citizens. In a similar vein, workfare policies are the welfare state's equivalent of an authoritarian law and order position: those who work hard are 'deserving' of support, whereas those who are not should be punished by state force (Ennser-Jedenastik 2016, Rathgeb 2021a, Chueri 2022). At the same time, the progressive appeals of social investment policies—social mobility and equal opportunities—clash with authoritarian values based on order, tradition, and convention, which explains why the radical right's voters are the fiercest opponents of such welfare recalibration (Busemeyer et al. 2022, Enggist and Pinggera 2022). Seen in this way, it becomes clear that the radical right is in fact remarkably outspoken on its policy priorities, as they are consistent with its nativist and authoritarian worldview.

Taken together, the (1) pro-welfare view and the (2) position-blurring view share two important features. First, they both focus on the electoral class composition of radical right parties. Whereas the pro-welfare view emphasizes growing working-class support as an important causal factor, the position-blurring view highlights the enduring diversity of the radical right's electoral class basis. While the former argues that growing working-class support sends a clear signal in favour of left-wing policies on the socio-economic dimension, the latter argues that this could disrupt the radical right's cross-class coalition, held together by nativist-authoritarian stances on the sociocultural dimension. In consequence, they both downplay how the radical right's sociocultural ideology affects their socio-economic policy preferences in the multidimensional context of contemporary distributive conflict.

Second, they both focus on the Western European context. Hence, they do not capture the *variation* in the policy impacts of radical right parties. Since the 2000s, the rise of the radical right is by no means geographically restricted to the cases of Western Europe (Mudde 2019). For example, Eastern European mainstream right parties like the Hungarian Fidesz and the Polish PiS are by no means less radical than the Norwegian Progress Party (FrP) or the British UKIP (Mudde 2016: 15). These parties share a nativist agenda with a strong law and order orientation that is characteristic of the radical right's core ideology. In a similar vein, the Tea Party represents an American mirror image of the European radical right (Minkenberg 2011) that has managed to radicalize the Republican Party, which culminated in the presidency of Donald Trump (Skocpol and Williamson 2011, Hacker and Pierson 2020). Trump's tenure can thus be seen as a functional equivalent of the European radical right in mobilizing similar voters—lower-educated white males—through an American nativist-authoritarian platform with anti-establishment appeals (Mudde 2018). Yet, we know very little about the cross-national differences between the policy influences of the radical right in diverse country contexts. This book draws on the central insight of these contributions that the electoral class composition of radical right parties is an important causal factor to understand their policy influence in government. In doing so, I will use the 'pro-welfare view' and 'position-blurring view' as alternative theoretical approaches to sharpen and nuance my own claim on how welfare state contexts mediate the radical right's deservingness perceptions in power. The next chapter will develop this argument in greater detail.

3

Policy Preferences and Impacts of Radical Right Parties in Diverse Welfare State Contexts

This chapter presents the theoretical framework of this book. It starts from the observation outlined in the previous chapter that the radical right had overall downgraded its neoliberal credentials before starting to assume office in the twenty-first century. Whereas in the Keynesian post-war era these parties had used anti-elitist free market appeals to attack the 'party cartel' from which they felt excluded, they gradually developed a focus on putting 'our own people first' in response to the globalization-*cum*-liberalization era. In this more recent context, previous studies have started to consider radical right parties as new 'pro-welfare parties' that expand the welfare state as a way of retaining (and expanding) high levels of working-class support (e.g. Afonso 2015, Eger and Valdez 2015, Ivaldi 2015, Harteveld 2016, Lefkofridi and Michel 2017, Afonso and Rennwald 2018). By contrast, other contributions argue that radical right parties pursue a strategy of 'position-blurring' in order to enhance the salience of sociocultural issues on which they mobilize most of their voters (e.g. Rovny 2013, Rovny and Polk 2020).

My theoretical framework deviates from these two approaches by distinguishing between (1) policy preferences and (2) policy impact. First, I will argue that the radical right's ideological core—i.e. nativism and authoritarianism—translates into distinct deservingness conceptions that favour labour market insiders, male breadwinners, and the elderly. The emerging preference structure typically attracts high levels of electoral support from formerly well-protected social groups who have experienced declining economic prospects in the post-industrial knowledge economy. Second, I will argue that regime-specific welfare state contexts mediate the policy preferences of radical right parties when they are in power, leading to distinct varieties of policy impact: chauvinist and familialist insider protection in Continental Europe, chauvinist insider protection in Northern

How the Radical Right Has Changed Capitalism and Welfare in Europe and the USA. Philip Rathgeb, Oxford University Press.
© Philip Rathgeb (2024). DOI: 10.1093/oso/9780192866332.003.0003

Europe, familialist protection and economic nationalism in Eastern Europe (Visegrád region), and trade protection in the USA.

Before outlining these two contentions, it is important to recognize the multidimensional space in which distributive conflict plays out today (Bonoli 2010, Häusermann 2012, Beramendi et al. 2015, Hemerijck 2018, Palier et al. 2022). A core insight of comparative political economy is that welfare states do not only (or even primarily) differ with regard to their relative size (i.e. how much public spending is devoted to areas of social policy), but also with regard to their institutional design and distributive priorities (see Esping-Andersen 1990 for an early contribution in this tradition). A central function of modern welfare states is to insure against social risks such as sickness, old age, unemployment, or needing care. The historical core of mature welfare states is therefore to provide social insurance via compensatory social spending on pensions, unemployment protection, social assistance, and similar transfer programmes.

Besides compensating for social risks via social transfers, welfare states have increasingly adopted an investment-oriented perspective. Social investment policies such as education, active labour market, and childcare policies aim to prevent the emergence of social risks before they materialize *ex ante* through human capital formation rather than compensating income losses *ex post*. There are important cross-national differences in regard to how much welfare states have moved towards the social investment approach, although this model has generally gained traction across the advanced capitalist countries (Beramendi et al. 2015, Hemerijck 2018, Palier et al. 2022). Finally, besides social transfers and social investment, welfare state institutions also intervene via regulatory policies, especially by making unemployment benefit receipt conditional on active job search, often called the workfare approach. Specifically, workfare refers to tightened obligations on the unemployed to take up any jobs deemed suitable, which Bonoli (2010) delineates from other active labour market policies by terming it 'incentive reinforcement', characterized by a strong employment orientation with no investment in human capital. Finally, social policy can be pursued by other means than social transfers and social investment, including for example trade protection or collective bargaining (Seelkopf and Starke 2019).

As a result, contemporary welfare politics is not necessarily about the preferred *size* of the welfare state as such ('more' versus 'less' welfare), but about the *kind* of welfare state that political actors want, including which social groups should be protected and what relative importance social transfers, social investment, workfare, or other means of income protection should have. Opening up the analytic space to disentangle the multidimensionality of contemporary distributive conflict allows us to move beyond the current terms of the debate, which is mostly organized around the question of whether the radical right has become more 'pro-welfare' and 'left-wing' or 'centrist' and 'blurry'. This way we are able to identify the distributive impact of the radical right in power and can expose the ways in which it uses socio-economic reforms to legitimize authoritarian rule.

Policy preferences: The role of nativism and authoritarianism

Democratic politics is not only a contest about winning elections; it is also a struggle over popular beliefs. The role of ideology distinguishes such a long-term hegemonic conception of politics from a short-term electoral conception. Without a strong ideological orientation, challenger parties may adapt to the terms of political debate, but they cannot change them. That the radical right's discourse has become mainstreamed and normalized over time testifies to its ideological consistency in activating race, ethnicity, and law and order as central focal points of twenty-first-century politics (Mudde 2019, Art 2022).

Drawing on the party politics literature, my theory of the radical right's socio-economic policy preferences starts from the premise that it has a core ideology consisting of nativism and authoritarianism, often combined with populism (e.g. Arzheimer 2012, Mudde 2007, Rydgren 2008, Art 2022). While this ideology centres on the sociocultural dimension of political conflict, it affects the socio-economic dimension with regard to questions of 'distributive deservingness' (Häusermann and Kriesi 2015: 206; see also Ennser-Jedenastik 2016, Rathgeb 2021a). According to this argument, radical right parties should typically endorse a particularistic conception of deservingness, drawing sharp distinctions between in-groups deserving welfare support versus out-groups that do not.

These ideological features—nativism and authoritarianism—help us to understand the radical right's deservingness conceptions and thus have clear distributive implications. First, *nativism* can be understood as a nationalist and xenophobic response to globalization. In the welfare state domain, it promotes a policy of welfare chauvinism that creates divisions in welfare entitlements between citizens versus non-citizens. More specifically, I follow Goul Andersen and Bjørklund (1990) as well as Kitschelt and McGann (1995) in conceptualizing welfare chauvinism as selective welfare cuts targeted at the social rights of non-citizens, while prevailing welfare arrangements for citizens remain untouched. By contrast, recent contributions define welfare chauvinism as a *combination* of support for (1) economic redistribution on the one hand, and (2) a preference for the exclusion of immigrants from it on the other (for an overview, see Careja and Harris 2022). The reason why I adopt the original conceptualization of welfare chauvinism is that the radical right's particularistic deservingness conceptions are at odds with a redistributive policy platform. As I will discuss below, its ideology promotes tightened screws on the unemployed and the poor as well as an opposition to an investment-oriented welfare recalibration that would cover new social risks (Rathgeb and Busemeyer 2022). Related to welfare chauvinism, nativism also stimulates a pro-natalist policy agenda aimed to foster the reproductive capacity of the native population without relying on immigration (Ennser-Jedenastik 2022). As the native nuclear family is central to the nativist worldview of the radical right, the welfare state should contribute to the reproduction of the native population while excluding immigrants from welfare entitlements. The economic mirror image of welfare chauvinism can be an economic nationalism that aims to reward and expand domestic businesses while discriminating against foreign-owned businesses, including for example the renationalization of key industries or special taxes and other regulations imposed on non-domestic companies. Seen in this way, nativism may have clear social and economic policy implications.

Second, *authoritarianism* translates into a preference for the punishment of out-groups that are perceived to break with traditional social norms such as 'hard work', authority, and heteronormativity. The role of authoritarianism in shaping deservingness conceptions has a long history in social science. Drawing on their studies of early twentieth-century fascism, Adorno et al. (1950) define authoritarianism as a 'personality syndrome' consisting of conventionalism, authoritarian submission, and aggression, as well as anti-intellectualism. Altemeyer (1981) developed a 'right-wing authoritarianism' scale, which measures a preference for submission, conventionalism, and authoritarian aggression as defining traits of an authoritarian ideology. His work shows how authoritarians want the state to enforce their desire for order, conformity, and homogeneity by force if necessary. Feldman (2003) highlights how authoritarianism re-emerged in the late twentieth century when values of social conformity (authoritarianism) and personal autonomy (liberalism) appeared increasingly in tension to each other. More recently, political science scholarship demonstrates how authoritarianism leads to negative stereotypes of ethnic minorities (Parker and Towler 2019), less support for gay rights and abortion (Barker and Tinnick 2006), less support for welfare recipients deemed fit to work (Blanchet and Landry 2021, Attewell 2021), and increased support for far-right parties (Aichholzer and Zandonella 2016).

As authoritarianism implies a strong law and order approach to ensure conformity with established social norms, it translates into a punitive approach with strong deservingness conceptions in the welfare state domain. In this view, social policy represents a political tool to reward 'hard-working' people as well as conservative gender relations within the nuclear family. As a result, the unemployed and social assistance claimants often get associated with 'lazy freeriders' that are undeserving of welfare support as opposed to pensioners who have demonstrated their willingness to work hard over their lifetime (Afonso and Papadopoulos 2015, Ennser-Jedenastik 2016, Rathgeb 2021a, Attewell 2021, Busemeyer et al. 2022, Chueri 2022).

A long and uninterrupted employment record indicates a willingness to be 'hard-working' in principle, which fosters a perception of deservingness and achievement (Feather 1999, Van Oorschot 2006). Hence, radical right parties cater more to the social demands of labour market insiders than those of labour market outsiders. In policy terms, they should thus be less supportive of welfare entitlements for employees with short and discontinuous employment records who have not yet 'earned' the right to strong state support (labour market outsiders), whereas they are likely to defend the established social insurance rights of workers with long and uninterrupted contribution records (labour market insiders). In a similar vein, the elderly are an obvious group deemed 'deserving' of welfare support, because they can be considered unable to work rather than unwilling to work after a long life of 'hard work'. Moreover, the radical right's preference for a punitive workfare approach to unemployment and social assistance is underpinned by the nativist subtext that the 'lazy freeriders' are mostly immigrants who exploit out-of-work benefits without seeking paid employment (Rathgeb 2021a).

It may be useful to distinguish between 'authoritarianism' and 'producerism' when capturing the radical right's ideological emphasis on the social norm to be 'hard working'. For example, Abts et al. (2021) make a case for arguing that producerism is a more accurate concept to capture the radical right's strong welfare deservingness conceptions. Following Kazin (1995), I define producerism as an ideology stipulating that self-serving groups from both below *and* above the social hierarchy are depriving middle-class citizens of the fruits of their productive work—from below by the welfare entitlements enjoyed by lazy freeriders unwilling to work, and from above by high taxes set by corrupt government elites. As a result, producerism not only refers to harsh deservingness conceptions in social policy; it also promotes a preference for tax cuts in economy policy (cf. Steffek and Lasshoff 2022 on 'productive capitalism'). A producerist ideology may be compelling in country contexts with enduring problems of elite collusion and corruption. For example, the Austrian Freedom Party argued that its policies would help to liberate tax-paying 'makers' from the economic burden imposed by self-serving 'takers' from above (corrupt elites) and below (immigrants) (Rathgeb 2021a). However, cutting taxes across the board is no longer a universally salient feature among radical right parties. By contrast, the concept of authoritarianism captures a preference for the punishment of out-groups perceived to break with the social norm to be 'hard-working' (i.e. the 'takers' from below), but it does not imply a preference for tax cuts to remove power from 'corrupt' government elites (i.e. the 'takers' from above). Moreover, authoritarianism as a conceptual lens has the advantage of identifying how the radical right influences family policies and thus horizontal inequalities in gender relations.

In the area of family policy, authoritarianism endorses conservative gender hierarchies and divisions of labour between men and women, i.e. the role of men should be to operate in the public domain and in full-time employment, while the role of women should be to reconcile (part-time) employment with greater caring responsibilities (Mudde 2007, 93). Akkerman's (2015: 56) analysis of the radical right's party positions on gender issues concludes, '[t]hese parties are the most conservative of all parties', whereas recent liberal frames on gender issues are primarily instrumental to underpin anti-Islam positions. Ennser-Jedenastik (2022) demonstrates how radical right parties in government are associated with a relative increase in social spending on child benefits compared to childcare, which contributes to restore the traditional division of care work between men and women by incentivizing the latter to assume a greater role as caregivers. Following Leitner's (2003) varieties of familialism typology, the radical right should thus be in line with a policy of 'explicit familialism', which aims to strengthen the care capabilities of nuclear families—which in practice means women—by prioritizing monetary family support (child benefits and tax breaks for families) over service support (childcare). The resulting familialism inherent in an authoritarian ideology weakens the economic prospects of working women as it prioritizes traditional hierarchies within the household over gender equality on the labour market. By contrast, a de-familialist policy would prioritize the expansion of childcare services as a way of facilitating equal opportunities in employment and welfare. At the same time, authoritarianism typically opposes greater LGBTQ+ rights while upholding conservative gender and family relations.

To be sure, radical right parties have room for agency and may deviate from such a worldview. For example, the Dutch PVV has developed a strategy labelled 'homonationalism', which describes an acceptance of LGBTQ+ rights as part of what defines a nation, thereby lending further legitimacy to the exclusion of (Muslim) immigrants from non-Western countries (Spierings 2021). Hence, Table 3.1 summarizes the policy implications that result from the deservingness conceptions of a nativist and authoritarian ideology, without producing explicit hypotheses on the party positions of radical right parties across different countries. As I will argue in the next subsection, the similarities and differences in the radical right's actual policy choices in power depend in large part on the welfare state contexts in which they assume power.

The policy implications of nativism and authoritarianism described above have attracted electoral support from white males with lower levels of formal education, especially production workers in the manufacturing sector (Häusermann et al. 2013, Beramendi et al. 2015, Oesch and Rennwald 2018, Häusermann et al. 2022). First, although welfare chauvinism—i.e. selective cuts in social protection targeted at immigrants—does not provide direct material benefits to native workers, it may restore the *relative* social status of previously dominant political groups who have experienced declining economic prospects (Gest 2016, Hochschild 2016, Gidron and Hall 2020). Second, insurance-based pension rights reward the core male workforces—i.e. labour market insiders—who have had long contribution records. The radical right's key electorate may feel threatened in its economic prospects due to deindustrialization and globalization, but it has traditionally had the continuous and uninterrupted employment biographies from which

Table 3.1 The deservingness conceptions of nativism and authoritarianism

Ideology	Deserving groups	Non-deserving groups	Policy implications
Nativism	Natives	Immigrants	Welfare chauvinism, pro-natalism, economic nationalism
Authoritarianism	Labour market insiders	Labour market outsiders	Insurance-based pension rights, elderly care, workfare instead of training-based active labour market policy
	Traditional male breadwinner families	LGBTQ+, working women	Monetary family support (child benefits, tax credits) instead of childcare

it derives relatively generous pension rights (Häusermann 2020). Related to that, production workers tend to display less support for social investment policies than middle-class voters, as they want the welfare state to sustain their current status quo rather than enabling them to find another job through education-related human capital formation (Häusermann et al. 2022). Third, and related to above, the radical right's conservative family policy based on child benefits rather than care stabilizes (or even reinvigorates) traditional gender norms and hierarchies. It is thus no wonder that radical right parties place little emphasis on social investment policies because they imply claims to greater social mobility and progressive gender values (Busemeyer et al. 2022). Taken together, the radical right primarily protects the ability of the 'deserving' core (male) workforce to protect themselves and their families from income losses when out of work—akin to what Häusermann (2012) calls 'old social policies' (earnings-related social insurance, child benefits) as opposed to 'new social policies' (social investment, inclusive welfare coverage for new social risk groups). As a result, the radical right does not primarily cater to those already 'left behind' by structural shifts in the economy; it responds to the *fear* rather than the *outcome* of economic decline among previously well-protected groups.

The above discussion makes clear that the perceived decline in social status among radical right voters (Engler and Weisstanner 2021, Gidron and Hall 2017, Kurer and Palier 2019, Kurer 2020) does not necessarily turn them into a political force against increasing levels of inequality, poverty, and precarity. In fact, more than fifty years ago, Lipset (1959) observed how economic insecurity can activate authoritarian predispositions rather than an opposition to the socially corrosive effects of austerity and liberalization. The policy preferences of radical right voters must therefore be placed in the broader historical context about the intimate relationship between the rise of authoritarianism and the demise of (neo-)liberalism (Polanyi 1944 [2001]). Recent studies underline how the socioculturally laden ideological features of the radical right can inform their socio-economic policies beyond the issues of immigration, law and order, and crime prevention (Ennser-Jedenastik 2016, Rathgeb 2021a, Busemeyer et al. 2022, Rathgeb and Busemeyer 2022, Chueri 2022). Despite these findings about how ideological values can shape social and economic policy preferences, there is little, if any, research on cross-national *variation* in the resulting impacts on national models of capitalism and welfare. In the next section, I will therefore theorize how different welfare state contexts mediate the radical right's policy preferences in shaping diverse policy choices in office.

Policy impacts: The role of welfare state contexts

While the radical right shares a similar ideology of nativism and authoritarianism, it also pursues widely different policy choices in government. To explain variations in policy impact we have to recognize the diverse welfare state contexts in which radical right parties have come to power. Drawing on comparative political economy and welfare state research, I distinguish between the conservative Continental European regime, the social democratic Northern European regime, the liberal American regime, and the post-communist Visegrád regime (Esping-Andersen 1990, Bohle and Greskovits 2012, Thelen 2014, Beramendi et al. 2015, Manow et al. 2018). My focus is on these four political-economic contexts. The Southern European welfare regime shares affinities with the Continental European welfare state context due to its heavy reliance on insider-oriented social insurance systems and pronounced male breadwinner legacies (Guillén et al. 2022), but in these countries the radical left has been in office more often than the radical right (Manow 2018, Hopkin 2020).[1] In what follows, I will discuss how these four diverse models provide different sets of opportunities and constraints for radical right parties in legislating a nativist-authoritarian agenda.

On the one hand, the *authoritarian* preference for familialism and against LGBTQ+ rights is likely to receive greater levels of political support in countries with conservative gender relations and family policies. It is difficult to conceive that the radical right would pursue a familialist policy regardless of the domestic preference structures in the broader electorate. For example, the entrenchment of a more gender egalitarian dual career model is likely to cut off political support for a conservative family policy in the Nordic welfare state context. In a similar vein, the authoritarian valorization of 'hard work' at the expense of labour market outsiders is easier to realize in mature welfare states where labour market insiders have traditionally enjoyed access to generous benefit entitlements.

On the other hand, the *nativist* preference for putting 'our own people first' may activate different policy reactions to globalization. As national societies are exposed to globalization in diverse ways, these policies have also taken very different forms in different welfare state contexts. In generous welfare states with high levels of immigration, the radical right is likely to prioritize a policy of welfare chauvinism to reserve social rights for native citizens.

---

[1] Italy is an exception in this regard, as the radical right Lega has been in a coalition government with the populist *Movimento Cinque Stelle* (M5S) from 2017 to 2019 (Rathgeb and Hopkin 2023). I will therefore use Italy as a shadow case study in Chapter 4.

By contrast, high levels of dependence on foreign direct investment (FDI) can promote an economic nationalism that favours domestic businesses at the expense of foreign-owned companies, whereas recurring current account deficits can stimulate a nationalist turn in trade relations on behalf of domestic industries. In other words, the nativist mirror image of welfare chauvinism may be economic nationalism and trade protectionism. The following discussion emphasizes how different preference structures in the electorate and exposures to globalization are crucial in promoting different varieties of radical right policy impact.

(1) Chauvinist and familialist insider protection in Continental Europe

The *Continental European context* features generous earnings-related social insurance systems and used to place the family at the centre of the welfare mix between state, market, and family. Hence, it stratified by gender and occupation by reproducing labour market inequalities into the welfare system. As these countries represent manufacturing-dominated export-led growth models, they have provided industrial male breadwinners and their employers with a pivotal economic and political position, which helped to entrench earnings-related social insurance systems and conservative gender norms (Hassel and Palier 2021).

With the demise of the so-called 'golden age', the Continental European regime faced sluggish employment rates due to high non-wage labour costs, which in turn called into question the fiscal viability of social insurance systems, also known as the 'welfare without work' problem. In response, governments liberalized labour markets and welfare systems for non-standard workers while leaving prevailing protections for the core (male) workforce largely in place (Palier and Thelen 2010, Emmenegger et al. 2012, Thelen 2014). Although this policy path enhanced employment rates in the low-value-added service sector, it reinforced inequalities between labour market insiders in relatively well-protected full-time jobs on the one hand, and labour market outsiders in precarious jobs or out of work on the other. The result was a new social cleavage across the political economy: a dual labour market, a dual welfare system, and a society even more divided between insiders and outsiders than it was before (Palier 2021: 841).

The radical right's key constituency of production workers has retained a relatively well-protected position in this welfare state context, as it typically displays long and uninterrupted employment biographies that provide high levels of job and social security. However, governments have gradually attempted to incorporate the social demands of new social risk groups outside the industrial core workforce. First, the expansion of public childcare arrangements aimed to reconcile work–family life for working women, as the male breadwinner model seemed no longer viable in a context of increasing female employment and the demise of the Fordist family wage (Naumann 2012). However, there is still considerable cross-national variation with respect to the prevalence of childcare arrangements, with higher levels of public provision in Belgium, France, and the Netherlands compared to the German-speaking countries. This variation may well influence the degree to which radical right parties push for gender-conservative family policies.

Second, governments retrenched early retirement options and long-term unemployment benefits to rein in public debt, but also to create fiscal leeway for social investment reforms (Ebbinghaus 2006, Manow and Schwander 2017). The emergence of new social risks—work–family reconciliation for working women as well as in-work poverty and insufficient benefit entitlements for labour market outsiders—has therefore received increased attention among governments, especially those on the left. However, the post-industrial paradigm of social investment catered primarily to the new middle class, whereas production workers typically prefer status protection in their current job rather than the prospect of a new job thanks to social investments in human capital formation (Williams 2017: Ch. 10).

At the same time, these countries have seen growing immigration rates, which the radical right could use to 'culturalize' distributive conlict. Due to their inclusive design of social assistance and healthcare arrangements, the Continental European political economies provide relatively generous minimum benefits to foreign newcomers. This context of high levels of immigration coupled with high levels of social security for non-citizens is likely to stimulate a nativist reaction against globalization in the form of welfare chauvinism. By contrast, nativist values are unlikely to promote policies of economic nationalism in Continental Europe, because these growth models typically benefit from export surpluses that help to generate fiscal resources for the insider-oriented benefits from which the voters of the radical right have benefited disproportionally (Hassel and Palier 2021, Baccaro and Höpner 2022).

Taken together, we may expect from the Continental European radical right a combination of defending insider protection and male breadwinner policies on the one hand (authoritarianism), and welfare chauvinist cuts targeted at non-citizens on the other (nativism). In essence, the radical right's policy impact here is conservative in nature, as it aims to uphold institutional legacies inherited from the past, while blocking immigrants and other new risk groups from gaining access to welfare entitlements.

(2) Chauvinist insider protection in Northern Europe

The *Northern European context* also features generous social insurance systems whose earnings-related character have been strengthened in the wake of fiscal strains and economic crises. Unlike in Continental Europe, however, the Northern European social insurance systems go hand in hand with large-scale efforts towards social investment in education and work–family reconciliation, leading to relatively large public sectors. Despite growing social divides in employment and welfare, this welfare state context has managed to hold together an electoral coalition of new middle-class and low-wage service workers on the one hand (pro social investment and redistribution), and production workers in manufacturing on the other (pro social insurance and insider benefits), which was facilitated by encompassing unionization rates. Overall, the Northern European growth model relies on high levels of social investment that underwrite knowledge-intensive manufacturing *and* services while securing the public sector a larger share in the economy at the same time (Hassel and Palier 2021).

Most importantly in our context, the Northern European dual-earner model deviates from the Continental European male breadwinner legacy. Whereas Continental European countries relied on foreign labour ('guest workers') to meet growing labour demand in the booming post-war economy, Northern European countries mobilized women to enter wage labour by expanding public childcare arrangements (Huber and Stephens 2001, Bonoli 2007). The earlier labour market entry of women had entrenched the dual-career model long before radical right parties came close to power in the early twenty-first century (ibid.). With the absence of conservative family relations, a resurgence of political demands for a conservative family policy becomes less feasible in political terms.

In other words, the authoritarian preference for traditional gender relations and hierarchies lacks electoral support in this context, such that radical right parties are unlikely to mobilize on such an agenda. This should therefore be a major difference between the policy impacts of Continental European and Northern European radical right parties. While the Northern welfare state context is likely to prevent familialist policies aiming to re-traditionalize gender relations, it does display insider-oriented welfare entitlements and pro-elderly policy arrangements the radical right very much supports, including for example early retirement arrangements for blue-collar workers with long contribution records. Hence, the radical right is likely to prioritize insider-oriented and pro-elderly policies as a matter of deservingness, while paying less attention to social investment areas that are crucial to this growth model.

The Northern European welfare state context is vulnerable to welfare chauvinism in the context of growing immigration rates because its benefit arrangements are very generous and inclusive to the margins of the (non-native) labour force. Figure 3.1 shows the increasing average share of foreign citizens in Continental and Northern Europe in comparison to the Visegrád region. As the Northern European countries relied more on the recruitment of female labour than foreign labour in the booming post-war economy, they have overall lower levels of foreign citizens than Continental European countries (see Figure 3.1). Whereas nativism translates into welfare chauvinism in the high-immigration and high-welfare contexts of Continental and Northern Europe, it is more likely to promote mobilizations against ethnic minorities in the low-immigration contexts of Eastern Europe (Bustikova 2019) and white supremacy in the racialized low-welfare context of the USA (Belew 2022).

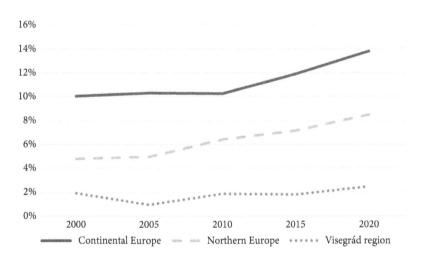

Figure 3.1 Average share of foreign citizens in Continental Europe, Northern Europe, and the Visegrád region, 2000–2020.

Notes: Five-year intervals of the following country clusters: Continental Europe (Austria, Belgium, France, Germany, the Netherlands, and Switzerland); Northern Europe (Denmark, Finland, Norway, and Sweden); Visegrád region (Czech Republic, Hungary, Poland, and Slovakia)

Source: Eurostat (2023)

The reliance on a highly skilled and specialized workforce in the Northern European context, underpinned by strong social investment in human capital formation, complicates the integration of low-skilled foreign newcomers into the labour market (Boräng 2018). This provides the ideal breeding ground for the politicization of immigration along welfare chauvinist lines. In contrast, nativism should not lead to the contestation of economic openness to foreign goods or foreign businesses. Similar to Continental Europe, their small open economies overall benefit from trade-related globalization, and their generous welfare systems compensate those who lose out from economic competition at the same time (Katzenstein 1985). As a result, we would expect from the Northern European radical right an insider-oriented and pro-elderly welfare policy in tandem with pronounced welfare chauvinism (similar to Continental Europe), but without strong backing for a conservative family policy (dissimilar to Continental Europe).

(3) Familialist protection and economic nationalism in the Visegrád regime

The *Visegrád context* of 'embedded neoliberalism' deviates from the Continental and Northern European contexts in a number of ways (Bohle and Greskovits 2012: Ch. 4). First, while these countries have relied on relatively generous early retirement arrangements to compensate the losers of the post-communist transition process, their welfare states overall remained much less generous and inclusive than those in Continental and Northern Europe (Vanhuysse 2006, Cerami and Vanhuysse 2009). In fact, fiscal overspending in response to the social costs of post-communist transition called into question the sustainability of generous pension insurances for labour market insiders. As a result, the expansion of insider-oriented pension rights such as early retirement might be complicated by fiscal constraints in shrinking and ageing societies. Second, and related to that, these countries have faced emigration rather than immigration (Krastev 2017). We may thus expect that low immigration rates reduce demands for welfare chauvinist legislation, which contrasts with the Continental and Northern European countries that are characterized by higher immigration rates and generous welfare states.

However, the problem of demographic decline may translate a nativist ideology into a pro-natalist and conservative family policy. Already during communist rule, Central and Eastern European (CEE) countries placed emphasis on family policy to facilitate ethno-nationalist state-building (Rat and Szikra 2018). With the fall of communism, the Visegrád countries strengthened their Bismarckian roots of social insurance–based welfare systems, which had originated from their membership in the Habsburg Empire before the First World War (Aspalter et al. 2009). Survey analyses from Kulin and Meulemann (2015) suggest that the communist legacy of what Claus Offe called 'authoritarian egalitarianism' has contributed to the restoration of conservative as opposed to universalist welfare state values. This may explain why gender-mainstreaming initiatives and gender equality legislation from the EU lacked political support in the new member states of the former Soviet Union (Szelewa and Polakowski 2022). In this context, the authoritarian preference for traditional gender relations should find strong political support, leading to a policy of pro-natalist (nativist) and conservative (authoritarian) familialism. As Tables 3.2 and 3.3 show, such an approach seems to be in line with electoral majorities.

Table 3.2 shows that support for the dual care model is lowest among respondents of the Visegrád region, which contrasts heavily with public opinion in Northern Europe. More than 60 per cent of respondents in the four Visegrád countries state that mothers should take over paid parental leave for children entirely, whereas this figure is at less than 4 per cent in the Northern European countries. The numbers for Continental Europe and the USA are somewhat in between these two regions. A similar picture of pronounced variations emerges when we shift our focus to Table 3.3 on the question of how preschool childcare should be arranged.

More than 60 per cent of respondents in the Visegrád region prefer family-based ('familialist') arrangements, whereas in Northern Europe, more than 70 per cent of respondents prefer public government-funded childcare arrangements. Again, Continental Europe and the USA are somewhat in

Table 3.2 Public opinion on family policy: What is the ideal division of paid leave between parents (percentage)?

	Continental Europe	Northern Europe	Visegrád region	USA
Mother entire, father not any	19.1	3.8	61.6	32.4
Mother most, father some	38.5	45.9	23.8	30.4
Mother and father half	42	49.8	14.1	36.7
Other	0.5	0.5	0.5	0.6

Notes: Continental Europe: Austria, Belgium, France, Germany, and the Netherlands. Northern Europe: Denmark, Finland, Norway, and Sweden. Visegrád region: Czech Republic, Hungary, Poland, and Slovakia.
Source: ISSP 2012 (2016)

Table 3.3 Public opinion on family policy: Who should be the primary provider of care for preschool-age children (percentage)?

	Continental Europe	Northern Europe	Visegrád countries	USA
Family members	45.3	14.2	62.2	56.5
Government agencies	22.6	72.2	32.8	7.8
Private/non-profit care	28	12.9	4.25	28.8
Other	4.1	0.6	0.8	6.9

Notes: Continental Europe: Austria, Belgium, France, Germany, and the Netherlands. Northern Europe: Denmark, Finland, Norway, and Sweden. Visegrád region: Czech Republic, Hungary, Poland, and Slovakia.
Source: ISSP 2012 (2016)

between these two regions, with larger support for state-provided childcare in the former compared to the latter. However, it is interesting to observe that on this question—preschool childcare—public support for familialism in Continental Europe and the USA is closer to the numbers found in the Visegrád region than those found in Northern Europe. The Continental European and American legacies of the male breadwinner model may thus have an enduring influence on public opinion (Leitner 2003). Notwithstanding, the data clearly suggest that a pro-natalist and conservative family policy expansion is likely to receive most support in the Visegrád region, whereas the opposite is the case in Northern Europe. Therefore, in the Visegrád region, the social protection of labour market insiders and male breadwinners is likely to take the form of familialist protection by supporting the ability of male core workers to sustain themselves and their families.

In economic policy terms, the Visegrád countries can be considered dependent market economies in which economic growth relies in large part on FDI and strong ties to the German production model (Nölke and Vliegenthart 2009, Bohle and Greskovits 2012, Ban and Adascalitei 2022). Low immigration rates in a less generous welfare state may preclude the legislation of welfare chauvinist measures, but nativism has different implications in the Visegrád region's foreign-led capitalism. In the 1990s and 2000s, these countries managed to 'build capitalism without capitalists' (Eyal et al. 2002) by attracting growing shares of FDI and foreign currency loans from Western Europe and North America. However, the global financial crisis exposed the vulnerability of these economies to their structural dependence on Western banks and sudden stops in capital inflows. Unlike in Western Europe where nativism stimulated opposition to the cross-border movement of people (welfare chauvinism), this region has faced economic vulnerabilities from the cross-border movement of capital (economic nationalism). In this context, we can expect nativism to shift the costs of economic adjustment onto foreign businesses rather than foreign welfare claimants. At the same time, post-communist countries may face structural limits in the extent to which they can sustain high levels of economic growth without relying on the large-scale attraction of foreign capital (Ban and Adascalitei 2022). Taken together, this welfare state context creates opportunities for the authoritarian preference for a conservative family policy expansion while the vulnerabilities of its FDI-led growth model may stimulate a nativist reaction against its strong dependence on Western multinational companies.

(4) Trade protection in the USA

The *American context* lacks generous (public) welfare states and family sup-port systems. Its welfare state follows a pronounced deservingness logic by providing pension insurance benefits in favour of labour market insiders (Social Security) and national healthcare for the elderly (Medicare), whereas social safety nets for the working-age population and especially poorer fam-ilies have been massively retrenched and made more punitive over time (Waddan 2014). The corresponding insistence on deservingness reflects the radical right's preferred logic of social policy provision, but America's wel-fare state does not encompass the working-age population at large, as it focuses on the protection of the elderly more exclusively. Financial deregula-tion was a way to substitute state- and employer-provided benefits with easier access to private financial instruments as a way of allowing, or in fact com-pelling, lower-income citizens to take out loans at their own risk with which to pay for their education or housing as potential sources of future prosperity ('privatized Keynesianism') (Crouch 2009). To compensate for the declining scope and generosity of America's social insurance, *private* social expendi-ture increased and eventually surpassed all OECD countries, whereas *public* social expenditure remained below the OECD average, especially for younger and poorer citizens (OECD stats). Taken together, employer-based and pri-vate welfare arrangements thus play a much more important role than in Europe's welfare states.

We may expect that the radical right would *not* expand public welfare arrangements for labour market insiders or traditional families in this con-text. Unlike in the European welfare states, a (white) nativist ideology rein-forces the long-standing 'racialization' of American social policy, whereby white workers traditionally benefited from their integration into social insurance (Lieberman 2001) and homeownership programmes (Thurston 2018), whereas black Americans—then as now disproportionately poor— relied on decentralized, often racially charged, social assistance programmes (Michener 2018). Survey analyses suggest that US whites are indeed more likely to support spending cuts for working-age benefits when they hold negative attitudes about African Americans and Latino immigrants (Spies 2018). At the same time, middle-class families are typically against tax increases as they are invested in *private* social programmes as opposed to *public* social welfare (Lynch 2014). By implication, the authoritarian impetus to reward traditional male breadwinner families through a conservative family policy expansion faces political and fiscal limits. Moreover, welfare chauvinism is likely to be less prominent in America due to the lack of generous welfare entitlements for foreign newcomers, which contrasts with the Western European welfare states.

I argue that trade protection may turn into a *functional equivalent* of social protection in this context, because it aims to protect the incomes of threatened labour market insiders and male breadwinners by other means than social policy, namely limits to foreign economic competition. Nativism may therefore turn against the trade-related impact of globalization, given that America has suffered from chronic current account deficits, which has affected the job security of American manufacturing workers (Autor et al. 2013). Figure 3.2 shows that the USA has had chronic current account deficits since the early 1980s, as it absorbed excess savings and profits from abroad, especially from Western Europe and China, at the expense of domestic production (Klein and Pettis 2020). By contrast, the Continental and Northern European economies have achieved on average persistent current account surpluses thanks to positive net exports with the opening of world markets, whereas the Visegrád region had large current account deficits by importing large shares of (Western) capital from abroad during the post-communist transition process. Unlike in the USA, the Visegrád region's economic convergence with Western Europe helped to improve the current account.

From a demand-side perspective, the US dollar's status as the global reserve currency has led to enormous capital imports from abroad, which push up the value of the dollar (thus hurting export competitiveness) and provide cheap credits for working- and lower-middle-class citizens as well as huge financial profits for high-income elites (thus increasing economic inequality) (Klein and Pettis 2020, Reisenbichler and Wiedemann 2022). The fallout of chronic current account deficits has been the loss of factory jobs to China and Europe at the expense of American manufacturing workers. From a

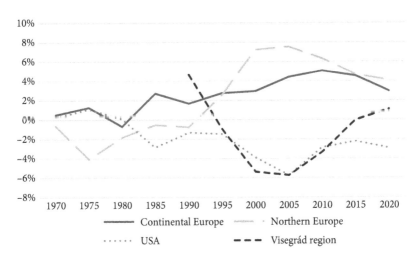

Figure 3.2 Average current account balances in Continental Europe, Northern Europe, the USA, and the Visegrád region measured in percentage of GDP.

Notes: Five-year intervals of the following country clusters: Continental Europe (Austria, Belgium, France, Germany, the Netherlands, and Switzerland); Northern Europe (Denmark, Finland, Norway, and Sweden); and Visegrád region (Czech Republic, Hungary, Poland, and Slovakia)
Source: World Bank (2023a)

supply-side perspective, America's lack of investment in vocational training and active labour market policy made US manufacturing vulnerable to low-cost competitors from emerging economies, whereas higher levels of industry-specific specialization and skill formation have made Europe's manufacturing bases more resilient to international economic competition (Iversen and Stephens 2008).

Taken together, whereas insider-oriented benefit expansion and familialist policies are likely to attract less political support in the USA than in Europe, we may assume that chronic trade deficits, especially vis-à-vis rivalling China, turns the nativist focus of putting 'our own people first' towards a policy of trade protection as opposed to social protection. This argument draws on previous insights about how America's lack of a European-style welfare state has traditionally reduced political support for high levels of foreign trade (Rieger and Leibfried 2003: Ch. 3). By contrast, generous welfare arrangements made Continental and Northern European economies susceptible to a different nativist reaction to globalization, namely welfare chauvinism. Despite this diversity in policy instruments, trade protectionism in the American context caters to a similar group of voters, i.e. threatened labour market insiders and male breadwinners in declining economic sectors. Table 3.4 summarizes my theoretical expectations about how different welfare state

Table 3.4 Welfare state contexts and varieties of radical right policy impact

		Welfare state generosity	
		Strong	Weak
Family conservatism	**Strong**	Chauvinist and familialist insider protection (Conservative regime)	Familialist protection (Visegrád regime)
	Weak	Chauvinist insider protection (Social democratic regime)	Trade protection (USA)

contexts mediate an ideology of nativism and authoritarianism in the policy choices of the radical right.

The Continental European context stimulates the radical right to defend the relatively privileged status of labour market insiders and male breadwinners through old-age protection, welfare chauvinism, and familialism; a policy approach that can be termed *chauvinist and familialist insider protection*. The Northern European context also promotes an insider-biased social policy and an even more pronounced welfare chauvinism, but without strong support for monetary family support due to the absence of conservative family policy legacies, which amounts to *chauvinist insider protection*. The Visegrád context allows for expansive family policies that underpin conservative family relations, but fiscal strains may complicate the establishment of Western European–style insider-oriented benefit arrangements while low levels of immigration cut off demand for welfare chauvinism. However, the reliance on Western FDI may promote a nativist reaction against foreign economic dependence in favour of the domestic business classes. Hence, we would expect the radical right to push for a policy of *familialist protection* alongside economic nationalism. By contrast, in the USA, *trade protection*—i.e. limits to foreign economic competition—can be geared towards 'deserving' citizens as a functional equivalent of social protection.

Case selection and method

To examine the argument outlined above, I compare the social and economic policy choices of radical right parties in Austria (Continental Europe), Denmark (Northern Europe), Hungary (Visegrád region), and the USA. I selected these countries because they capture cases in which the radical right has assumed the longest periods of government responsibility within the four respective regions described above. This way I ensure an empirically observable policy influence across different policy areas. The Austrian FPÖ was in coalition governments from 2000 to 2006 and from 2017 to 2019 with the Christian democratic-conservative Austrian People's Party ÖVP.[2] The Danish DF was the pivotal support party for a centre-right minority government from 2001 to 2011 and from 2015 to 2019. The Hungarian Fidesz party and its satellite Christian Democratic People's Party (KDNP) have formed a majority government since 2010, whereas the Trump administration was in power from 2016 until 2020. These primary case studies will be supplemented with secondary case studies: the German AfD and Italian *Lega* (compared to the Austrian FPÖ), the Norwegian FrP and Swedish SD (compared to Danish DF), and the Polish PiS (compared to Hungarian Fidesz). If my argument were correct, we should observe similar policy choices within a particular welfare regime from those radical right parties who assumed office (i.e. *Lega*, FrP, PiS) or the absence of such policy influence when radical right parties did not come to power (i.e. AfD, SD).

Investigating policy choices in office allows me to identify the radical right's direct influence on public policies as well as their priorities developed over time when faced with strategic trade-offs in the policymaking process. Drawing on Korpi (2006), I will distinguish between reforms in which the radical right has been either a 'consenter' or 'protagonist' in coalition governments (Rathgeb and Klitgaard 2022). Consenters initially voice concerns over policies initiated by other parties and demand compensations in return for parliamentary support. By contrast, protagonists initiate a policy through agenda-setting and thus achieve their first-order preference once it is legislated. In the cases of Austria and Denmark, we would thus expect the radical right to be a protagonist behind insider-oriented pension policies, but only in Austria should the radical right be a protagonist of expanding monetary family support at the same time (i.e. child benefits, tax breaks for families). In Hungary and the USA, the radical right has formed single-party majority governments, which allows me to identify the radical right's policy choices without paying attention to underlying negotiations between coalition partners.

To enhance the validity of my argument, I first address competing hypotheses by analysing the electoral class compositions of radical right parties through survey data. Let us recall that the 'position-blurring view' expects a divided electoral coalition between small shop owners (right-wing) and blue-collar workers (left-wing) to cause a blurry positioning and thus little

---

[2] As Switzerland represents a mixture between a liberal and conservative welfare regime, I select the Austrian FPÖ rather than the Swiss SVP as the primary case for the conservative Continental European regime (Esping-Andersen 1990).

impact on national models of capitalism and welfare. By contrast, the 'pro-welfare view' expects growing working-class support to cause a redistributive pro-welfare impact. When the actual policy choices of radical right parties are inconsistent with the predictions of these two competing hypotheses, I move on to develop my own argument about how welfare state contexts mediate the ideologically derived policy preferences of radical right parties once in power.

In the empirical chapters, I first present evidence from secondary case studies to underscore that nativism and authoritarianism constitute the core ideology of the radical right in a given country. I then show how these ideological features translate into distributive policy choices that correspond with the expectations outlined above. My argument would expect the radical right to justify their policy choices on nativist-authoritarian grounds as outlined in Table 3.1. To capture how radical right parties legitimize their policy choices, I rely on speeches, parliamentary debates, and official party documents. I used direct quotes when they illustrated the radical right's core rationale for their policy choice. The Austrian case study (Chapter 4) relies in large part on data collected for two previous research articles (Rathgeb 2021a, Rathgeb and Gruber-Risak 2021). For the Danish case study (Chapter 5), I draw on official party documents published from 1998 until 2021, with a particular focus on speeches from party leaders at annual party conventions, short policy papers (*Principprogram*), and extensive working papers from the party's parliamentary group (*Arbejdsprogram*). In the Hungarian case, I focused on Orbán's Annual State of the Nation speeches to capture how his government evaluates previous policy choices and sets the tone for future policy projects. By contrast, party manifestoes have become less comprehensive and policy-focussed after the 2010 election. In addition, I rely on parliamentary debates in the National Assembly to capture the legitimization strategies of the Fidesz–KDNP government on specific social and economic policy choices. For the American case (Chapter 7), I rely on primary sources consisting mainly of speeches by Donald Trump prior to and during his presidency (2015–2021). As the 2016 and 2020 Republican election manifestoes are identical (i.e. the party released the same platform for both elections), I pay greater attention to Trump's speeches and written remarks than the GOP's manifestoes.

I used primarily public opinion data and macroeconomic indicators to show how different welfare state contexts create diverse opportunities and constraints for radical right parties in legislating a policy of status protection in favour of social groups considered 'deserving'. For example, I look at attitudes on foreign trade in the wake of America's growing trade deficit to substantiate my claim about how trade protection can be a functional equivalent of social protection for 'deserving' (but threatened) labour market insiders in America's racialized and market-based welfare state context. In the Hungarian case, I emphasize how the economic fallout of the global financial crisis complicated the maintenance of insider-oriented early retirement options and put strong external constraints on domestic policymaking autonomy, whereas conservative attitudes in the broader electorate facilitated familialist policies under the Orbán cabinet. In the Danish case, I show how a booming economy helped the DF to avoid difficult distributive policy choices in the 2000s, whereas in the face of the global financial crisis, it supported cuts for the unemployed while prioritizing the benefit and service entitlements of the more 'deserving' elderly and labour market insiders throughout. In the Austrian case, we can see how the FPÖ aimed to protect these groups from fiscal austerity in similar ways, but the conservative legacies of the country's male breadwinner model and related attitudes in public opinion were conducive to a more familialist policy impact. I am indebted to Patricia Rodi and Anna KissPal for their research assistance in the data collection process.

4

Chauvinist and Familialist Insider Protection in Continental Europe

Austria used to receive international attention when the Freedom Party of Austria (FPÖ) gained electoral success and public office. In a small state context of high political and economic stability (Katzenstein 1985), the party's conversion into a pioneer of the European populist radical right proved to be a source of recurring disruption for Austria's political establishment. From 1986 to 1999, the FPÖ increased its vote share from 5 to almost 27 per cent in general elections. The subsequent government formation with the Christian democratic/conservative People's Party of Austria (ÖVP) stimulated a wave of street demonstrations, international protests, and even diplomatic sanctions imposed by the fourteen EU partners—all very unusual in Austria's consensus democracy. Although the FPÖ imploded around internal conflicts in the 2002 election, it recovered its vote share back to 26 per cent in 2017, leading to the formation of another coalition government with the ÖVP. This time, however, the party's entry in office was met with little, if any, domestic or international political outcry. On the contrary, the FPÖ, it seems, has become a mainstreamed party in a historical context characterized by the rise of similar nativist-authoritarian parties across the world (Mudde 2019: Ch. 2).

The FPÖ is an interesting case not only because it has been relatively successful in electoral terms and therefore entered government twice; it is also a prototypical case of the so-called 'proletarization' of the radical right (Betz 1993). According to the 'pro-welfare hypothesis' described in Chapter 2 (e.g. Eger and Valdez 2015, Lefkofridi and Michel 2017, Afonso and Rennwald 2018), the FPÖ should have had a strong electoral incentive to shift to the left on the economy as a way of catering to its sizeable working-class base. As Figure 4.1 shows, the share of production workers within the FPÖ's electorate hovered between 25 and 44 per cent and the share of service workers between 14 and 32 per cent from 2002 until 2019.[1] Two thirds of its voters

---

[1] Both surveys—AUTNES and ESS—contain ISCO-codes, which I transformed into Oesch's eight-class schema (2006). Unlike AUTNES, the ESS also contains information on the occupation of the respondent's

How the Radical Right Has Changed Capitalism and Welfare in Europe and the USA. Philip Rathgeb, Oxford University Press.
© Philip Rathgeb (2024). DOI: 10.1093/oso/9780192866332.003.0004

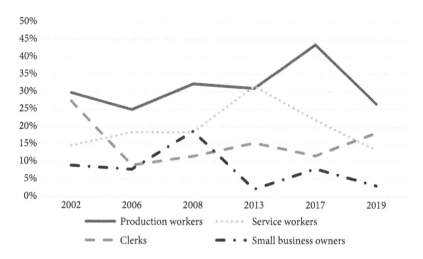

Figure 4.1 Share of votes from production workers, service workers, clerks, and small business owners within the FPÖ's electorate, 2002–2019 (percentages).

Sources: ESS (2002, 2006, 2008, 2014, 2020) for 2002–2013 and 2019 elections, Aichholzer et al. (2018) for 2017 election.

had been production and service workers before the party entered government for its second time in 2017. In addition, office clerks, often counted as working-class voters too (Afonso and Rennwald 2018, Häusermann et al. 2022), make up another sizeable group within the FPÖ's electorate. By contrast, the share of small business owners stayed below 10 per cent throughout, except for the 2008 election. While the electoral support base of radical right parties often rests on two electoral strongholds with diverse socio-economic policy preferences—production workers and small business owners (Ivarsflaten 2005)—the 'proletarization' of the FPÖ's electoral composition should make this tension less acute.

Yet, despite such strong working-class support, the FPÖ's policy impact was by no means pro-welfare in a redistributive sense. Austria's radical right catered more specifically to the social demands of labour market insiders by prioritizing generous social insurance rights and monetary family support, whereas it paid little attention to new social risk groups, including women (i.e. lone parenthood and work–family reconciliation), the young (i.e. temporary employment), and the low-skilled (i.e. long-term unemployment).

partner as well as ISCO-codes of the last job the respondent's partner had. For unemployed and retired respondents, I used the class position of the last job. I used the partner's class position when the respondent's class position was still missing—i.e. the respondent never had a job—and the partner lives in the same household. I excluded respondents who were not in work when the data were collected or refused to give an answer. Data is weighted.

In essence, the FPÖ in government defended the social rights of the (male) core workforce while retrenching those of immigrants and sustaining male breadwinner legacies, a policy combination that may be termed *chauvinist and familialist insider protection.*

Understanding this policy combination requires detailed attention to the conservative welfare state context. As Continental European countries have experienced relatively high levels of immigration, the radical right's *nativism* promotes a welfare chauvinism that reduces the benefit entitlements of immigrants and thereby helps to defend traditional social hierarchies between the native core workforce and non-native precarious fringes. The radical right's ideology of *authoritarianism* also underpins a policy of status protection on behalf of labour market insiders. The long and uninterrupted employment biographies of labour market insiders indicate not only a willingness to be 'hard-working' in principle, which fosters a perception of deservingness and achievement in an authoritarian worldview (Feather 1999); it also characterizes the contribution records of blue-collar workers, who typically constitute the radical right's electoral stronghold (Häusermann et al. 2013: 229; see also Häusermann 2020). The radical right thus defends the established social insurance rights of labour market insiders, while disregarding the welfare entitlements of labour market outsiders with short and interrupted employment patterns. At the same time, the radical right's authoritarianism implies political support for the conservative legacies of the male breadwinner model, i.e. child benefits and tax breaks for families that help to sustain conservative family relations and gender hierarchies, characterized by full-time employment for men and part-time employment with caring responsibilities for women.

The FPÖ's ideological preference for a chauvinist and familialist insider protection draws on regime-specific support coalitions. In the Continental European context, industrial male breadwinners and their employers have traditionally enjoyed a pivotal electoral position, which entrenched earnings-related social insurance systems and conservative gender norms in the long run (Beramendi et al. 2015, Manow et al. 2018). For example, survey results suggest that Austrian citizens are significantly more likely to prefer a gendered distribution of parental leave than Swedish citizens (Valarino et al. 2018), albeit conservative attitudes are even more pronounced in the post-communist countries of Eastern Europe (Pongracz 2005; see Chapter 6). At the same time, the open and universal design of social assistance and family benefits facilitated the successful politicization of the welfare state along chauvinist lines (Ennser-Jedenastik 2018). In other welfare state contexts, radical right parties are likely to use other policy instruments to reward the 'deserving' core workforce, as they may face little public support for familial-ism (Northern Europe, Chapter 5) or little fiscal space for insider protection (Eastern Europe, Chapter 6), or middle-class preferences for private rather than public social protection arrangements (USA, Chapter 7).

While the Austrian story of the radical right is in part a more general one about similar nativist-authoritarian parties in conservative welfare states, it is also a specific one about a challenger party using neoliberal economic policies to disrupt a cartelized political establishment. A core feature of the Austrian political system is the close institutional and personal linkage between the social democratic SPÖ and Christian democratic/conservative ÖVP on the one hand, and the social partner camps from the labour and employer side on the other. Given its outsider status in this system of corporatist power sharing, the FPÖ has retained an anti-corporatist and anti-labour position that informs demands for attacks on union power and cuts in tax rates. Austria's enduring problems of clientelism, party patron-age, and corruption are thus important contextual features to understand how the FPÖ's chauvinist and familialist insider protection has gone hand in hand with recurring neoliberal demands for tax cuts and trade union disempowerment, portrayed as efforts to disempower 'corrupt elites' in the interest of the 'common man'. Ironically enough, the FPÖ itself failed in gov-ernment around corruption plans in the wake of the so-called Ibiza affair in 2019.

This chapter proceeds as follows. First, it briefly reconstructs the histori-cal origins and ideological legacies of the FPÖ, before analysing the political and economic context in which the party challenged the SPÖ and ÖVP in the 1990s. I then analyse the programmatic development and policy choices of the FPÖ when entering government with the ÖVP. The chapter pays partic-ular attention to how the FPÖ justified its policies in order to show how the party geared its ideology of nativism and authoritarianism to the Continen-tal European welfare state context, leading to a policy approach of *chauvinist and familialist insider protection*. A final section concludes.

The national-liberal roots of the Freedom Party

Traditionally coined the 'Third Camp' (*Das Dritte Lager*) in Austrian politics, the FPÖ was founded in 1956 as a pan-German, anti-Marxist, anti-clerical, and libertarian political party with roots dating back to the nineteenth cen-tury. Its predecessor, the VdU (*Verband der Unabhängigen*, 1949–1956), had already positioned itself as a counterweight to Austria's two historical major parties. In this way, the VdU aimed to reintegrate those former Nazis (*Ehemalige*), who had already joined the NSDAP when it was still an illegal political movement, into Austria's emerging post-war democracy (Reiter 2019). However, the party's market-liberal orientation under Herbert Kraus and Viktor Reimann caused looming tensions with its nationalist wing rooted in the pan-German movement. The subsequent formation of the FPÖ was thus an attempt to reconcile the internal contradictions within the 'Third Camp', even though recent historical works, stemming from different ideological vantage points, emphasize programmatic continuity over change in this transition process (Höbelt 1999, Reiter 2019).

While retaining its pan-German nationalist identity, the FPÖ under the leadership of Friedrich Peter (1958–1978), a former SS officer, started to emphasize its liberal roots in an effort to move closer to political power. Proof of this ambition came in the 1970 elections when the FPÖ (5.5 per cent) provided the SPÖ (48.4 per cent) with a majority in parliament, to the great disappointment of the ÖVP (44.7 per cent). Between 1971 and 1983, the SPÖ formed a single-party majority government across three consecutive elections, thereby turning into the most successful social democratic party alongside the Swedish SAP (Bartolini 2000: 304–305), followed by a short-lived SPÖ-FPÖ coalition government until 1986.

The collaboration between the SPÖ and FPÖ originated from a political deal between Bruno Kreisky and Friedrich Peter: the former supported a reform of the election system in favour of smaller parties like the FPÖ, whereas the latter agreed to secure political support for the SPÖ in the absence of a clear parliamentary majority. Kreisky considered the political entrenchment of the FPÖ instrumental to split the 'bourgeois camp' at the expense of the ÖVP, a power-strategic calculation he had learnt in Stockholm during his exile as a Jewish socialist in the Nazi period. Indeed, the Austrian post-war party system resembled the Swedish context by featuring a united political left (SPÖ) and a fragmented political right (ÖVP and FPÖ) (on the origins of Austria's working-class unity in the nation building period, see Lipset and Rokkan 1990: 132; and Bartolini 2000: 552). At the same time, Kreisky's permissive position towards the pan-German FPÖ remained highly controversial, culminating in the political and personal feud between Kreisky and the Nazi hunter Simon Wiesenthal around ministerial appointments and the SS past of Friedrich Peter, which had been revealed by Wiesenthal (*Kreisky-Peter-Wiesenthal Affäre*).

In electoral terms, the FPÖ did not manage to challenge the hegemonic position of the SPÖ and ÖVP before the takeover by Jörg Haider in 1986 (see Figure 4.2). Previously hovering between 5 to 6 per cent, the FPÖ turned into

Figure 4.2 Vote shares of the FPÖ, 1956–2019.

Source: Bundesministerium für Inneres (2023)

a vote-winning machine by disempowering the liberal wing and downplaying its pan-German identity in favour of an Austrian patriotism and a populist anti-establishment strategy targeting the party cartel formed by the SPÖ and ÖVP (Heinisch 2004). In response, the SPÖ terminated its social–liberal coalition with the FPÖ (1983–1986) and formed consecutive grand coalitions with the ÖVP, which aided Haider's portrayal of the two historical major parties as self-serving elites out of touch with the populace. Internal conflicts around the FPÖ's participation in government put an end to its electoral rise with the 2002 elections, but the party quickly recovered throughout the 2000s and 2010s, before facing another blow from the Ibiza affair in 2019.

As Ennser-Jedenastik (2019) shows, the party underwent an ideological trajectory from a more neoliberal anti-establishment position in the 1980s and 1990s towards a classic radical right agenda of nativism and authoritarianism since the 2000s. Party manifesto data suggest that over this period the FPÖ also increased its support for pro-welfare positions (Afonso and Rennwald 2018: 176). While these data are useful to capture the party's preferred *size* of the welfare state, they provide little insight into the *kind* of welfare state the FPÖ wants, for example which social groups should be protected and what relative importance social consumption (e.g. pensions, unemployment benefits) and investment (e.g. education, childcare) should have. Perhaps even more importantly, party positions tell us little about the *direct* influence of parties on the material resources and life chances of citizens through welfare state reform. The subsequent analysis will therefore analyse the policy priorities and choices of the FPÖ across different periods in time and situate their influence in the respective political and economic contexts.

Against the party cartel and immigration (1990s)

The Austrian party system of the 1990s provided the FPÖ under Haider with a number of favourable opportunity structures. First, the SPÖ's refusal to cooperate with the FPÖ due to Haider's ambiguous stance on Austria's past in the Nazi regime paved the way for recurring grand coalition governments that facilitated the public perception of a party cartel held together by clientelistic and corporatist power-sharing. As Kitschelt and McGann (1995: 161) argued, Austria and Italy may be considered 'partocracies', defined as 'the fusion of state, party, and economic elites in politico-economic networks characterized by patronage, clientelism, and corruption', which provided a fertile breeding ground for the FPÖ's anti-establishment campaign.

In this context, Haider's neoliberal policy demands—e.g. a uniform flat tax system, the privatization of state-run industries, the decentralization of collective bargaining, the abolition of mandatory employee/employer representation in the Chamber system—had an insurgent quality by removing power from the political establishment in the management of these non-market institutions. As Austria's post-war capitalism excluded the FPÖ from political influence and patronage, Haider came to gear its economic policy along power-strategic calculations that would dismantle the entrenchment of the two historical major parties and their affiliated social partners in industrial relations, welfare systems, and state-run industries. In his political pamphlet *Die Freiheit, die ich meine*, for example, Haider (1993) argued, 'Austria's social policy is without mete and moral. It is a self-service store for political functionaries and managers' (p. 158). 'Functionaries as parasitic elements of the welfare state need to be disempowered or put in their place' (p. 165).

In addition to long-standing problems of clientelism and patronage in Austrian post-war capitalism (Treib 2012, Ennser-Jedenastik 2016), the challenge of reducing public debt in line with the Maastricht criteria drove an increasing wedge between the SPÖ and ÖVP, thereby undermining their common reform capacity. The successful accession of Austria to the EU in 1995 was arguably the grand coalition's last common political project, but the fiscal policy demands posed by the Maastricht criteria led to the negotiation of austerity packages that created recurring reform deadlocks and made the government appear increasingly ineffective in policymaking (Rathgeb 2018: Ch. 3).

Despite its traditionally market-liberal outlook, the FPÖ's vote maximization targeted blue-collar workers in urban areas traditionally dominated by the SPÖ (Luther 2008). Haider calculated that the blue-collar vote represented a sizeable electorate that had become dissatisfied with the SPÖ's fiscal consolidation agenda and its technocratic policy style geared to meet the Maastricht criteria under Vranitzky's Chancellorship (Heinisch 2004: 254). However, the 1995 election sent a clear signal to the FPÖ that the SPÖ would be hard to beat in the area of social policy (ibid., 255). As the issue of public pensions dominated election debates, the SPÖ achieved a great election victory against both the ÖVP and FPÖ on a campaign pledge to keep the generosity of public pensions untouched, widely distributed in letters to Austrian households (*Pensionistenbrief*). In response, the FPÖ doubled down on an anti-immigration platform it had developed with the mobilization of its 'Austria first' petition in 1993, denounced as an 'anti-foreigner' petition by the other parties. The reaction from civil society organizations against the FPÖ's petition involved the largest street demonstration in Austrian history (*Lichtermeer*), which suggested a fertile breeding ground for the cultivation of a new wedge issue that would split the (social democratic) electorate. From the mid-1990s, the FPÖ thus broke with its remaining liberal spokespeople inside the party and prioritized nativist-authoritarian demands aimed at the attraction of blue-collar voters (Höbelt 2003: Ch. 2), similar to other West European radical right parties mobilizing production workers mainly through cultural protectionism rather than economic demands (Oesch 2008).

However, Haider's new strategic focus on blue-collar workers and broad dissatisfaction with the grand coalition's fiscal austerity put constraints on the electoral viability of a purely neoliberal agenda. The FPÖ instead gradually carved out a selective pro-welfare position for labour market insiders, which catered to the core (male) workforce in production sectors with long and uninterrupted employment biographies. In essence, Haider thereby not only claimed to reward hard-working people with tax cuts as before, but also to protect them from welfare cuts. Whereas the unemployed were typically considered suspicious of welfare abuse in the FPÖ's election manifestoes of the 1990s and 2002 (Ennser-Jedenastik 2016: 421), the 'hard-working' Austrians with long contribution records should be entitled to generous welfare support, according to Haider.

As I argued elsewhere (Rathgeb 2021a), this programmatic reorientation may be best understood as a producerist agenda that pits 'makers' against 'takers': while the makers are considered hard-working citizens that are responsible for the creation of a country's wealth (i.e. employees, employers), the 'takers' are considered self-serving parasites who live off this wealth without contributing to it (i.e. immigrants, corrupt elite). In other words, the FPÖ argued that high levels of taxation no longer serve the 'makers' in society, but instead provide excessive benefits to immigrants as well as corrupt elite networks (for a similar logic, see De Koster et al. 2013). By cutting public resources for the self-serving 'takers' from above (corrupt elite) and below (immigrants), the state would have the fiscal space necessary to reward the truly hard-working 'makers' with tax cuts and welfare benefits, typically production workers and small shop owners.

Entering government, facing austerity (2000–2006)

The rise of the FPÖ under Jörg Haider provided the ÖVP with a welcomed opportunity to break away from the role of a junior coalition partner in a grand coalition that lost a great deal of popular support. Although the economic outlook of the FPÖ was in line with the fiscal consolidation agenda of the ÖVP, Haider went further on neoliberal reform by calling for the introduction of a uniform flat tax system and the dismantling of compulsory membership in the Chamber system. In the 1999 election, the FPÖ became the second strongest party (26.9 per cent; +5 percentage points) at the expense of the ÖVP, ranking behind with a few hundred votes (26.9 per cent; −1.4 percentage points), while the SPÖ took the largest vote share in spite of considerable losses (33.2 per cent; −4.9 percentage points). Once again, the strongest party, the SPÖ, invited the ÖVP to form a grand coalition, but the negotiations failed and thus paved the way for the formation of a centre-right coalition between the ÖVP and FPÖ (Müller 2000a).

An important objective of the FPÖ in government was to reshape economic governance at the expense of organized labour. It thereby took advantage of public grievances against personal privileges and excessively high incomes enjoyed by representatives of the Chamber of Labour (BAK) and the Chamber of Commerce (WKÖ) in Austria's social partnership (Karlhofer 2010: 108). While the FPÖ has traditionally been opposed to the privileged integration of organized interests in public policymaking, it developed a union-hostile agenda in particular when the FPÖ came to compete for working-class votes with the SPÖ (Karlhofer 2010, Rathgeb and Klitgaard 2022). The SPÖ's refusal to form a coalition with the FPÖ due to Haider's controversial statements on Austria's past in the Nazi era reinforced the confrontational stance of the FPÖ against the red bloc of Austria's political system, including the SPÖ in tandem with the Chamber of Labour (BAK) and the trade union confederation (ÖGB). The Economic Chamber (WKÖ), by contrast, could bet on its privileged influence through the ÖVP's government participation.

The FPÖ thus attributed the trade unions the role of self-serving 'takers' that need to be disempowered in the interest of tax-paying 'makers'. Asked about the social policies the party leadership had in mind in 1999, Lothar Höbelt, a collaborator of the FPÖ's vice chancellor, Susanne Riess-Passer, and member of the drafting committee of the 1997 programme, referred to early retirement and child benefits, but,

> We had had 30 years of socialist government participation, in which they [the SPÖ] had already implemented any benefits one can imagine, if there were any funds around at all. The FPÖ could only say: Against the apparatuses—for example, the mandatory contribution payments to the Chamber of Labour—against the privileges of functionaries.
>
> **(Rathgeb 2021a: 647)**

The above description of the party's anti-establishment outlook resonates with public opinion research and sheds light on the party's efforts in undermining corporatist power sharing. As much as 65 per cent of FPÖ voters indicated that they vote the FPÖ because it fights scandals and privileges, which the party associated with the close linkages between the historical major parties and the social partner organizations (Müller 2000b: 44). That the domain of corruption and scandals had become one of the five most important issues in 1996 and 1997 underscores the FPÖ's successful articulation of this new issue (Müller 2000b: 42).

The attempt to reorganize the Federation of Social Insurance Providers, an organization based on corporatist self-administration, shows how the FPÖ's declared fight against scandals and privileges created opportunities for the government to attack institutional union power (Obinger and Tálos 2006: 81–84). Immediately after taking office, the ÖVP–FPÖ government could agree to provide the FPÖ with an influential role in the social insurance boards and restructure the balance of corporatist representation at the expense of union delegates. While the Constitutional Court annulled large parts of this reform as it breached the principle of self-administration, the government still managed to shift the balance of power from union delegates to employer representatives (Obinger and Tálos 2006: 84).

In a similar vein, the FPÖ legitimized privatization as a way of undermining the power base of social democratic politicians and union representatives. While the SPÖ urged the government to maintain blocking minorities among the remaining public enterprises to prevent hostile takeovers (e.g. in energy, communication, transport), the ÖVP called into question the economic viability of public ownership and considered privatization an opportunity for fiscal consolidation. The FPÖ, by contrast, was explicit in connecting privatization with party patronage among the red bloc of Austria's political system. In the words of Thomas Prinzhorn, the FPÖ's main spokesperson on economic affairs, during the parliamentary debate on the government's major privatization package legislated in March 2000:

> But I need to tell you something else: What really hurts you is the loss of power in state-run industries. That's what it is about: Privileges, Proporz [proportional representation of ruling parties]. All this had your handwriting! [...] Now the party is over, now a new government is here! It will make a different kind of politics and return the taxpayer what you [the SPÖ] took from him.
>
> **(Sten. Prot., XXI. GP, 15. Sitzung: 29–30)**

Although union exclusion and privatization were widely welcomed, the internal contradictions of the party's economic policy platform led to widening divides between the government team and the party base at the grass-roots level. While the FPÖ's government team under its minister of finance, Karl-Heinz Grasser, endorsed putting fiscal consolidation front and centre, it contradicted the party's image to fight for the cause of the 'common man'. The FPÖ should thus be considered a consenter to the ensuing welfare retrenchment, whereas the protagonist behind a number of social spending cuts—the legislation of new charges on hospital outpatient fees, the taxation of accident-related pensions, increases in patient's contribution fees—was the ÖVP under its Chancellor, Wolfgang Schüssel (Heinisch 2003: 103). Notably, these cuts caused internal opposition, as they arguably broke with the ideological premise of the FPÖ to protect the 'hard-working' (and thus deserving) makers from income losses (see e.g. Heinisch 2003, 116). According to Ewald Stadler, former member of the party's federal executive committee, the policy of welfare retrenchment was a first step towards the party's subsequent implosion (Rathgeb 2021a: 649).

The FPÖ's internal reaction against cuts in social insurance rights is consistent with two welfare expansions that the party considered its main successes in social policy during its first coalition with the ÖVP (2000–2002): the introduction of a new child benefit scheme (*Kinderbetreuungsgeld*) and early retirement scheme (*Hacklerregelung*) (ibid.). The male breadwinner bias of the child benefit scheme stems from the associated incentives for women to leave—or not enter at all—the labour market for an extended period.

Compared to the previous benefit scheme (*Karenzgeld*), it implied a universalization in coverage, regardless of the previous employment record; an extended benefit duration from 18/24 months to 30/36 months; an expansion in generosity from 4000 to 6000 Austrian Schilling (= 436 euro); and a relaxed limit on additional income to be earned alongside child benefit receipt (*Zuverdienstgrenze*) (Obinger and Tálos 2006: 162–167). In other words, the FPÖ's response to the new social risk of reconciling work–family life was 'to give women the possibility to stay at home', whereas the social protection of workers in non-standard employment was 'not an issue' in the party's policy agenda (Rathgeb 2021a: 649). While the ÖVP was generally in line with the FPÖ's demands for child benefit expansion, it moderated initial demands from Jörg Haider in the interest of fiscal sustainability (see also Müller 2000b: 35). Finally, the early retirement scheme created the option to retire after 40/45 years (female/male) of paid employment at the age of 55/60 years, which benefits full-time workers with long and uninterrupted employment records (*Hacklerregelung*).

Yet, a series of election defeats at the regional level reinforced the looming disaffection with the government team's austerity agenda and the ensuing social insurance cuts, which contributed to the party's internal implosion at its congress in Knittelfeld in March 2002 and led to the resignation of most of the FPÖ's team in government (Heinisch 2003). Wolfgang Schüssel thus called for new elections in response to the opposition of the FPÖ's grass roots against the government team. The 2002 re-elections led to an unprecedented victory of the ÖVP (+15.4 percentage points) and defeat of the FPÖ (−16.9 percentage points), followed by a new ÖVP–FPÖ government with a greatly diminished role of the FPÖ. The FPÖ's lesson has been to call into question the dictates of balanced budgets in order to avoid welfare cuts that might alienate their working-class base. As the FPÖ gave in to the postponement of a long-promised tax reform, the new agenda of Haider's grass-roots camp was to moderate the degree of welfare cuts in the 2003 pension reform. At the same time, the FPÖ did not call into question the need for a pension reform as such, because cost reductions in the area of public pensions were an indispensable part of the government's ambition to consolidate the federal budget (Müller and Fallend 2004: 815).

While consenting to large-scale retrenchment primarily at the expense of non-standard workers with discontinuous employment biographies (Rathgeb 2018: 80–82), the FPÖ achieved moderate compensations for employees with long and uninterrupted contribution records, which, once again, benefited primarily the male core workforce (Obinger and Tálos 2006: 99). In short, while consenting to a number of welfare cuts demanded by the ÖVP as a matter of fiscal discipline, the FPÖ aimed to defend the social insurance rights of full-time workers with permanent employment in order to protect themselves and their families from income losses in the event of old age (*Hacklerregelung*) and child-rearing (*Kinderbetreuungsgeld*).

When the government had finished its large-scale pension reform, the FPÖ pushed for tax cuts. Notably, the party tied its previous consent to the pension reform to the legislation of a tax reform—arguably the core of its previous election campaigns (Grillmayer 2006: 348)—with the overall aim to decrease the total tax and contribution ratio from the peak level of 45.1 (2001) to below 40 per cent until 2010 (FPÖ election manifesto 2002: 90–91). In an interview with the weekly finance and business magazine *Format*, Jörg Haider described the FPÖ's position in the reform negotiations in July 2003. When the interviewer asked about the reform's benefits for the party's 'much-heralded little man'—an often-used term by the FPÖ for working-class and low-income voters—Haider responded, 'We want a tax reform with introducing a few low tax rates towards a flat tax system, with exemption limits for families according to their number of children. This is what we should finally tackle' (Rathgeb 2021a: 660). It is interesting that Haider associated the party's flat tax programme—which reduces the progressiveness of the tax system in favour of high-income groups—with benefits for the lower strata of the income distribution. However, such a position is precisely what we would expect from a producerist ideology. The main point of contention with the ÖVP was the timing rather than the content of tax reform itself, because the FPÖ wanted to deliver tax cuts as soon as possible, also with a view on Haider's election in Carinthia in March 2004. The ÖVP and FPÖ agreed to divide the distribution of a net tax cut of 2.6 billion euro among employees and employers through a 50:50 ratio.

We may conclude that the FPÖ was at least in part successful in attacking the Austrian party cartel (reorganization of social insurance administration, privatization, union exclusion), albeit the critics of the Knittelfeld party congress would have gone much further in targeting para-public institutions. At the same time, the austerity paradigm provided little room for tax cuts and welfare improvements for deserving 'hard-working' labour market insiders—leading to internal turmoil around the dictates of balanced budgets. The FPÖ's remaining role was to mitigate the costs of austerity for the core workforce. The 2006 elections led to a rather unexpected victory of the SPÖ (35.3 per cent) against the ÖVP (34.3 per cent), which lost 8 per cent of their voters from 2002, and a fragmentation of the populist radical right between the FPÖ (11 per cent) and its breakaway group, the BZÖ (4.1 per cent).

With the new leadership of Heinz-Christian Strache (2005–2017), the FPÖ doubled down on nativism while relegating some of Haider's neoliberal rhetoric. Welfare chauvinism thereby turned into a dominant theme across social policy areas in subsequent election manifestoes (Ennser-Jedenastik 2016: 419). The FPÖ's rebranding as the 'social homeland party' underscored this reorientation aimed to consolidate its electoral support among working-class voters, given that Austria's 'radical right has gained the greatest support among sociological groups previously associated with social democracy' (Aichholzer et al. 2014: 131). With Strache, the party also regained internal stability and unity after its tumultuous years in office and the breakaway of the more market-liberal BZÖ. Whereas Strache resembled his predecessor in pursuing a confrontational strategy in opposition, he was considered more predictable and approachable among the party base. Asked about the difference between Haider and Strache, the response by the FPÖ's long-standing ideologue, Andreas Mölzer, was in many ways telling: 'We've tried with the Messiah. Now we have a good comrade' (Profil 2013).

The exhaustion of the grand coalition (2007–2017)

The decade from 2007 to 2017 was a period of political compromise between the two major historical parties that formed consecutive grand coalitions. Although the grand coalition managed to offset the socio-economic effects of the Great Recession quite effectively, it faced a number of major problems that paved the way for the re-entry of the FPÖ into office. First, mounting internal conflicts in combination with low economic growth rates haunted the cohesiveness of the grand coalition and led to frequent reform deadlocks, which negatively affected their approval ratings in public opinion. At times, the grand coalition circumvented open conflicts by delegating policymaking negotiations to their affiliated social partners, thereby providing interest group and bureaucratic elites a high level of policy autonomy (Rathgeb 2018: Ch. 3). While the declining ability of the government to find common grounds allowed the social partners to regain influence, in the eyes of voters the grand coalition became increasingly ineffective and conflictual. Proof of this lack of popular support came with the first round of Austria's presidential election in April 2016, whereby the candidates of the ÖVP and SPÖ fell way below the 15 per cent mark, receiving less than one third of the vote altogether (Rathgeb and Wolkenstein 2016). In all of the presidential elections that had gone before, the candidates of the two historical major parties together received far more than two thirds of the vote, sometimes even more than 90 per cent.

Second, and related to this, the 2015 refugee crisis drove a wedge between the grand coalition partners and created opportunities for the FPÖ to mobilize around its core issues of immigration, asylum, and law and order. With an influx of 90,000 refugees, the country recorded the second highest number of asylum seekers in Europe relative to its population size, ranking only behind Sweden. 'Integration and asylum' had thus turned into the most important issue of Austrian politics, with the FPÖ leading the polls between autumn 2015 and spring 2017 (Plasser and Sommer 2018: Ch. 10). In this context, the ÖVP under its new party leader, Sebastian Kurz, had given up on the idea to restore the reform capacity of the grand coalition, whereas the SPÖ under Christian Kern advocated for a 'New Deal' with the ÖVP. In response, the ÖVP called for re-elections in May 2017.

Haunted by very low approval ratings, the regionally and occupationally fragmented party elites provided Sebastian Kurz with much leeway to rebrand the ÖVP as the 'New People's Party' and prepare for re-elections. In programmatic terms, the most marked change came with the adoption of a tighter position on immigration and an ultimate rejection of another crisis-ridden grand coalition. Aided by Kurz's popularity and a professional PR campaign, this programmatic strategy ultimately proved successful. The 2017 elections yielded an enormous victory for both the ÖVP (31.5 per cent; +7.5 per cent) and the FPÖ (26 per cent; +5.5 per cent), with the SPÖ stagnating at 26.9 per cent. As a result, a broad consensus emerged on the political right to collaborate on a nativist agenda that puts 'Austrians first' and reframe virtually any debate of socio-economic character into a culturally laden problem around the integration of non-Western refugees and immigrants into Austrian society. It thus came as no surprise when the ÖVP and FPÖ could swiftly agree on the formation of a coalition government under the Chancellorship of Sebastian Kurz after the 2017 elections.

Less austerity, more chauvinism—and the Ibiza affair (2017–2019)

In electoral terms, the ÖVP–FPÖ government rested on a cross-class coalition between large employers, small business owners, and the higher-grade service class (i.e. managers, technicians, and technical experts) supporting primarily the ÖVP on the one hand, and blue-collar workers and lower-grade service workers supporting primarily the FPÖ on the other. Whereas the

ÖVP had traditionally drawn on high levels of support among business groups, the FPÖ attracted an unprecedented 62 per cent of blue-collar workers in the 2017 elections (Aichholzer et al. 2018).

What united this diverse class coalition was a preference for a nativist and authoritarian approach to immigration and asylum in combination with moderate tax cuts for middle- and high-income earners alongside the defence of welfare entitlements for 'deserving' social groups. Notably, the ÖVP came to share the FPÖ's long-standing ambition to target the welfare entitlements of non-citizens in response to shifts in public opinion during the refugee crisis, but strong working-class support required the FPÖ to protect the employment and welfare standards of labour market insiders.

At the same time, the FPÖ had developed a new economic programme that included once again demands for cuts in progressive taxation and social insurance contributions amounting to 13.2 billion euro (3.5 per cent of GDP), which was broadly in line with the ÖVP (Das freiheitliche Wirtschaftsprogramm 2017). The programme had a consistently welfare chauvinist outlook while the election manifesto included a demand for a minimum pension of 1200 euro for workers with forty years of paid employment and higher annual increases of family benefits. Strongly borrowing from earlier populist campaigns of Haider, the FPÖ claimed to finance the remaining loss of tax revenues in large part with spending cuts targeted at public administration systems under control of a self-serving party cartel (Rot-schwarzer Verwaltungsspeck). In this context, the costs of labour and welfare reform had to be shifted to non-citizens and the precarious margins of the workforce, which in the previous grand coalition government could bet on the support of the SPÖ.

While welfare chauvinism was absent in the previous ÖVP–FPÖ government record in the early 2000s, it was a major feature of social policy reforms between 2017 and 2019. In the presentation of the 2018/2019 budget, Chancellor Kurz (ÖVP) claimed that the government would put an end to sixty-four years of accumulating public debt (Schuldenpolitik), whereas Vice Chancellor Strache (FPÖ) highlighted that, 'We cut back money for non-Austrians, because the point is to make immigration into our welfare system less attractive' (Kronen Zeitung 2018). First, the government legislated an indexation of family benefits (Familienbeihilfe) for children of foreign workers living outside Austria. In effect, the reform links the levels of family benefit payments to the cost of living in the home countries of foreign workers. In response, the European Commission initiated an infringement procedure before the European Court of Justice. In June 2022, the Court ruled that indexation was unlawful as it constituted an indirect discrimination on

grounds of nationality and a breach of the Regulation on freedom of movement for workers within the European Union. Hence, the indexation had
to be abolished on legal grounds. Second, the government significantly cut
the levels of social assistance for refugees and required immigrants from EU
countries to obtain a permanent residency for at least five years to qualify for
social assistance entitlements. When the Constitutinal Court overturned this
legislation, the government adjusted its social assistance reform by making
full benefit eligibility conditional on language requirements or the com-
pletion of compulsory schooling in Austria—two criteria refugees typically
could not fulfil. In December 2019, however, the Constitutional Court ruled
that making social assistance benefits conditional on a rather high command
of the German (B1) or English language (C1) would violate the Constitution
as it is objectively unjustified. The Constitutional Court also annulled cuts
in social assistance levels for families with more than two children, arguing
that the necessary living conditions for couples with multiple children are
not guaranteed.

The FPÖ once again pursued policies that targeted the influence of
organized labour in corporatist administration boards. Notably, the ÖVP
consented to the FPÖ's long-standing demand to merge the occupationally and regionally fragmented social insurance providers from twenty-three
to only five. Similar to the institutional reorganization in the early 2000s,
the reform implies a reduction in the influence of organized labour on
corporatist administration boards in favour of employers and state actors.
Not surprisingly, the interest organizations of labour protested against this
reform, whereas the government emphasized the efficiency-enhancing effect
of reducing the number of health insurance providers. The Constitutional
Court, once again, annulled some minor parts of the reform, but the
enhanced role of employer representatives remained untouched. Borrowing from earlier populist campaigns, the FPÖ's spokesperson for welfare
affairs, Dagmar Belakowitsch, legitimized the reform as a way of enhancing
the quality of healthcare providers by removing influence from self-serving
corporatist officials:

> Long waiting times for necessary medical examinations or even a lack of medi-
> cations necessary—created by an outdated system of political sensitivities—now
> belongs to the past. All involved stakeholders must now realize that the patient is
> at the forefront and not the system as a self-service store for political functionaries.
> (FPÖ-Parlamentsklub, 26.10.2018)

The FPÖ also continued to exert pressure on the Chamber system. The
government programme stated that the Chambers need to reduce their

expenditures to create leeway for a reduction in compulsory membership fees in the interest of a lower tax and contribution ratio. Whereas the WKÖ announced it could 'live well' with such a cut as it had already managed to reduce costs for its members, the BAK reacted strongly against the government (*Kleine Zeitung* 12.12.2017). However, the sudden and unexpected fall of the government in the wake of the Ibiza affair scandal in 2019 prevented legislative changes in the funding of the Chambers.

Most important for the government's 'new fairness' appeal, it could swiftly agree upon significant tax relief for families amounting to 1.5 billion euro per year (*Familienbonus*), benefiting high-income groups with higher tax burdens more than low-income groups. Rather than expanding public child-care to reconcile work–family life for working mothers, the *Familienbonus* reflects a familialist ideology according to which the earnings of one parent in full-time employment – i.e. mostly the 'male breadwinner' in practise – should be sufficient for a family's income if necessary (Das Freiheitliche Wirtschaftsprogramm 2017: 34). In fact, 70 per cent of the beneficiaries were male and 80 per cent of the tax breaks went into the pockets of men in 2019, as the Chamber of Labour documented (Salzburger Nachrichten, 20.10.2021).

Another part of the government's new fairness appeal was the FPÖ's achievement to legislate a minimum pension of 1200 euro for workers with forty years of paid employment, which, however, implied extra costs of only 40 million euro per year. However, the deservingness notions of both parties implied that public pensions, sickness benefits, and elderly care should remain untouched. In this way, the government deprived the SPÖ of one its main issues, because it used to enjoy high levels of credibility on public pensions and thus strong support among older voters.

Yet the FPÖ's image as the party of the 'little man' came under pressure by the statutory liberalization of working time regulations, against fierce protests of trade unions, allowing employers to require employees to work twelve hours a day and sixty hours a week, irrespective of collective agreements. When public opinion turned largely negative, the FPÖ added a clause providing employees with the possibility to reject longer working hours for private reasons. In a similar vein, the FPÖ opposed plans to follow a German-like Hartz-IV reform that would have reduced the maximum duration of unemployment benefits for workers with long contribution records. In response to intra-coalitional conflicts and open questions about the design of unemployment benefit reform, Strache made clear on his Facebook account that, 'Those who work for a longer time deserve a higher unemployment benefit for a longer duration! [...] And also the socialist German Hartz-IV model will certainly not arrive in Austria under the Freedomites' (HC Strache, 18.11.2018).

Shortly after the government had agreed upon a series of moderate tax cuts for employees and employers that should have come into effect from 2020 to 2022, the Ibiza affair put an abrupt end to the ÖVP–FPÖ coalition. Kurz called for re-elections in May 2019 as German newspapers published extracts from a video that led Strache to resign from office. The video documents how he discussed plans to undermine the independence of Austria's largest tabloid newspaper (*Kronen Zeitung*) and generate party donations in exchange for public sector contracts once the FPÖ were in government. Strache at one point said he wanted to remodel Austria's media system along the lines of Hungary under Viktor Orbán, who undermined media pluralism and independence in favour of pro-government campaigns. In the subsequent re-elections, the ÖVP made significant inroads among disappointed FPÖ supporters, which led to a resounding election victory and the formation of a coalition with the Greens. Whereas Strache had resigned immediately after the publication of the 'Ibiza video', Kurz himself faced accusations of corruption, bribery, and embezzlement, as the Ibiza affair led to subsequent revelations of private telephone chat conversations, which, for example, suggested that he and his inner circle abused tax money to pay for the commissioning and publication of favourable opinion polls in tabloid newspapers (Heinisch and Werner 2021). In response, the ÖVP tried to discredit the judiciary by claiming that the relevant prosecutors are part of 'red' (i.e. social democratic) circles that would aim to undermine Kurz's popularity. Hence, the ÖVP–FPÖ's period in power challenged important elements of Austria's liberal democracy, but the judiciary managed to hold the relevant actors accountable, which led Kurz to resign too, following increasing pressure from the Greens within the coalition.

In the welfare state domain, similar to the early 2000s, the FPÖ pushed for cuts in progressive taxation, trade union disempowerment, and the defence of welfare entitlements for labour market insiders and the elderly when re-entering government in the late 2010s. At the same time, however, welfare chauvinism has gained a much more prominent place in the wake of the refugee crisis. The ensuing instances of welfare chauvinism—i.e. in social assistance and child benefits—not only illustrate the policy impact of the radical right on benefit schemes that are inclusive to non-citizens; they also demonstrate the constitutional limits of welfare chauvinism in a liberal democracy and EU member state. In other words, the Austrian experience shows how the liberal-constitutional component of a democracy may put legal constraints on the introduction of divisions between citizens and non-citizens in social policy.

Shadow case studies: Germany and Italy

To lend additional credibility to my claim about how the Continental European conservative welfare state context promotes a policy of chauvinist and familialist insider protection among radical right parties, I will now provide cursory evidence from Germany and Italy ('shadow case studies'). If my claim about the regime-specific logic of the radical right's policy impact were correct, we should find similar policy choices from a Continental European radical right party in government elsewhere (Italy) and the absence of such a policy influence in a country where the radical right has never been in government (Germany).

Although the *Italian* welfare state has traditionally differed from the Continental European regime due to its lack of minimum income protection schemes and social services, it does share an insider-oriented social insurance system with strong male breadwinner legacies (Ferrera 1996, Guillén et al. 2022). In this context, it comes as little surprise that the Italian *Lega* had exactly the same policy priorities as the FPÖ when entering office with the populist *Movimento Cinque Stelle* (M5S) from 2017 to 2019. First, like the FPÖ, the *Lega* successfully pushed for the reintroduction of early retirement at the age of sixty-two years after thirty-eight years of contributions, also known as *Quota 100* (Afonso and Bulfone 2019). Similar to the insider-oriented *Hacklerregelung* in Austria, the male core workforce, especially in the Northern manufacturing-dominated regions of Italy, benefited from the scheme due to well-protected permanent contracts and thus long and uninterrupted employment biographies (ibid., 248). Second, again like the FPÖ, the *Lega* demanded increased child benefits that would sustain traditional gender roles, but was partly blocked by the M5S inside the government (Meardi and Guardiancich 2022). Third, the *Lega* also retained a low taxation agenda that had initially been devised to disempower corrupt elite networks in *Roma ladrona* ('Rome, the thief'). In both Austria and Italy, we therefore see a clearly insider-oriented and familialist social policy impact with enduring claims to tax cuts from radical right parties that originated as challenger parties opposed to a cartelized political establishment (Kitschelt and McGann 1995: Ch. 5).

However, the absence of inclusive and generous social assistance reduced the relevance of welfare chauvinism in Italy, because newly arrived immigrants often work in the shadow economy and lack access to welfare rights, especially in the South of Italy (Pellizari 2013). In other words, the nativist ideology of the *Lega* could not translate into welfare chauvinism in legislative terms, because immigrants had little to gain from the Italian welfare state, which contrasts with Austria's universal and generous family support scheme (*Familienbeihilfe*) and means-tested social assistance scheme. Only when the M5S demanded the introduction of a minimum income scheme (*Reddito di cittadinanza*) in favour of its state-dependent constituencies in the Southern regions, the *Lega* was keen to disadvantage newly arrived non-EU immigrants (Landini 2022). As a result, the case of the *Lega* resembles the FPÖ's insider-oriented and familialist impact, but its welfare state context in large part precluded a policy of welfare chauvinism.

In Germany, the AfD (*Alternative für Deutschland*) has never been in government and continues to be treated as a pariah by the centre-left SPD as well as the centre-right CDU/CSU. The absence of the AfD in government would imply the absence of a policy of chauvinist and familialist insider protection. First, similar to the FPÖ, the AfD has pushed for welfare chauvinist measures in the wake of the refugee crisis (Marx and Naumann 2018), but the other parties have so far opposed the selective cuts we observed in the Austrian case. Second, the AfD has also demanded higher minimum pension entitlements for workers with long and uninterrupted contribution records (AfD 2020: 34), reminiscent of the FPÖ's introduction of a minimum pension of 1200 euro for workers with forty years of paid employment. Third, similar to the FPÖ, the AfD has also catered to labour market insiders by demanding a stronger link between the maximum duration of unemployment benefit receipt and the individual contribution record of a jobseeker (Rathgeb and Klitgaard 2022), which resonated with Strache's criticism of ÖVP demands in unemployment protection analysed above. This way, the AfD would reverse those aspects of the hotly contested Hartz IV reform that hit the entitlements of labour market insiders with long contribution records, i.e. a group of voters from which it received disproportionate electoral support, especially in the manufacturing-dominated regions (Manow 2018). In short, whereas non-citizens should face welfare cuts, native labour market insiders should receive better protections, a policy combination of chauvinist insider protection perfectly in line with the FPÖ.

The exclusion of the radical right from power arguably contributed to a divergence between Austria and Germany in family policy. Austria continues to display legacies of the male breadwinner model—i.e. generous child benefits, long maternity leave periods, and residual childcare provision (at least outside Vienna)—but German governments of different partisan complexions have gradually expanded childcare facilities and enhanced gender equality in parental leave arrangements. As Leitner (2011) shows through a case study comparison, this divergence emerged in the early 2000s when the FPÖ's welfare minister, Herbert Haupt, introduced the *Kinderbetreuungsgeld* in a coalition with the ÖVP, whereas German grand coalition governments started to expand public childcare arrangements instead. The title of this study – 'Germany outpaces Austria in childcare policy' – seems vindicated by recent OECD statistics according to which 39.2 per cent of German versus 20.2 per cent of Austrian children between 0 and 2 years old are enrolled in early childhood education and care services (OECD 2023). Without a strong radical right party in government, there was not enough political support to sustain the conservative legacies of Germany's family policy. Notably, the AfD (2020: 65) has recently called for an end to the 'discrimination of full-time mothers' to make sure women can take over a greater role as caregivers without further reliance on public childcare facilities. This policy would clash with the Scandinavian-style turn taken by German governments to reconcile work–family life by expanding childcare rather than child benefits.

The German case therefore provides a sound factual scenario from which we can derive a counterfactual claim: Without the radical right in power, immigrants are less likely to face selective welfare cuts, whereas working women are more likely to benefit from greater childcare expansion. By contrast, the cases of Austria and Italy show that the radical right in power contributes to (1) greater protections for the core (male) workforces, (2) familialist policy measures sustaining traditional gender divisions in employment and welfare, and (3) selective welfare cuts for non-citizens in previously inclusive benefit schemes.

Conclusion

The FPÖ is a case of how conservative institutional legacies translate an ideological agenda of nativism and authoritarianism into insider-oriented and, more recently, welfare chauvinist social policy choices. Hence, the party defended the employment and welfare standards of labour market insiders, whose traditionally well-protected status has come under pressure from technological change (Kurer 2020), welfare state recalibration (Häusermann 2020), and low-wage competition (Engler and Weisstanner 2021). In this way, the FPÖ catered to its core male working-class constituency that has traditionally benefited from insider-oriented welfare entitlements thanks to long and uninterrupted contribution records (Häusermann 2020). At the same time, the new social risks of women (i.e. lone parenthood and work–family reconciliation), the young (i.e. temporary employment), and the low-skilled (i.e. long-term unemployment) played only a marginal role, given that the FPÖ showed little interest in social investments in childcare facilities, minimum benefit entitlements, and active labour market policy when in office. Whereas the male core workforce has clearly been the material winner of the FPÖ's social policy impact, the opposite can be said about immigrants and those without steady and secure employment, leading to a policy combination of *chauvinist and familialist insider protection*. Although the FPÖ certainly used to be an anti-system force in Austria's consensus democracy, its policy impact helped to sustain the historically evolved institutional system of the conservative welfare state. *So how can we explain this policy impact?*

As Austria has experienced relatively high immigration rates that proved to be a point of contention among its citizens, especially during the refugee crisis of the mid-2010s (Plasser and Sommer 2018), the radical right's *nativism* politicized inclusive welfare schemes that are open to non-citizens. It thus comes as little surprise that the FPÖ mobilized for selective welfare cuts in social assistance and family support. The social assistance scheme turned into an obvious target, given that its inclusive design makes benefit receipt conditional on need rather than employment or citizenship. In this context, the FPÖ also achieved cutbacks in the child benefit entitlements (*Familienbeihilfe*) for parents who raise their children outside of Austria, targeted at commuters from Austria's Eastern European neighbour countries. Although the FPÖ under Strache may be considered the protagonist behind welfare chauvinism, the ÖVP was quick to endorse these policies when it seemed clear that the radical right managed to reshape public opinion in this direction.

Whereas the Constitutional Court and the European Court of Justice annulled welfare chauvinist measures on the grounds of equal treatment, the FPÖ's familialism had a more lasting impact on Austria's gender relations. In a conservative welfare regime, the radical right's *authoritarianism* translates into a preference for the maintenance and expansion of conservative family policies. While its familialist rhetoric lost some relevance over time, the FPÖ pushed for child benefit expansion through the legislation of the *Kinderbetreuungsgeld* (previously introduced as 'children cheque' in Carinthia under Haider), which strengthened incentives for families, and thus women in practice, to extend maternity leave and reduce working hours to care for children.

Increased spending for child benefits and tax breaks for families (*Familien-bonus*) went hand in hand with the sluggish expansion of public childcare facilities (at least outside Vienna), thereby entrenching traditional gender divisions in paid employment and unpaid care work. Austria's conservative family policy buttresses ongoing disadvantages for working mothers when it comes to career prospects, gender pay gaps, and pension levels in retirement (Rathgeb and Wiss 2020). However, it is important to bear in mind the variation *within* the Continental European welfare states on family policies and gender roles. Whereas the German-speaking countries and Italy display stronger male breadwinner legacies, the opposite can be said about France and the Benelux countries. Hence, we need more research on the question of whether radical right parties in the latter group of cases use their government influence in similarly familialist ways.

In addition to this chauvinist and familialist insider protection, the FPÖ upheld a long-standing preference for trade union disempowerment and tax cuts that complemented a producerist logic pitting the 'makers' (small employers and employees in private sector) against the 'takers' from below (immigrants) and the 'takers' from above (corrupt elite networks) (Rathgeb 2021a). Perhaps unsurprisingly, the Covid-19 pandemic and the party's Ibiza affair undermined the political feasibility of a low taxation agenda aimed to disempower 'corrupt elites'. It remains to be seen whether these developments put an end to the party's neoliberal legacies in tax policy and industrial relations.

When shifting our attention to the radical right in Northern Europe, we may observe similar policies of (1) welfare chauvinism when social transfers are open to non-citizens without employment requirements (e.g. social assistance) and (2) insider protection when the 'hard-working' core workforce enjoys generous benefit entitlements (e.g. early retirement). At the same time, however, the Nordic social democratic context of the dual career model cut off political support for a conservative family policy from the radical right, as we will see in the next chapter.

5
Chauvinist Insider Protection in Northern Europe

The Danish People's Party (*Dansk Folkeparti*, DF) emerged as a breakaway group from the Progress Party (*Fremskridtspartiet*, FrP) in 1995. Similar to the Austrian FPÖ, the Danish radical right followed a programmatic trajectory from a neoliberal anti-establishment agenda under the Progress Party towards nativism and authoritarianism under the Danish People's Party (Jupskås 2015, Pappas 2019). At the same time, the DF also experienced relatively strong working-class support, which would suggest an incentive to pursue a pro-welfare policy that caters to this group of voters (e.g. Eger and Valdez 2015, Lefkofridi and Michel 2017, Afonso and Rennwald 2018). Drawing on Oesch's class schema (2006), Figure 5.1 provides insights into the DF's class composition by showing its four largest electoral constituencies, i.e. production workers, service workers, clerks, and small business owners.

From 2001 to 2015, the DF's share of votes from production workers gradually declined from 38 to 20 per cent, while its share of service workers fluctuated between 25 to 35 per cent. Therefore, between 45 and 73 per cent of the DF's voters had a working-class background in production or service jobs, while the respective shares of small business owners and clerks hovered between 5 and 12 per cent in this period. The 2015 election was an exception, as fewer than one in two DF voters had a working-class background, compensated by a growing share of votes from higher-grade managers and administrators. Whereas the DF gained votes from the centre-left Social democratic party (*Socialdemokraterne*, S) in the 1990s and the 2001 election, it attracted electoral support mainly from the centre-right Liberal Party (*Venstre*, V) in the 2015 election (Kosiara-Pedersen 2020: 315–316). The two subsequent general elections brought heavy defeats for the DF in a context of internal turmoil and splits, their vote share declining from 21.2 per cent in 2015 to 8.7 per cent in 2019 and 2.6 per cent in 2022. In this context, the ISSP 2020 (2022) data on the DF's class composition in the 2019 election should be interpreted with caution, because it includes only fifty-six respondents who voted for the DF *and* indicated their occupational background. Among

How the Radical Right Has Changed Capitalism and Welfare in Europe and the USA. Philip Rathgeb, Oxford University Press.
© Philip Rathgeb (2024). DOI: 10.1093/oso/9780192866332.003.0005

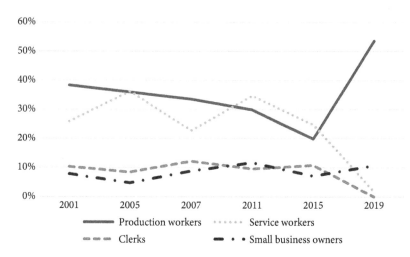

Figure 5.1 Share of votes from production workers, service workers, clerks, and small business owners within the DF's electorate, 2001–2019 (percentages).

Sources: ESS (2002, 2006, 2008, 2012) for 2001–2011 elections, ISSP (2017, 2022) for 2015–2019 elections.

them, more than every second was a production worker. Judging from the relatively similar compositions of the FPÖ's and DF's electoral support base, we could expect similar policy choices from these two parties. However, as I will show below, there are important differences in the ways that these parties have influenced welfare state reform.

This chapter argues that understanding the similarities and differences in the FPÖ's and DF's social policy impact requires an appreciation of the institutional contexts and historical legacies that characterize the Northern European social democratic and Continental European conservative welfare states. Notably, the Danish welfare state traditionally provided generous early retirement for labour market insiders with long contribution records, that is, the *efterløn* scheme. Production workers often benefit from this type of social protection, as they typically display the continuous and uninterrupted employment biographies necessary to become eligible for early retirement (Häusermann 2020). The DF indeed prioritized the maintenance of early retirement in the interest of the 'deserving' (male) core workforce, comparable to the FPÖ's expansion and defence of early retirement (*Hackler-regelung*), which we could observe in the previous chapter. Again, similar to the FPÖ, the DF also pushed for enhanced financial support for low-income pensioners and elderly care, thereby solidifying a pro-elderly image alongside its anti-immigration platform. Given the more redistributive legacy and institutional design of the Danish state pension system, the DF's pension support had, however, more redistributive implications (*Ældrechecken* in Denmark vs minimum pension for long-term employed in Austria). Moreover, the universal design of the Danish welfare state led the DF to promote a policy of welfare chauvinism at a much earlier point in time than the FPÖ, targeting in particular the benefit entitlements of non-citizens in the country's relatively generous social assistance scheme.

While the DF and FPÖ have had overall a relatively similar pro-elderly and welfare chauvinist policy impact, they markedly diverged in the area of family policy. Unlike in the case of the FPÖ, the DF has not supported a strategy of 'explicit familialism' (Leitner 2003) that would allow (and expect) families, mostly women in practice, to reduce working hours in order to care for children. An important reason for this is that the Nordic welfare states have traditionally promoted high levels of gender equality via the public provision of encompassing childcare, shared parental leave, and individual taxation. This legacy goes back to the 1950s and 1960s. Whereas the Northern European social democratic welfare states mobilized female labour in response to labour shortages during the booming post-war years, the Continental European conservative welfare states sustained the male breadwinner model by discouraging female employment and instead attracting immigrants through what were known as state-sponsored 'guest worker' programmes (Afonso 2018). Hence, women in the Nordics entered the labour market in larger numbers and in higher full-time rates (Orloff 1993). The dual career model, whereby women are less reliant on their spouses' income and child benefits, is therefore more entrenched in Northern than in Continental Europe, which makes a strategy of 'explicit familialism' much less feasible for radical right parties operating in a social democratic welfare state context.

Existing analyses are less attuned to how welfare regime legacies mediate the social policy choices of the radical right. First, the 'position-blurring' hypothesis (Rovny 2013) would expect from the radical right a strong emphasis on immigration while de-emphasizing welfare policies with (re)distributive implications. Indeed, the DF's core issue is immigration, and its mobilization efforts explain in large part why Denmark features the strictest asylum regime in Scandinavia (Garvik and Valenta 2021). In fact, even the Social democratic party under the leadership of Mette Frederiksen (since 2015) has co-opted the DF on its restrictive stance on immigration, which demonstrates the indirect impact of the DF on policy change in these areas (Rathgeb and Wolkenstein 2022). However, the DF has also had clear and consistent priorities with regard to the welfare state, and not only on immigration.

At the same time, the emphasis of the 'pro-welfare hypothesis' (Eger and Valdez 2015, Lefkofridi and Michel 2017, Afonso and Rennwald 2018) on the role played by growing working-class support—which is confirmed in Figure 5.1—helps us to understand why the DF has abandoned the neoliberal orientation of its predecessor, the Progress Party. However, it downplays that the DF's impact was by no means pro-welfare in a redistributive sense, but rather geared towards groups of voters that are typically considered 'deserving' in the ideology of radical right parties—i.e. the elderly and labour market insiders—while paying little, if any, attention to the demands of new social risk groups and social investment measures.

This chapter will briefly reconstruct the policy outlook of the DF's predecessor, the Progress Party, before analysing the programmatic origins and policy influence of the DF when it constituted the pivotal support party of centre-right minority governments from 2001 to 2011 and from 2015 to 2019. It will pay particular attention to how the DF justified its policy choices to show how the party geared its ideology of nativism and authoritarianism to the Nordic welfare state context, leading to a policy approach I term *chauvinist insider protection*: cuts in welfare for non-citizens while expanding social security for labour market insiders and the elderly. A final section concludes.

The neoliberal-populist roots of the Danish radical right

The programmatic outlook of the Danish Progress Party illustrates the neoliberal anti-establishment orientation of West European radical right parties during the Keynesian class compromise of the post-war era. Founded in 1972, the party's *raison d'être* was to resist the high levels of taxes that sustained the Danish welfare state. Notably, tax rates had not only increased under left-wing governments in the post-war era; the Danish political right raised taxation even more from 1968 to 1971, similar to their Norwegian counterparts (Goul Andersen and Bjørklund 1990: 198). In this context, the tax lawyer Mogens Glistrup broke away from the Conservative Party and created the Progress Party in August 1972. He had previously gained broader prominence thanks to an interview on national television where he declared, on the last day for sending in tax returns, that he had not paid any income taxes. During the interview, he went on to praise tax fraudsters as the 'freedom fighters of our times' and compared them with railway saboteurs during the German occupation. Glistrup's tax revolt disrupted Danish politics thereafter as his Progress Party became the second largest party in the 1973 earthquake election, with a vote share of 15.9 per cent and twenty-eight seats of 179, ranking behind the Social democrats with 25.6 per cent and forty-six seats (see Figure 5.2).

Despite a moderate drop in electoral support, the Progress Party managed to consolidate its position in the two subsequent elections. However, internal splits between more pragmatic and fundamentalist wings emerged in the late 1970s, contributing to a heavy defeat in the 1984 election. Glistrup started to mobilize against immigration from non-Western countries at that time, declaring a 'Mohammedan-free Denmark' as one of the party's new goals in 1980, before being sentenced to jail for tax fraud three years later. As Denmark admitted a growing number of asylum seekers during the 1980s, the Progress Party under its new leader, Pia Kjærsgaard, mobilized on suspicions that many of them were not in danger of persecution at home and came to Denmark for purely economic reasons instead. As a result, in the late 1980s, the defining feature of Progress Party voters in both Denmark and Norway was a preference for 'welfare chauvinism', i.e. social spending should be restricted to native citizens, which set them apart from the attitudes of centre-right and centre-left voters (Goul Andersen and Bjørklund 1990: 211–212). Similarly, both the Danish and Norwegian Progress Parties were distinct in opposing economic aid to developing countries (ibid.). That the universal tax-financed design of the Nordic welfare regime would be prone to a policy of welfare chauvinism became clear already in the 1980s.

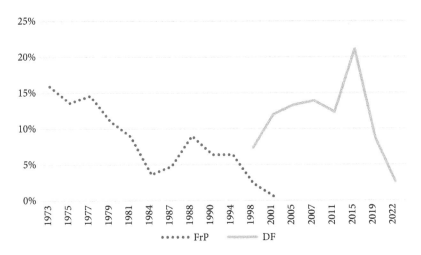

Figure 5.2 Vote shares of Danish Progress Party (FrP) and Danish People's Party (DF), 1973–2022.

Source: Folketingets Oplysning (2023)

Although the Danish Progress Party regained some of its share in 1988, it suffered from ongoing internal power struggles. In response, Pia Kjærsgaard founded the Danish People's Party with three other MPs as a breakaway group from the Progress Party in October 1995. Whereas Mogens Glistrup, after being released from prison in 1987, wanted to retain a pronounced anti-tax and anti-establishment strategy, Pia Kjærsgaard and her followers stood for a more pragmatic outlook aimed at greater political collaboration, including a more centrist agenda in economic and social policies. The DF's strategy proved to be successful, while the Progress Party failed to reach the 2 per cent threshold required to stay in parliament in the 2001 elections. While the two parties resembled each other on the sociocultural dimension, they differed on the socio-economic dimension (Figures 5.3 and 5.4).

Figure 5.3 shows that the Progress Party's manifestoes displayed much stronger support for neoliberal reform than those of the DF, whereas Figure 5.4 indicates that the DF advocated for a larger welfare state than the Progress Party. As I will show below, the DF pushed, however, for a specific *kind* of welfare state that catered to 'deserving' benefit groups and thereby attenuated the redistributive and social investment–oriented design of the Danish welfare state. The subsequent analysis will therefore analyse the policy choices of the DF across different periods in time and situate their influence in the respective political and economic contexts.

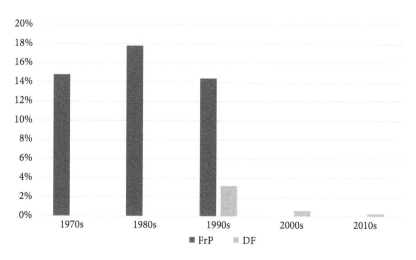

Figure 5.3 Support for neoliberalism in the election manifestoes of the Danish Progress Party (FrP) and the Danish People's Party (DF), 1970s–2010s.

Notes: The score combines the share of manifesto statements (quasi-sentences) in support of the free market (per401) and economic orthodoxy (per414).
Source: Comparative Manifesto Project (Volkens et al. 2021)

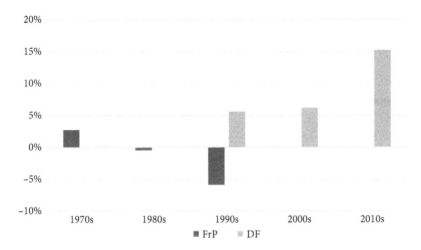

Figure 5.4 Support for the welfare state in the election manifestoes of the Danish Progress Party (FrP) and the Danish People's Party (DF), 1970s–2010s.

Notes: The score shows the share of manifesto statements (quasi-sentences) in support of welfare state expansion (per504) minus statements (quasi-sentences) in support of welfare state limitation (per505).
Source: Comparative Manifesto Project (Volkens et al. 2021)

Anti-immigration and pro-elderly: The Danish People's Party (1995–2001)

The founding of a radical right party with a moderate positioning on socio-economic issues came at a moment when the social democratic–led government (1993–2001) pursued welfare state reforms that alienated some of its traditional blue-collar and lower white-collar base (Arndt 2013; see also Green-Pedersen 2002: Ch. 7). Specifically, the centre-left government pursued a Third Way–oriented reform strategy that no longer attributed unemployment to a lack of Keynesian aggregate demand management, but to structural supply-side problems (Larsen and Goul Andersen 2009). Faced with an unemployment rate of 12.4 per cent in 1993, the Social democrats thus implemented a turn from 'decommodification' towards labour market activation, cuts in marginal taxes, and tightened eligibility conditions for early retirement. Their focus on labour supply also motivated a strong expansion of training-based active labour market policy (ALMP) in the interest of skill enhancement, which benefited workers with greater unemployment risks due to low (or obsolete) skills. This way, the Danish labour market model became associated with the 'golden triangle' of its Flexicurity model, whereby: (1) a strong focus on ALMPs complemented previous legacies of; (2) strong unemployment protection; and (3) weak employment protection (Rathgeb 2018: Ch. 4). The Social democrats' embrace of a market-conforming reform strategy catered to new middle-class voters (via social investment measures) and helped low-skilled workers to enter the labour market (via training-based ALMP), but it had little to offer for their traditional support base which rejected tightened eligibility criteria for insurance-based out-of-work benefits (Arndt 2013).

While retaining the Progress Party's anti-immigration stance, the DF developed a selective pro-welfare position on behalf of 'deserving' benefit recipients—i.e. the elderly and the sick—while downplaying social investment and education-related policies in its platform. For example, in the DF's annual meeting in October 1997, Pia Kjærsgaard outlined the party's social policy platform, thereby ruling out support for tax increases (similar to the Progress Party), but expressed strong support for public pensions and elderly care as these areas are dedicated to 'deserving' welfare groups (unlike the Progress Party):

> [W]e will not help to save a single penny when it comes to taking care of the citizens who are unjustifiably unable to fend for themselves. On the contrary, in many cases we will be prepared to increase public services for these vulnerable groups. It makes no sense that the old-age pensioners, who in their working lives have toiled and dragged for the benefit of Denmark, must find themselves in a situation where there is hardly enough money for the basic needs. We want a proper economy for the pensioners. [...] As old-age pensioners have great financial difficulties, so do early retirees. These are people who, as a result of physical or mental disabilities, have suddenly found themselves in a situation where they are no longer able to support themselves. [...] As mentioned, the Danish People's Party's social responsibility became one of the main points in the program of principles, which we then finally completed.
>
> **(Kjærsgaard 1997)**

After its 1998 election victory, the Social democrats came under attack around issues on which the DF mobilized its voters. First, the treatment of immigrants and refugees turned into the 'most important problem in Denmark' according to opinion polls conducted during the election campaign (Bjugan 1999: 173). Second, the Social democrats broke their election promise to keep the popular early retirement scheme (*efterløn*) untouched, by cutting its benefit generosity and restricting eligibility criteria, while further tightening activation demands for unemployed workers at the same time. In essence, the reform was in line with the government's overall strategy to increase labour force participation rates, especially among older workers.

At the same time, the scheme itself had become the 'target of experts, economists, and conservative politicians' for the increased costs it imposed on the pension system (Petersen 2020: 546), but the Social democrats themselves had used to present themselves as ardent defenders of early retirement entitlements. The Prime Minister, Poul Nyrup Rassmussen, however, argued that the government's reform had secured the fiscal sustainability of the scheme in the face of demographic ageing and secured its political survival thanks to a cross-bloc agreement with the mainstream centre-right parties (Green-Pedersen 2002: 127–128). Yet, this narrative backfired in public opinion: the Social democrats lost almost one half of their voters from the March election to December 1998 (Larsen and Goul Andersen 2009: 255).

This context played into the hands of the DF. While immigration became a key issue in Danish politics, the DF solidified a pro-elderly image in elderly care, healthcare, and public pensions at a time when the Social democrats lost some of their credibility on these issues. In the words of Pia Kjærsgaard at the party's annual meeting in October 1998:

> Instead of dealing with foreign expenditure [i.e. spending for non-citizens], the ongoing debate about what the Danish welfare society can afford has, unfortunately, developed into a discussion about how much money is to be taken from pensioners. [...] The Danish People's Party has, however, a completely different starting point. We do not believe that pensioners should come crawling asking for alms. Their pension and other benefits should not be seen as help, but as well-acquired rights after a long life's efforts. [...] It is those Danes who built up the welfare state.
>
> **(Kjærsgaard 1998)**

The political right celebrated a landslide victory in the 2001 elections, with the centre-right Liberal Party gaining fourteen seats (31.2 per cent of votes) and the radical right DF gaining nine seats (12.0 per cent), whereas the Social democrats lost eleven seats (29.1 per cent), even though the latter's government record had been very successful in reducing unemployment and public debt rates. An important reason behind the Liberals' election success lay in its moderation on welfare state issues and economic redistribution. In response to the party's election defeat in 1998, the party leader, Anders Fogh Rasmussen, wanted to avoid any explicit assault against the Danish welfare model that could have provoked electorally unfavourable discussions about the distributive effects of welfare retrenchment (Klitgaard and Elmelund-Præstekær 2013). Hence, scholars of Danish politics observed a subsequent convergence between the centre-left and centre-right on the socio-economic dimension (e.g. Larsen and Goul Andersen 2009, Goul Andersen 2019, Arndt 2013, Arndt 2014), which arguably facilitated the DF's politicization of the immigration issue. At the same time, the Socialist People's Party (SF) could not capitalize on the Social democrats' election losses, given that it supported the centre-left minority government's reform agenda (Arndt 2013).

Goul Andersen (2003: 192) thus comes to the conclusion that 'the immigration issue gave voters more incentive to vote for a bourgeois party in 2001 than in 1998, whereas the welfare issues gave them fewer incentives, if any, to vote for the Social Democratic government'. While a strong relative majority of production and service workers supported the Social democrats, it is interesting to observe that working-class voters had become overrepresented in the DF's electorate. According to ESS data, 38.3 per cent of DF voters were production workers (24.8 per cent of electorate) and another 25.9 per cent service workers (20.7 per cent of electorate) in the 2001 election.

Into the mainstream (2001–2008)

Before the 2001 election, Poul Nyrup Rasmussen famously declared the DF would never be part of the political establishment due to its radical positioning on immigration (*salonfähig*)—this statement proved remarkably short-lived however. The DF entered a support agreement with the ensuing Liberal–Conservative minority government and thereby kept the right-wing bloc in power from 2001 to 2011. What facilitated the stability of the so-called 'VKO government' (V = Liberals, K = Conservatives, O = DF) was the favourable economic situation inherited from the Social democratic–led government, which meant that there was little, if any, structural pressure to pursue unpopular welfare cuts. At the same time, the Social Liberals (*Radikale Venstre*, RV), a party that would have come closest to the Conservatives and Liberals on the socio-economic dimension, ruled out a support agreement with the new government due to its liberal position on immigration. Hence, the ensuing centre-right minority government pursued a centrist position on the socio-economic dimension in tandem with a restrictive approach on immigration, broadly in line with the DF's platform (Rydgren 2004: 496–497; Jupskås 2015: 29–30). Being the third largest party now, the DF was thus in a position to become a more mainstreamed party that would assume government responsibility and thereby acquire greater policy influence.

In the area of welfare state reform, the DF traded its parliamentary support for the centre-right government's economic policies in return for: (1) welfare chauvinist measures; (2) enhanced spending for the elderly, while; (3) try-ing to put constraints on pension cuts targeted at labour market insiders. Notably, the DF presented its anti-immigration position not only in cultural terms around national identity, but connected it to the viability of the Dan-ish welfare state, a position the Social democrats have come to share in the mid-2010s under Mette Frederiksen:

> The welfare state is seen as heaven-sent, so that no harm could come to it in the future. People believe—or hope—that a Danish welfare system can be freely combined with open borders and mass immigration. A society based on solidarity presupposes a reasonably uniform, stable society like the Danish one, where citi-zens have a large degree of community around language, culture and religion. Only in a nation with a sense of cohesion and shared responsibility can true solidarity exist. The more the national community is broken down in favour of a multicultural or borderless Europe, the more the basis for solidarity with one another disap-pears. [...] The ideology of globalism, which has come in the wake of immigration, is undermining the national community.
>
> **(Kjærsgaard 2001)**

Immediately after the government assumed office, the DF used its pivotal position to push for tightened immigration laws and social assistance cuts that targeted family types in which non-Danes constituted the majority of recipients. In response, the government introduced a new benefit scheme for immigrants from non-EU countries, who had not satisfied the criteria of legal residence in the country for a minimum of seven out of the last eight years. According to Anker et al. (2009: 13f.), this 'start assistance' scheme was 35 to 50 per cent less generous than the ordinary social assistance rates. Second, the government introduced a benefit ceiling for families with 'extraordinary' expenses, i.e. it capped the maximum level of social assistance benefits for people out of work. As Careja et al. (2016) show, subsequent labour market reforms disproportionally affected the benefit entitlements of immigrants, which the authors consider 'indirect' measures of welfare chauvinism. In the area of immigration law, the '24-year-rule' (introduced in 2003) implied new requirements on permanent residence, including: (1) a minimum age of twenty-four years for spouses; (2) formal ties to Denmark as a new host country; (3) minimum income/savings conditions; and (4) proof of resi-dence (Bech et al. 2017). The declared goal was to cut down forced marriages and immigration via family reunification.

Second, the DF used the annual budget negotiations to strike concessions for the elderly. Of particular importance to the DF was the introduction of supplementary pension benefits for low-income pensioners, who rely on the state pension without savings in occupational or private pension plans (*Ældrechecken*). At the same time, the DF regularly received side payments from the government in annual budget negotiations through enhanced spending on long-term elderly care, including elderly housing in care units and home help, resonating with the party's pro-elderly deservingness conceptions (Greve 2020). Kristian Thulesen Dahl, who became the DF's party leader in 2012, considered the annual budget agreements one of the most important pathways for policy influence (Christiansen 2016: 104).

Third, the party tried to strike a delicate balance between its policy priority to retain pension entitlements for labour market insiders on the one hand, and the VK government's ambition to rein in social spending on public pensions on the other. This tension resembled the political context of the Austrian 2003 pension reform analysed in Chapter 4, where the FPÖ's role was to moderate the degree of pension cuts. Hence, in 2003, the VK government appointed an expert commission to zoom in on pension reform, but the DF wanted it to focus mainly on the welfare costs of immigration (Petersen and Petersen 2009) and was particularly sceptical on announcements to raise the statutory retirement age and abolish the early retirement scheme (*Efterløn*) (see also Klitgaard and Nørgaard 2009):

> When the Danish People's Party announced at the beginning of the year that we were prepared to make minor adjustments to the early retirement pension, it was not a decision taken lightly. We believed—and still believe—that with minimal adjustments, we can afford the early retirement pension.
>
> **Kjærsgaard (2006a)**

In response, the DF made its support for pension reform conditional on the incorporation of the Social democrats in the reform negotiations, thereby hoping to avoid an electoral setback among labour market insiders. Aided by a broad cross-bloc alliance, the DF consented to the ensuing 2006 Welfare Agreement, which gradually raised the statutory retirement age and made early retirement less attractive. In this way, the DF managed to water down initially more far-reaching recommendations from the expert commission and thereby avoid the complete abolition of early retirement. Pia Kjærsgaard thus claimed credit for the party's influence in front of its delegates at the annual party meeting in September 2006:

I can personally guarantee you all that if the Danish People's Party had not been glued to its chairs in the welfare negotiations that stretched into June, the government, together with the extremely reform-minded Social democrats and Social Liberals, would have happily cut the welfare benefits. And not least, early retirement would have taken a real punch to the gut.

Kjærsgaard (2006b)

In return for the policy concessions described above, the DF supported the government's 'tax freeze' (*skattestoppen*), which meant that neither direct nor indirect taxes could be increased during the government's tenure. As the Danish economy boomed during this period, the freezing of taxes had little effect on sound public finances. In the area of labour market policy, the DF also supported the government's agenda of tightening activation demands for the unemployed and liberalizing the union-administered unemployment funds, which had a detrimental impact on institutional union power and led to the proliferation of non-political 'yellow' unions (Rathgeb 2019, Rathgeb and Klitgaard 2022). Taken together, the DF's influence implied moderate improvements for 'deserving' benefit recipients on the one hand, and tightened activation demands for the unemployed as well as significant cuts for non-citizens on the other.

Giving in on austerity (2008–2011)

The first seven years as support party of the Liberal–Conservative minority government provided the DF with policy influence in 'almost all legislation, except EU policies that the government had agreed upon with other parties' (Christiansen 2016: 103). Yet, the DF's problem was that it focused rather narrowly on immigration and social policy, as it delegated authority over economic policymaking to the centre-right parties. As a result, the party lacked a macro-economic policy platform, which put it in a weak position relative to the government when the global financial crisis hit the Danish economy (Christiansen 2016: 99).

While during the economic boom of the early 2000s the Liberal Party moderated its economic stance for vote-seeking reasons, the onset of the Great Recession in the late 2000s provided a window of opportunity to legitimize cutbacks on labour market protections and social spending. As the Liberal prime minister, Anders Fogh Rasmussen, had decided to leave Danish politics and not run in another election campaign, he opted for a more policy-seeking agenda that was closer to his earlier ideological convictions, which he laid out in an ultra-liberal pamphlet called 'From Social State to Minimal State' (*Fra socialstat til minimalstat*) in 1993. In this context, the VK government put the DF under pressure to provide the votes necessary to pursue an austerity agenda by threatening to dissolve their parliamentary support agreement if they do not give in on an austerity package (Christiansen 2016). This proved ultimately successful. In response, the DF aimed to present itself as a 'responsible' mainstreamed party in economic terms, by supporting the government's economic agenda, in return for tightened border controls to Germany.

As the DF accepted the government's fiscal consolidation agenda, it came up with a compromise that retrenched the social rights of the unemployed and lowered family benefits by 5 per cent (Goul Andersen 2012: 178). The ensuing 'recovery package' led to the following changes in unemployment protection: (1) the benefit duration was cut from four to two years and the period for calculating the benefit level was extended from thirteen weeks to twelve months; (2) the requalification period to obtain access to unemployment insurance was doubled, to fifty-two weeks; the period of the so-called adult education support for unskilled or uneducated persons was halved, from eighty to forty weeks (ibid.). As a result, 33,900 insured unemployed workers lost their benefit entitlements when the reform came into effect in 2013 (Klos 2014). At the same time, the DF also supported the government's proposal for significant tax breaks in favour of higher income earners, thereby lowering the top statutory tax rate on labour from 63 to 56 per cent (Christensen 2017: 155). Given the redistributive profile of the tax cuts in favour of high-income earners, the trade unions denounced it as the government's 'red wine reform' (Rathgeb 2019).

In line with the radical right's deservingness conceptions, the DF shifted the costs of fiscal austerity on to the unemployed. This is consistent with the party's previous prioritization of the benefit entitlements for social groups typically considered 'deserving'. However, the austerity drive did not stop at this point. As the DF had clearly developed an office-seeking calculus that provided the government with greater leeway in economic policymaking, the new Liberal prime minister, Lars Løkke Rasmussen, took advantage of the widespread perception that the global financial crisis hit the Danish economy hard. According to nationwide representative survey data conducted between July 2009 and the general election in November 2011, the share of respondents stating that the Danish economy faces a 'quite serious' crisis more than doubled from 29 per cent to 60 per cent, while 14 per cent were of the opinion that the economy would be in a 'very serious' crisis (Goul Andersen and Møller Hansen 2013: 140–143).

To the great disappointment of the DF, Lars Løkke Rasmussen thus unilaterally announced in his New Year's Eve speech his determination to phase out the *efterløn* scheme and gradually increase the statutory retirement age from sixty-five to sixty-seven years as a way of bringing the Danish economy back on track. He thereby directly contradicted the previously declared position of Pia Kjærsgaard to defend early retirement and public pension entitlements:

> Early retirement allows older, worn-out workers to leave the labour market a little earlier than they would otherwise be able to do. They are the bus driver, the cashier, the blacksmith, the mechanic, the bank assistant, the home help—all those working groups who find that everyday life just gets too hard and stressful, as they get older. These people need to know that, if the Danish People's Party has its way, their early retirement and public pension entitlements will not be at risk.
>
> **Avisen DK (13.05.2011)**

Perhaps unsurprisingly, the DF spoke little about its support for the Liberals' social spending cuts and tax breaks during the campaign, but instead doubled down on its key positions of immigration control, welfare chauvinism, social transfers for the elderly (*Ældrechecken*), and greater domestic autonomy from EU integration (Kjærsgaard 2011). The fallout of the Great Recession created opportunities for the Social democrats to unite with the peak trade union confederation LO and mobilize voters on their campaign call for a 'Fair Solution' (*En Fair Løsning*). Central to their platform was to roll back welfare cutbacks and find a negotiated tripartite response to the economic crisis with the unions and employers. The trade unions in particular were keen to regain policy influence in the wake of the government's austerity agenda (Rathgeb 2018: Ch. 4). Indeed, the socialist bloc won the election with a narrow majority in October 2011, thus forming a social democratic–led government for the first time after ten years in opposition. The DF, by contrast, lost 1.5 percentage points and three seats in parliament, which was overall a relatively moderate drop in support, given that the campaign was dominated by questions of economic recovery and job creation, and the DF had supported austerity measures hitting its working-class base.

No more austerity in opposition (2011–2015)

When the Social democrats returned to power in 2011, the DF under its new party leader, Kristian Thulesen Dahl, aimed to broaden its policy profile in the economic domain. This was a central lesson from the Great Recession, as the Liberal Party caught the DF under Pia Kjærsgaard off guard on economic crisis management (for a similar assessment, see Christiansen 2016). Thulesen Dahl's previous role in chairing the Finance Committee of the Danish parliament (*Folketing*) from 2001 to 2011 provided him with a solid background in this regard.

In addition, the policy performance of the incoming social democratic-led government under Prime Minister Helle Thorning-Schmidt (2011–2015) required the DF to take a stance on policy strategies for economic recovery. Notably, the centre-left minority government immediately broke its election promises by stating it would continue the economic reform policy of the previous Liberal–Conservative government in its government programme (Regeringen 2011: 9). Social democratic spokespeople pointed to the pivotal position of the market-liberal Social Liberals within the centre-left coalition, arguing that they made government participation conditional on this written declaration. Indeed, the Social Liberals had already pointed out that they were in favour of the cuts that had been made by the previous government in the election campaign, and they thereby outmanoeuvred the promises of the 'Fair Solution' campaign already prior to Election Day. However, the Social democrats remained the key political operators of the government, and its minister of finance, Bjarne Corydon, carved out the entire economic reform policy in close cooperation with his civil servants. Drawing on interview evidence from Rathgeb (2018: Ch. 4), the Social democrats were convinced that an export-led recovery strategy would generate the economic growth rates necessary to win the subsequent election (on the relevance of neoliberal ideas in Danish Social democracy, see also Klitgaard 2007, Larsen and Goul Andersen 2009). In other words, the government's goal was to raise labour supply and cost competitiveness at the expense of public consumption (Goul Andersen 2019: 192).

As a result, the Social democrats not only implemented the reforms previously announced by the Liberal–Conservative minority government shortly before the election, including cuts in unemployment protection and the phasing-out of early retirement. Bjarne Corydon also broke off negotiations with the powerful metalworkers' union (*Dansk Metal*) and other LO-affiliated unions, who had previously backed the 'Fair Solution' campaign. The reason for this was that the Social democratic leadership demanded an increase in working time in order to finance future investments in education, job creation, and welfare. The unions, however, were only willing to agree to an increase of working days under the condition of rising labour demand, but not when the unemployment rate more than doubled to almost 8 per cent.

Instead of continuing any further negotiations with the unions, the Social democrats under Thorning-Schmidt pursued a strategy that could be coined 'progressive neoliberalism' (Fraser 2019), revoking tightened immigration laws and embracing cosmopolitan liberal values, while embarking on neoliberal reform against union demands. In 2012, the Social democrats introduced another round of moderate tax cuts in favour of higher-income-earners in employment, partly financed through welfare cuts legislated through a reduced indexation mechanism of social transfers for the non-employed, except for pensioners. The government also legislated cuts in the student loan scheme SU, again with the declared goal to enhance labour supply in the face of projected shortages. In fact, a similar rationale had informed the party's Third Way reorientation under Poul Nyrup Rasmussen in the 1990s.

Perhaps unsurprisingly, these reforms rested on cross-bloc agreements with the centre-right parties, as the mainstream right as well as the employers' associations welcomed the reforms to the disappointment of the trade unions and the radical left Red–Green Alliance. This agenda almost invariably created tensions with the Socialist People's Party (SF) inside the coalition, but the final straw came when the Social democrats and the Social Liberals proposed to sell DONG energy shares to Goldman Sachs in 2014. In response, the SF left the coalition, but it kept the government's parliamentary majority intact by ruling out a vote of no confidence.

The DF, by contrast, did not provide parliamentary support for welfare cuts, tax cuts, and the sale of large parts of DONG energy to Goldman Sachs, even though it had paved the way for those changes through the 2010 austerity package. In his annual party convention speech, Thulesen Dahl (2012) argued that the problem of labour supply had turned out to be less severe than expected, which would call into question the government's economic strategy: 'What politicians are we, what leaders of the country are we if we do not have enough courage to say: We were wrong! The preconditions did not hold. It looked like this at Pentecost 2010, but the reality in 2012 and 2013 is different.' In September 2014, Thulesen Dahl presented one of the DF's central pledges for the subsequent 2015 general election. It is interesting to observe how consistently the DF prioritized the social needs of the elderly, which suggests that their deservingness perceptions are more long-term and ideological in nature:

> Let me now just review some of the important tasks that I see that we have ahead of us to ensure just that [i.e. security & trust]. First, about our elderly. Because we want proper care for the elderly. And there must be the financial resources needed to ensure this. It was therefore thought-provoking that the Prime Minister did not mention the elderly in the speech at the opening of Parliament last year. Nor was

there any money for better conditions for the elderly in the government's finance bill last year. [...] That is why we are now saying to the government: let's boost the elderly area with a real billion. A billion that will go directly to benefit, to warm hands, to the elderly who need it. A billion that the municipalities cannot then shave from the budget. This is an important part of our proposal for next year's budget. It will create more security!

Thulesen Dahl (2014)

In the 2015 election, the DF achieved its best election result with 21.1 per cent and 37 seats (+15 seats), followed by the Liberal Party, which suffered a heavy setback (19.5 per cent) down to 34 seats (−13 seats). Although the Social democrats remained the strongest party, partly by claiming credit for enhanced economic recovery, the Socialist People's Party and Social Liberals lost eighteen seats combined. As the red bloc no longer had a majority, the political right took over from 2015 to 2019.

Similar to the early 2000s, Thulesen Dahl quickly reaffirmed the idea that the DF should not enter government despite its electoral success. This way, so the logic went, the party would again achieve high levels of policy influence, without having to take responsibility for unpopular decisions, however (Kosiara-Pedersen 2020a). This argument must also be seen in light of Denmark's fragmented and flexible parliamentary majority building style, offering opposition parties relatively high levels of policy influence in annual budget negotiations. In policy terms, the DF made government participation conditional on its key positions to reintroduce border controls, tighten immigration and asylum laws, and increase pro-elderly spending, but this time it also insisted on a 0.8 percentage growth in annual public spending. This was a notable deviation from the 'zero growth' strategy implemented from 2010 and clashed very obviously with the Liberal Party and especially the Liberal Alliance. Hence, the DF stayed outside government, but backed a Liberal single-party minority government that came to power with a vote share of only 19.5 per cent.

Winning the argument, losing the vote (2015–2020)

Whereas the past Liberal–Conservative minority government (2001–2011) had been able to rely on a support agreement with the Danish People's Party, the Liberal government (2015–2019) has seen itself dependent on parliamentary support from all three centre-right parties or cross-bloc agreements with the left-of-centre parties. The apparent job of Lars Løkke Rasmussen has therefore been to administer a durable political compromise across the left–right divide.

Despite this unprecedented party system fragmentation, the DF's positions on immigration reached an almost hegemonic status in the wake of the 2015/2016 refugee crisis. With the appointment of Mette Frederiksen as new party chair (since 2015), the Social democrats co-opted the DF on immigration and returned to a more protection-oriented social policy approach (Rathgeb and Wolkenstein 2022). At the same time, the Liberal Party mustered a parliamentary majority for long-standing DF demands within less than a year. In other words, the ensuing degree of legislative change was not merely a short-term electoral outcome; it rather reflects the DF's long-term success in reshaping the public 'common sense' on immigration and asylum.

With regard to welfare chauvinism, the government reinstated a general ceiling on the level of social assistance, cut social assistance for residents who had not been in Denmark in seven of the past eight years ('integration allowance'), and introduced an employment requirement of at least 225 hours a year to gain eligibility for social assistance benefits (Denmark Government 2016). Based on a cross-bloc agreement with the Social democrats, the 'Jewellery law' (*Smykkelov*) in particular reached international headlines in allowing authorities to seize valuables worth more than the equivalent of 1500 euro from immigrants and refugees, alongside cuts in development aid and reinstated border controls to Germany (Kosiara-Pedersen 2020a). This package (L87) also implied that family reunification for refugees only became possible after three years instead of one, and the requirements for obtaining a permanent residence permit were raised for all foreigners to six years of legal residency in the country plus employment and higher language skills. Asylum seekers could also be legally required to sustain themselves and their families for a longer period. In the 2016 Finance Act, the DF also achieved its key demand for an additional billion Kronor spending for elderly care, while vetoing the tax cuts demanded by the Liberal Alliance (Regeringen 2016).

Notably, the Social democrats prepared themselves for the 2019 election by adopting the DF's narrative of ensuring the fiscal viability of the welfare state by tightening immigration laws. In the words of Henrik Sass Larsen, the social democratic parliamentary group leader:

Non-Western immigrants are historically more difficult to integrate into the labour market, and this is also true for those Syrians who are coming here these days. The more [there come], the more difficult [it is to integrate them], the more expensive. [...] We are going to do everything we can to limit the number of non-Western immigrants that come to this country. For this reason, we went far—and much further than we had imagined. This is because we do not want to sacrifice the welfare society in the name of humanism. For welfare society is social democracy's political project. This is a society built on principles of liberty, equality and solidarity. Mass immigration will undermine welfare society's building.

Politiken (18.12.2015) cited in Rathgeb and Wolkenstein (2022)

In this context, Thulesen Dahl announced the DF's intention to intensify cooperation in a widely noted interview with the Social democratic party chair, Mette Frederiksen, and the chair of the trade union for blue-collar and (lower-skilled) service workers (3F), Per Christensen, in 2017. It is easy to see why: although there are certainly ongoing differences in the areas of social investment and climate change, when it comes to tightened immigration laws and improved social protection for 'deserving' recipients, the DF and Social democrats had found common ground under the leaderships of Mette Frederiksen and Kristian Thulesen Dahl. Proof of this common ground came when the Social democrats and DF formed an alliance in reinstating early retirement for workers with long contribution records, together with the Socialist People's Party and the radical left Red–Green Alliance (Beskæftigelsesministeriet, 10.10.2020). The only point of contention was the question of whether immigrants should also have access to early retirement, but once the DF had dropped this condition, a cross-bloc agreement between the political left and DF was reached.

Despite the DF's success in shaping other parties' platforms, it suffered a heavy defeat in the 2019 election, losing more than half of its parliamentary seats. It is clear that the high salience of climate change and environmental sustainability hurt its mobilization efforts and instead created opportunities for left-wing parties (Kosiara-Pedersen 2020b). Moreover, the party competed with two new radical right challenger parties, i.e. the market-liberal New Right (*Nye Borgerlige*) and the extreme right Hard Line (*Stram Kurs*), and lost votes to both of them. In addition, however, the party also lost to the Liberal Party and, more unexpectedly, to the Social democrats (ibid.). In a post-election speech in front of party members, Thulesen Dahl argued that the DF finds itself in a paradoxical situation. According to him, the party's positions have become mainstream, but its vote share crashed down nevertheless:

In the best of all worlds, our party is redundant because the other parties have been convinced that they must pursue our policies. And when it comes to the combination of strict foreign policy combined with a proper welfare policy, it must be said that the election this time provided more opportunities. In 2015, the Liberal Party went to the polls on zero growth in the public sector. This time, they gave a welfare promise of 69 billion DKK until 2025. In 2015, the Liberal Party went to the polls for zero border control. This time, Lars Løkke Rasmussen stood by Kruså [i.e. Danish border region] together with Inger Støjberg [Minister for Immigration, Integration and Housing from 2015 to 2019] to promise that border control would continue. In 2015, the Social democrats, together with the Radicals [Social Liberals], went to the polls on a lax foreign policy. This time, they made a promise to continue our foreign policy—regardless of whether they are surrounded by parties that want the exact opposite. In 2015, the Social democrats had just made both top tax cuts and corporation tax cuts. This time, they promise gold and green forests to all government employees—almost paid without tax increases. [...] So in reality, the parties have claimed that they are broadly ready to ensure the implementation of our policy.

(Thulesen Dahl 2019)

The 2019 election led to a Social democratic single-party minority government under Mette Frederiksen while pushing the DF further into decline. Within the party, there was a growing sense that Thulesen Dahl's previous refusal to join the government was a strategic mistake. Whereas the 'one foot in, one foot out' strategy had helped the DF to achieve significant policy concessions and succeed in elections until the mid-2010s, this seemed no longer tenable as the political mainstream co-opted its core policy demands on immigration and integration, thereby calling into question the party's *raison d'être*. In this context, Thulesen Dahl stood down as party leader in early 2022. Yet, his successor, Morten Messerschmidt, faced even more resistance from the party's base for his leadership style and controversies related to the misuse of EU funds. Two months after his appointment, ten of the DF's Members of Parliament left the party to create a new alliance under the leadership of *Venstre*'s previous minister of immigration, Inger Støjberg, called Denmark Democrats party. Its early focus has been to combine anti-immigration appeals with Euroscepticism and demands for political-administrative decentralization. As a result, the Danish party system has featured three radical right parties in the 2022 election contest. The Denmark Democrats achieved the strongest result (8.1 per cent), followed by the New Right (3.7 per cent), and the DF (2.6 per cent). Taken together, these three parties received a collective vote share of 14.4 per cent, falling short of the 21.1 per cent the DF had gained in the 2015 election. By contrast, the Social democrats achieved their best election result since 2001 (27.5 per cent) and formed a novel cross-bloc government with the mainstream right (V) and its breakaway group, the Moderates (M). The official rationale for this grand coalition settlement was to ensure national unity in the face of international crises, with an immediate focus on the cost-of-living crisis and enhanced military spending in response to Russia's aggressive war in Ukraine. At the same time, the Social democrats confirmed that it would go ahead with plans to open asylum reception centres offshore in Rwanda while renewing residence permits only for those Syrian refugees who might help to ease labour shortages. Although the radical right may now appear fragmented and weakened from a short-term electoral perspective, the Social democrats' policy record under Mette Frederiksen testifies to the DF's long-term hegemonic success.

The conspicuous absence of family policy

This empirical chapter has identified similarities in the social policy impacts of the Austrian and Danish radical right parties: welfare chauvinism on the one hand, and labour market insider protection (i.e. early retirement) plus elderly care spending on the other. In contrast to the FPÖ, however, the DF did *not* pursue a familialist policy that would have created incentives for women to assume a stronger role as caregivers, even though the party clearly displayed similarly authoritarian values on crime prevention (Jupskås 2015: 30). First, the DF did *not* use its policy influence as support party of centre-right minority governments to strike familialist policy deals, focusing instead on welfare cuts for immigrants, enhanced pro-elderly spending, and the defence of benefit entitlements for labour market insiders.

Second, in its party documents, the party articulated mostly generic statements on the importance of the nuclear family for Danish society, with only a few policy-relevant exceptions. In its 1997 manifesto, the DF supported ongoing state support for the public provision of childcare for employed parents—excluding those who are unemployed—in light of Denmark's high tax rates, but also stated that parents should be in a position to care for their children themselves, if they wished to do so (DF 1997: 13). The 2001 working programme echoed this position: the party wants to sustain high-quality childcare and kindergartens, but 'public care cannot and should not replace the natural ties and networks of families and friendships' (DF 2001: 51). The 2009 working programme took a more progressive tone by emphasizing the relevance of public childcare as well as the expansion of flexible leave arrangements as instruments to achieve 'more equal opportunities between men and women and to better career opportunities for women in our society' (DF 2009: 102). Only in the 2020 annual party convention speech did party leader Kristian Thulesen Dahl voice a more conservative family policy demand:

We want to make it a real possibility for you to care for the little ones yourself, if you should wish so. Today, however, the only option is if one parent has a very well-paid job. By offering a daily allowance to one parent caring at home, we will ensure that it becomes a real option and choice for everyone.

(Thulesen Dahl 2020)

While the policy details do not come out clearly in the speech, the introduction of a daily child benefit allowance would incentivize parents, i.e. mostly women, to reduce working hours to take over childcare.

Overall, the party showed little interest in family policy, let alone the restoration of traditional gender roles within families, which contrasts with the policy agendas of radical right parties in the Continental European context (Chapter 4) and especially the Eastern European context (Chapter 6). This should not come as a surprise from a comparative perspective. As Denmark has the highest proportion of children being cared for outside the home worldwide, the dual earner/dual carer model is well entrenched in public opinion and receives widespread political support (Petersen 2020; see also Tables 3.2 and 3.3 in Chapter 3). According to the ISSP 2012 (2016) survey, almost 85 per cent of the Danish electorate think that mothers should work outside the home when they have a child below school age.

Shadow case studies: Norway and Sweden

To further assess my argument about how the Nordic welfare state context stimulates a policy of chauvinist insider protection, I will now supplement my primary case study on Denmark with additional evidence from Norway and Sweden ('shadow case studies'). If my claim about the regime-specific logic of the radical right's policy impact were correct, we should find similar policy choices from a Nordic radical right party in government elsewhere (Norway) and the absence of such a policy influence in a country where the radical right has been in opposition (Sweden).

First, the Norwegian Progress Party (FrP) retained a stronger neoliberal orientation than the DF when it comes to taxation and economic regulation (Jupskås 2015), thereby resembling the Danish Progress Party on the socio-economic dimension. However, the Norwegian FrP and Danish DF share a strong anti-immigration agenda that reshaped the political debate in both countries. According to Wiggen (2021), the Norwegian political left 'has almost copied FrP's anti-immigration strategy' when entering office in 2011. While the political mainstream had aimed to tone down the immigration debate in the wake of the 2011 Oslo and Utøya Terror Attacks, the politics and attitudes around immigration and Islam remained largely the same (Wiggen 2012). Similar to the DF, welfare chauvinism has thus been at the centre of the FrP's messaging, by pitting the welfare entitlements of 'our own' inhabitants against those of 'the others' (Bjerkem 2016).

The FrP came to power in a minority coalition government with the Conservative Party (*Høyre*) in 2013. Although the government's platform involved 'a series of tax reforms' and an opening to 'more private ser-vice providers to increase freedom of choice in the welfare system', it has not announced radical changes when it comes to the generosity of welfare benefits and sick leave schemes (Mühlbradt 2014). More controversial was the liberalization of temporary employment and working time regulations through the 'Working Environment Act', which the peak union confederation LO called a 'declaration of war' (Steen 2015). In the domain of social policy, however, the FrP was more reluctant to cut back on prevailing provisions.

Similar to the Danish DF, the Norwegian FrP instead claimed credit for welfare chauvinism and improvements for the elderly in need of care, whereas family policy played a more minor role. Following its withdrawal from government in 2020, the FrP's leader, Siv Jensen, described the party's seven main policy achievements in government (Aftenposten, 18.02.2021). In the area of social policy, she highlighted: (1) welfare cuts for non-citizens; (2) an expansion in pension entitlements for married/cohabitating couples (8000 NOK per year); and (3) the introduction of a pilot project on state-funded elderly care (ibid.). This suggests that the radical right's ideological deservingness perceptions in both Denmark and Norway have promoted a pro-elderly policy impact coupled with welfare chauvinist measures.

The Sweden Democrats (SDs) entered parliament with the 2010 election, but have been met with outright rejection from the political establishment in its early years. Sweden is therefore a 'negative case' in which the explanatory factor of interest—the radical right in government—remains absent across the 2010s. However, the 2022 *Tidö Agreement* among Sweden's right-of-centre parties paved the way for the SD to achieve greater influence under the current centre-right government (since October 2022). To show the distinc-tive impact of the radical right in the Nordic welfare regime context, we would expect (1) welfare chauvinist and (2) pro-elderly measures to be absent or at least less pronounced in degree during the 2010s. Perhaps unsurprisingly, this expectation can be confirmed with regard to welfare chauvinism, but it is more difficult to establish this impact with regard to pro-elderly measures.

It is clear that the SDs have been the sole protagonist behind welfare chauvinism, because the political mainstream had resisted such appeals and refused to legislate selective cuts for immigrants (Norocel 2016). As Jylhä et al. (2019) find, welfare chauvinism was an important factor for vote switches from the Swedish Social Democratic Party (SAP) to the radical right Sweden Democrats. Interestingly, the Swedish left and right did not follow welfare chauvinist appeals, even though there was a popular sentiment in favour of drawing stronger boundaries in the social entitlements between natives and immigrants (ibid.). In response, the SDs have portrayed themselves as 'the only Swedish-friendly' parliamentary party (Rydgren and van der Meiden 2019). The Swedish case thus buttresses the view that welfare chauvinism is not endogenous to the Social democratic welfare regime context per se, but a distinctive partisan impact from the radical right in relatively open and inclusive welfare states that experience growing immigration rates.

Similar to the DF and FrP, the SDs also hold pro-elderly positions with regard to the welfare state. For example, they made their support for a government conditional on benefit increases for low-income pensioners (The Local Sweden 2016). Indeed, old-age poverty has increased in Sweden, as for most other age groups, in the past two decades, which led the Social democratic–led government to find a cross-bloc agreement for an increase in the statutory basic pension for 200 Swedish Krona (SEK) per month in October 2019. It would, however, be difficult to attribute increased spending for low-income pensioners to the mobilization efforts of the SDs in opposition, given that the elderly are an electorally numerous group in Sweden and elsewhere in the ageing societies of the rich democracies. It is, however, uncontroversial that the SDs pushed for welfare chauvinism and pro-elderly measures in the social policy domain, which resembles what we could observe in the Danish case.

Conclusion

What explains the DF's policy impact of: (1) welfare chauvinism; (2) pro-elderly spending through enhanced elderly care spending and generous pension entitlements for labour market insiders; while (3) disregarding social investment policies that would cater to new social risk groups? My claim is that the Nordic social democratic welfare regime is an important factor to understand why the DF promoted this policy combination I call *chauvinist insider protection*.

The Danish case illuminates two points about the policy impact of the radical right. First, in the Nordic social democratic welfare state context, the observed defence of welfare entitlements for 'deserving' benefit recipients—i.e. the elderly and labour market insiders—while retrenching the social rights of immigrants at the same time resembles what we could observe in the previous chapter in the Continental European conservative regime context. Both in Austria and Denmark, early retirement schemes have appealed to deservingness perceptions that cater to the 'hard-working' people with long contribution records. A similar deservingness logic pertains to strong support for elderly care, because the beneficiaries of these schemes are typically native citizens who have demonstrated their willingness to work over their lifetime. By contrast, the social demands of the unemployed, the poor, and new social risk groups have not figured prominently in the policy priorities of the DF and FPÖ, which typically contrasts with the policy platforms of left-of-centre parties. At the same time, growing immigration rates in a universal and generous welfare state context stimulated a pronounced policy of welfare chauvinism that restricted prevailing benefit entitlements to native citizens, especially in the area of social assistance. Taken together, the Austrian and Danish radical right parties have had similar policy priorities, which is in line with the similarities of the welfare state contexts in which they operated: high levels of immigration and relatively generous and inclusive social assistance and healthcare schemes (promoting welfare chauvinism) in combination with generous early retirement schemes (promoting insider protection).

Second, in contrast to the Continental European conservative welfare state context, the progressive design of Nordic family policy and the related absence of a strong male breadwinner legacy implied that child benefit expansion and maternity leave options have lacked a strong popular basis. While the FPÖ toned down its familialist rhetoric over time, it always preferred child benefit expansion and tax breaks for families over childcare arrangements. By contrast, the DF has never developed a strong interest in family policy in annual budget negotiations, where it had had considerable policy influence. As we will see in the next chapter, radical right parties in the Eastern European welfare state context place much more emphasis on the family policy domain in an effort to reinvigorate traditional gender norms and reverse falling birth rates in countries haunted by high levels of emigration rather than immigration.

When we shift from an international comparative perspective to the temporal dynamics of the Danish case, it is interesting to observe how consistently the DF has pursued its social policy priorities over time, which is in line with my argument on the important role played by ideology in a given welfare state context. Over the entire period of investigation, the DF wanted spending increases for the elderly alongside benefit cuts for immigrants, whereas the policy preferences of mainstream parties have been more dynamic and aligned with short-term calculations. For example, the Social democrats broke their promises to defend generous early retirement before losing office (late 1990s) and to reverse welfare cuts and find a negotiated solution with the unions when re-entering office (early 2010s). The Liberals converged towards the centre ground on economic issues for vote-seeking reasons across the 2000s, but once the global financial crisis hit the economy, it pursued an austerity strategy more in line with its traditional policy goals, against union protests. What both mainstream parties have in common, however, is that they co-opted the radical right on immigration and integration policies, especially in the wake of the refugee crisis in 2015/2016. As a result, Denmark still features a welfare state that ensures relatively low levels of inequality, but with new social divides between citizens and non-citizens.

6

Familialist Protection and Economic Nationalism in the Visegrád Region

Despite its liberal roots in opposition to the ruling communist party, Fidesz's ideological outlook has become nativist and authoritarian in subsequent decades. While the mainstream right underwent a process of ideological radicalization towards the far-right across Central and Eastern Europe (CEE), the transformation of Fidesz is arguably the clearest expression of that process (Minkenberg 2013). According to Krekó and Mayer (2015: 198), Fidesz's reigns in power 'have a deep historical basis in the ideology of the Hungarian radical right. In turn, these elements did not appear out of the blue but can be observed in Orbán's statements going back some years as well'. Hungary is therefore one of the few Western countries where a nativist-authoritarian alliance has formed a majority government.

Since 2010, the Hungarian Civic Alliance (Fidesz) and its satellite Christian Democratic People's Party (KDNP) have ruled the country with a two-thirds majority and thereby entrenched its power through a process of democratic backsliding (Enyedi 2006, Levitsky and Ziblatt 2018). Although there are regular parliamentary elections, the ruling Fidesz party used its landslide victory in the 2010 election to undermine a fair party competition context in three consecutive tenures by tilting the electoral system, the media landscape, and the judiciary in its own favour. The Hungarian prime minister himself, Victor Orbán, did not hide his intention to turn his country into an 'illiberal democracy' that would resemble similar authoritarian regimes developed in Turkey, Russia, or China. With such a high concentration of power, it comes as little surprise that Fidesz–KDNP has had a broader and deeper policy impact than radical right parties in Continental Europe (Chapter 4) and Northern Europe (Chapter 5). Hence, this chapter not only covers the radical right's influence on welfare state reform, but also its economic policy impact more broadly.

Despite substantial differences in political power and context, the electoral class composition of Fidesz with its satellite KDNP resembles the working-class dominated electorates of the Austrian FPÖ and Danish DF.

How the Radical Right Has Changed Capitalism and Welfare in Europe and the USA. Philip Rathgeb, Oxford University Press.

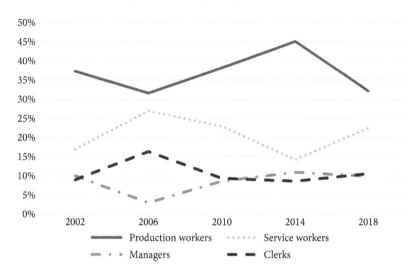

Figure 6.1 Share of votes from production workers, service workers, managers, and clerks within the Fidesz–KDNP electoral class composition, 2002–2018 (percentages).

Source: ESS (2002, 2006, 2010, 2014, 2018)

Figure 6.1 shows Fidesz–KDNP's class composition by showing its four largest electoral constituencies from 2002 to 2018, based on Oesch's (2006) class schema.[1]

From 2002 to 2018, the share of votes from production workers hovered between 31 and 45 per cent, and among service workers between 14 and 27 per cent. Two important sources of electoral support also come from office clerks (between 9 and 16 per cent) and managers (between 3 and 11 per cent), closely followed by small business owners and sociocultural professionals. Hence, more than 50 per cent of Fidesz voters had a working-class background in each general election since 2002. Let us recall that similar levels of working-class support can be found for the Austrian FPÖ since the 2008 election and the Danish DF since the 2001 election. Notably, Social democratic parties often remain the party family that receives the highest support among both production and service workers in Western European countries, but *within* the radical right's electorate, there is a growing and disproportionately high share of working-class voters (Abou-Chadi et al. 2021: 16–18).

---

[1] In the 2006 election, Fidesz and KDNP formed an electoral coalition for the first time. Hence, the numbers shown in Figure 6.1 for the 2002 election capture the electoral class composition of Fidesz only, excluding the KDNP.

The important point to bear in mind, however, is that there is a much greater share of production workers among the electorates of Eastern European countries, especially in the manufacturing-dominated Visegrád region (Bohle and Greskovits 2012: Ch. 4). Hence, the share of working-class voters is higher among the class bases of all Hungarian parties in comparison to their Western European counterparts. Figure 6.2 shows a comparative breakdown of the electoral class structures of Austria, Denmark, and Hungary, as measured by Oesch's schema (2006) with data from the ESS 8 (2018) and ISSP 2015 (2017).

We can immediately identify the large electoral size of production workers in Hungary compared to Austria and Denmark. With a share of 33 per cent, they represent more than twice the share found in the other two countries. This finding resonates with the Europe-wide class analysis of Hugrée et al. (2020), in which the authors observe that in Central and Eastern Europe (as well as in Southern Europe) 'the working class is predominant among people in work' (p. 27), partly due to the relocation of Western European manufacturing plants. By contrast, small business owners form a larger constituency in Austria, whereas a higher share of managers and sociocultural professionals can be found in Denmark. This is in line with Beramendi et al. (2015), who argue that managers and especially sociocultural professionals are typically larger electoral groups in Northern Europe than in Continental Europe, which helps understand higher levels of political support for social investment measures in the former region compared to the latter. Taken

Figure 6.2 Breakdown of electorates in Austria, Denmark, and Hungary by class.

Source: ESS round 8 (2018) for Austria and Hungary, ISSP (2017) for Denmark.

together, the Fidesz–KDNP alliance may indeed be better described as a *Volkspartei* ('people's party') rather than a 'workers' party', because it represents relatively evenly the social class structure of Hungary's electorate, which somewhat contrasts with Austria and Denmark, where radical right parties have gained a disproportionately high share of blue-collar working-class votes.

From a theoretical perspective, we could start from the assumption of the 'pro-welfare hypothesis' (Eger and Valdez 2015, Lefkofridi and Michel 2017, Afonso and Rennwald 2018) that the Fidesz–KDNP alliance has faced relatively strong electoral incentives to expand the welfare state as a way of catering to their sizeable working-class bases. In particular, the very high share of production workers illustrated in Figure 6.1 may incentivize Fidesz–KDNP to expand social insurance rights, because this group of voters typically comprises labour market insiders who benefit from insurance-based welfare benefits, thanks to long and uninterrupted employment biographies (Häusermann et al. 2013, Häusermann 2020). However, the Fidesz–KDNP alliance overall *decreased* social spending and *retrenched* social insurance rights, especially insider-oriented early retirement arrangements. In fact, the Orbán cabinet cut back even more on redistributive welfare schemes at the expense of the poor and the unemployed. As a result, the pro-welfare hypothesis about the crucial role played by blue-collar working-class support is not borne out by the evidence.

An alternative view would argue that the Fidesz–KDNP alliance might have an electoral incentive to downplay the salience of social and economic policies in favour of immigration control and other sociocultural issues. However, this 'position blurring' hypothesis (Rovny 2013, Rovny and Polk 2020) is not feasible for a majority government confronted with the task of macroeconomic management. In fact, Orbán was more than outspoken on his economic policy priorities, as well as on the material winners and losers his agenda would create. In other words, a purely electoral micro-level logic seems to be of little help to explain the Hungarian case, because the policy performance of Fidesz–KDNP was neither 'pro-welfare' nor 'blurry', as existing theories would predict. What we can observe in the Hungarian case instead is a policy logic of *familialist protection* aimed to reward the 'productive Magyar family', which complemented Orbán's selective economic nationalism that was aimed to restore domestic policymaking autonomy. The most distinctive welfare state impact of Fidesz–KDNP is an unprecedented expansion of a conservative family policy aimed at boosting fertility rates and preserving traditional gender relations. While Hungary's reinvigoration of familialism implies a cultural re-traditionalization, it should *not* be equated with a return of the 'male breadwinner' model that was predominant in Western Europe in the twentieth century. In fact, Hungarian women are increasingly required to assume a greater role as caregivers *and* seek full-time employment to gain access to social rights (Fodor 2022).

So, how can a comparative perspective focused on the interplay of radical right ideology and welfare state context explain Fidesz–KDNP's policy impact? First, unlike in Austria and Denmark, Hungary's radical right has not embarked on a comprehensive policy of welfare chauvinism in legislative terms despite its ideology of *nativism*. As I will outline below, the Roma minority has been in large part excluded, albeit indirectly, from the expansion of monetary family support, but as Hungary has faced high levels of emigration rather than immigration while its social assistance scheme offers relatively low benefits (Bahle and Wendt 2021: 632-634), the Orbán cabinet has not pursued the welfare chauvinist cuts targeted at non-citizens we could observe in Western European countries (Chapters 4 and 5). However, we can see the role of nativism clearly in display in Fidesz–KDNP's family policy that aims to respond to population decline and falling birth rates in the wake of post-communist transition. In other words, whereas nativist parties typically respond to high immigration rates primarily with welfare chauvinist cuts targeted at non-citizens in Western Europe, they are likely to respond to high emigration rates with pro-natalist measures in Eastern Europe. Although the Fidesz–KDNP government overall cut back on social spending, its reforms contributed to the second highest family spending rates across the OECD in 2017 (OECD 2021) and the subsequent 'Family Protection Action Plan' (2019) expanded on this area even more, thus strengthening Hungary's long-standing familialist legacy (Inglot et al. 2022).

Second, the *authoritarian* ideology of Fidesz means that its family policy should not only increase birth rates, but also reinvigorate traditional gender norms and hierarchies. Hence, the party has emphasized the role of women in taking over caring responsibilities through a policy logic of 'carefare', i.e. the access to and level of welfare support for women has become increasingly conditional on child-rearing alongside paid employment (Fodor 2022). Although unique in many ways unique, Orbán's familialist project draws on Soviet legacies of shifting care work to women and tying social citizenship rights to motherhood whilst rejecting Western feminist ideas and movements (Fodor 2022: 10–14). It is important to bear in mind the ongoing prevalence of culturally conservative attitudes in the Visegrád's welfare state context (Szelewa and Polakowski 2022), which contrasts sharply with the more liberal attitudes found in Northern Europe. It thus comes as little surprise that unlike the Danish DF, the Austrian FPÖ and especially the Hungarian Fidesz–KDNP have used their policy influence to strengthen conservative family policy elements.

Third, whereas the Austrian FPÖ and Danish DF defended early retirement and other benefits in the interest of labour market insiders with long contribution records, the Fidesz–KDNP government abolished it in response to tightened fiscal constraints, which reflects the weaker institutional and fiscal entrenchment of social insurance rights in the post-communist Visegrád context. Although radical right parties may well consider labour market insiders deserving of welfare support, they are in a more difficult position to sustain and expand early retirement options in the Hungarian context, because massive labour shedding during the post-communist transition phase caused recurring fiscal crises in social insurance systems (Vanhuysse 2006).

However, the authoritarian values of radical right parties that place strong emphasis on 'hard work' and 'deservingness' face no such fiscal constraint in labour market policy. This helps explain why authoritarianism has translated into workfare policy in Hungary, which came out clearly when Orbán declared that 'instead of the Western-style type of welfare state that is not competitive, a work-based society' was to be pursued by his cabinet (cited in Szikra 2018: 5). Following this notion, the government retrenched the social rights of the unemployed and introduced compulsory public works programme. While radical right parties tend to shift the costs of economic crises onto the unemployed more generally (Rathgeb 2021a, Busemeyer et al. 2022, Chueri 2022), the Hungarian case clearly stands out in implementing a comprehensive workfare regime under the Fidesz–KDNP government. This policy has also contributed to enhanced political loyalty for the government among rural mayors who gained quasi-feudal control over benefit claimants in local workfare programmes (Mares and Young 2019, Ch. 5).

Finally, in economic policy, the central feature of Hungary's economic model is that, unlike in Western Europe where nationalism stimulated opposition to the cross-border movement of people (welfare chauvinism), this region has faced economic vulnerabilities from the cross-border movement of Western capital in the form of foreign direct investment (FDI) (economic nationalism) (for a similar logic, see Manow 2018). In this context, Hungary's radical right has pursued a strategy of economic nationalism that shifted the costs of economic adjustment onto multinational companies and renationalize strategically important sectors (Bohle and Greskovits 2019).

This chapter proceeds as follows. I will first reconstruct the ideological origins and post-communist context in which the party platform of

Fidesz–KDNP under Orbán rose to power, before paying greater attention to its policy impact since its 2010 election victory (after its first tenure from 1998 to 2002). As in the previous empirical chapters, I will analyse how Fidesz–KDNP justified its policy choices to show how the government geared its nativist and authoritarian ideologies to the Visegrád welfare state context, leading to a policy approach I term 'familialist protection', i.e. a pro-natalist and conservative family policy expansion. In that context, I will elaborate on how the gender regime of the Soviet legacy in combination with the 2015 refugee crisis created a fertile ground for the Orbán cabinet to reframe family policy in demographic terms. The subsequent section provides a shadow case study of the Polish case to demonstrate the familialist similarities of the radical right within the post-communist welfare regime context of the Visegrád region. A final section concludes and situates the Hungarian case in a broader comparative perspective.

A liberal insurgent shifting towards the radical right

The historical roots of Fidesz go back to the late 1980s when an underground group of liberal students set out to challenge the ruling communist regime. With an upper age limit of thirty-five years, the party aimed to attract young dissidents committed to regime change at a time when any involvement in the opposition still put people's careers at risk. In 1989, Fidesz even won the Rafto Prize in memory of the Norwegian human rights activist for its liberal spirit and organizational efforts to facilitate the transition towards liberal democracy. Viktor Orbán rose to prominence thanks to a pronounced anti-communist speech at the reburial of Imre Nagy—the martyred prime minister (1953–1955)—in June 1989, where he demanded the introduction of democratic rights, national independence, and the withdrawal of Soviet troops from Hungary (Lendvai 2010: 15). His speech was widely considered the fiercest and most articulate in a series of statements voiced in the memory of Nagy, which attracted both national and international headlines, thus marking the beginning of Orbán's political career. According to the Hungarian essayist, Péter György, Orbán's speech lent this day historical significance by breaking political taboos at the expense of the communist regime (ibid., 16).

The 1990s and 2000s were a period of almost constant alternation between governments of the left and the right, with the exception of the left-liberal MSZP–SZDSZ coalition that achieved a second consecutive term in the 2006 election. Despite heightening conflicts on questions of economic competence, both sides followed a modernization consensus shared by post-communist neoliberal forces that implied a preference for Western integration, EU and NATO accession, and the attraction of FDI. At the same time, generous social policies, especially in the pension domain, targeted key electoral groups to create consent for neoliberal reform, even though they have proven insufficient to secure re-election (Bohle and Greskovits 2012: 161).

When Fidesz entered parliament in 1990, a centre-right coalition under József Antall (1990–1993) and Péter Boross (1993–1994) initiated the transition process towards liberal democracy and capitalism in a new multi-party political system. The 1994 election paved the way for a centre-left coalition under Gyula Horn between the socialist MSZP, the former communist party, with the liberal SZDSZ in an effort to modernize the Hungarian economy. The main problem faced by the Horn cabinet was the structural tension between Hungary's low tax regime coupled with sectoral/firm subsidies aimed to attract FDI on the one hand, and the maintenance (and selective expansion) of generous pension policies aimed to compensate the losers of the transition process on the other. Hence, the ex-communists saw themselves confronted with an emerging social insurance crisis that haunted Hungary's fiscal situation for decades to come (Inglot 2008: 282). In response, the left-liberal government introduced the country's most controversial austerity package—also known as 'Bokros package'—named after its architect and Minister of Finance Lajos Bokros. While previous governments began to establish tripartite consultations along corporatist lines, the Bokros package put an end to power-sharing to the detriment of organized labour (Bohle and Greskovits 2012: 149).

As Fidesz benefited from public disaffection with the left-liberal government's 'Bokros package' in the 1998 election, it was able to form a government with smaller centre-right parties (see Figure 6.3). While prominent liberal members had already left Fidesz due to the party's conservative turn, Orbán's ideological reinvention came in large part with the narrow 2002 election defeat. In spite of electoral gains, Fidesz lost its government majority for two consecutive tenures and created an alliance with the Christian democratic KDNP. In opposition from 2002 until 2010, Orbán managed to 'rebuild the right' (Greskovits 2020) by harnessing the civic activism of grass-roots organizations and educated middle-class supporters around a radical right agenda that would break with the Western liberal orthodoxy in important ways (Appel and Orenstein 2018: 160–165). In addition to economic grievances caused by another austerity package, the infamous leaked speech by the Prime Minister Ferenc Gyurcsány, in which he admitted fooling the electorate about the actual state of the economy, opened the door for a resounding election victory for the Fidesz–KDNP alliance in 2010. Since then, the Fidesz–KDNP government has enjoyed a two-thirds majority of seats due to a number of election laws designed in favour of the incumbent, even though it did not reach a majority of votes in 2014 and 2018.

In programmatic terms, Orbán's strategy was to capitalize on economic grievances as the mobilizing capacity of his civic circles movement faced limits in reaching out to working-class neighbourhoods in Budapest and other manufacturing-dominated strongholds during the 2000s (Greskovits 2020: 261). The Fidesz–KDNP government did not, however, embark on a broad pro-welfare agenda as such. It instead used the welfare state in a more selective way to reward the 'productive Magyar family' while at the same time imposing broad social spending cuts, institutionalizing a workfare regime, and underfunding social investment areas. The following empirical analysis will show how Hungary's welfare state context mediated the ideological agenda of Fidesz–KDNP and thereby led to a reform path that deviated from the insider protection and welfare chauvinism pursued by radical right

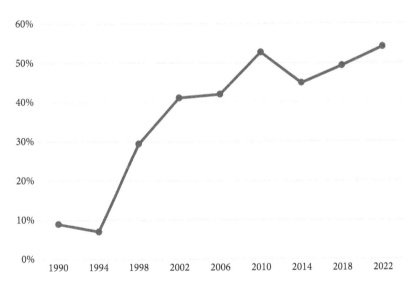

Figure 6.3 Percentage of list votes at parliamentary elections for Fidesz (1990–2002) and Fidesz–KDNP (2006–2022), 1990–2022.

Source: Nemzeti Választási Iroda (2023)

parties in Continental Europe (Chapter 4) and Northern Europe (Chapter 5). First, recurring problems of fiscal overspending and jobless growth put constraints on insider protection through early retirement arrangements and other forms of labour-shedding. As Fidesz–KDNP has been a majority government, it had to act more responsibly in fiscal policy terms than radical right-wing junior coalition partners (e.g. in Austria) or support parties of minority governments (e.g. in Denmark). Second, relatively low levels of immigration in a welfare state context characterized by weak minimum income schemes meant that welfare chauvinism was of minor importance in legislative terms. In this context, nativism and authoritarianism promoted instead a pro-natalist family policy that reinvigorated traditional gender hierarchies. However, realizing this agenda required first a policy response to the fallout of the global financial crisis that exacerbated pre-existing external constraints on the domestic policymaking autonomy of Hungary's foreign-led capitalism.

Orbán's 'war of liberation' during the financial-*cum*-fiscal crisis (2010–2014)

Understanding the policy impact of Fidesz–KDNP since 2010 requires an appreciation of the economic context in which it assumed office. As mentioned above, fiscal austerity was an endemic feature of the Visegrád region's 'embedded neoliberalism', which relied on relatively generous welfare systems to compensate the losers of post-communist transition and facilitate the institutionalization of an FDI-led growth model (Bohle and Greskovits 2012: Ch. 4). As the global financial crisis has aggravated this neoliberalism-*cum*-welfare tension, the first visits of Orbán as prime minister were to Brussels and Berlin asking for greater leeway with respect to the fiscal targets of the Stability and Growth Pact—without success (Csaba 2022: 3). The orthodox adjustment strategy devised in response to Southern Europe's sovereign debt crisis precluded concessions from the European Commission and the German government to Hungary. Hence, the new Orbán cabinet had to follow the bailout package negotiated by the previous left-liberal government with the IMF and the EU in October 2008. The domestic fiscal fallout of the global financial crisis led Hungary to sign another emergency financing package with the IMF in November 2011. At the same time, Hungary remained subject to the EU's excessive deficit procedure until 2013. Fiscal consolidation to keep the annual fiscal deficit below 3 per cent and reduce the debt/GDP ratio from 80 per cent was thus an unavoidable task facing the Fidesz–KDNP government. The government's overriding concern to reduce public debt comes out clearly in the preface of the *Széll Kálmán plan* that informed its economic programme during the early 2010s:

> Due to the almost unprecedented proportion of external debt in international comparison, Hungary has now become one of the most vulnerable countries in the world. It's as life-threatening as it is to have constant blood pressure above 200 for the human body.
>
> **(Government of Hungary 2011: 10)**

However, Orbán declared early on that the government will not adhere to budget plans coming from the IMF and the EU, preferring instead to carve out its own fiscal consolidation path (Bohle 2014). When rejecting the terms and conditions of the IMF's second loan, Orbán said that '[n]o one can restrict Hungary's economic sovereignty any more' (Reuters, 18.11.2011), thereby distancing himself from the 2008 IMF deal signed by the left-liberal government, which he had denounced as 'banker's government' already in 2004 (Sebök and Simons 2022: 1633).

Central to the government's fiscal consolidation strategy was to impose special taxes on banks, insurance companies, and other financial services to create revenues for support measures to help Hungarian households indebted in foreign currencies (Bohle 2014: 935). Prior to the global financial crisis, the widespread privatization of housing markets and the lack of domestic mortgage markets made borrowing in foreign currencies, especially in Swiss francs, much more attractive than in domestic Forint. However, Hungary's policymakers had underestimated the risks associated with the promotion of foreign currency loans (ibid., 931). In 2010, about two thirds of Hungarian household debt was held in foreign currency-denominated loans, reaching about 28 per cent of Hungary's GDP. As the Forint exchange rate devalued sharply whereas the Swiss francs acquired the status of a safe haven, the monthly repayment rates of Hungarian households increased by 60 per cent (ibid.). In response, the Orbán cabinet introduced multiple rounds of bailouts for indebted households, largely at the expense of the predominantly foreign-owned banking sector, 'which eventually footed the bill in almost every case when it was called upon to do so' (Sebök and Simons 2022: 1634). The government eventually even forced foreign banks to convert foreign currency mortgage loans into Hungarian forint. Taken together, these measures averted the ultimate risk of indebted households to lose their home while bringing much of the banking sector under 'Hungarian control' at the same time (ibid., 1636).

Another important part of Hungary's 'unorthodox' crisis management was the *de facto* nationalization of the second-pillar compulsory private pension fund to reduce the deficit below the Maastricht threshold of 3 per cent/GDP and to overcome the fiscal scrutiny of the IMF and EU, while also creating fiscal resources for a 16 per cent flat-rate personal income tax (Szikra 2014: 490–491). As the adoption of such a flat tax, which reduced the top personal income rate from 32 to 16 per cent, was a central election pledge that implied a further tightening of the budget, the government reached out to the vast assets of the private funded pension pillar accumulated since 1997. Following its previous rhetoric directed against multinational banks and insurance companies, the government made the conditions of the private funded pillar so unattractive that 97 per cent of its members 'opted' for a transfer of their pension assets to a newly created Fund for Pension Reform and the Decrease of the Deficit (ibid.). In effect, the reform eliminated the second private pension pillar and returned the pension system to its pre-1997 state with only one public pay-as-you-go pillar. That the government pushed through such a fundamental overhaul of the pension system within only a few months gave a sense of Orbán's commitment to override the parliamentary procedures and constitutional limits of a liberal-democratic welfare state.

The government connected short-term fiscal crisis management with a more long-term political strategy to relegate Hungary's external economic dependence in favour of a newly created domestic business class that would prove loyal supporters of Hungary's ensuing 'illiberal' regime (Johnston and Barnes 2015, Scheiring 2020). Hence, Orbán directed his so-called 'war of liberation' not only against the fiscal control exercised by the EU's Excessive Deficit Procedure and the IMF's bailout conditions, but also against Hungary's heavy reliance on Western finance in its FDI-dependent growth model (Sebök and Simons 2022). In doing so, he could draw on growing disillusionment in public opinion about the outcomes of the recent post-communist past: the share of the Hungarian population approving the transition to market economy declined from 80 per cent in 1991 to 46 per cent in 2009, according to Pew Research Centre (Scheiring 2020: 166–167). Interestingly, this disappointment was not restricted to a nostalgic sentiment among older age cohorts, but widely shared across generations (ibid.).

Whereas right- and left-wing governments had relied on technocrats and transnational capital to 'build capitalism without capitalists' (Eyal et al. 2002) in the earlier transition period, the subsequent Fidesz–KDNP government fostered the emergence of a national class of capitalists (Scheiring 2022). The following quote from a parliamentary debate, in which the minister of economic affairs (2010–2013) and current head of the Hungarian National Bank (since 2013), György Matolcsy, explains the introduction of special taxes on foreign-owned banks, illustrates the government's case for a domestic business class:

> We Hungarians believe that as a small nation, as a small country, we have to comply with everyone, be it the International Monetary Fund or the European Union, we used to look at other countries, other capitals, and now we think that we have to comply with the whole world. Let's be honest, the successful nations of the world want to live up to themselves: politicians for their own voters, and the business sector following the national interest for the goals of their own country. I think that the compulsion to comply must be ended, this is what a series of points of the first action plan [i.e. Szell Kalman plan] is about.
>
> (Országgyűlési Napló [Parliamentary Protocol], 7 June 2010, page 714)

Two sets of measures reflected the government's economic nationalism aimed to 'magyarize' the economy in favour of Hungary's native business class: (1) special sectoral taxes imposed on foreign-owned enterprises in banking, energy, retail, telecommunication, and advertising companies, and (2) the nationalization of some companies and redistribution of others to native business actors (Bohle and Greskovits 2019: 1075). This way, Orbán could, at least in part, decouple Hungary's model of capitalism from its reliance on Western capital and build a loyal network of oligarchs in support of his government, leading to what scholars of Hungarian politics have called a 'mafia state', due to recurring corruption among business–state elite networks (Magyar 2016). At the same time, however, the government remained very active in nurturing investment promotion from the German car industry. In fact, the FDI stock in manufacturing as a percentage of the GDP doubled between 2010 and 2019 (Scheiring 2022). Bohle and Greskovits (2019) therefore speak of a *selective* economic nationalism to account for the apparent distinction made by the Fidesz–KDNP government between 'good' FDI (e.g. manufacturing) and 'bad' FDI (e.g. banking).

In terms of welfare state reform, the government's fiscal consolidation agenda not only hit the welfare entitlements of the unemployed and the poor; it also made access to disability pensions more difficult and abolished early retirement as a social right for labour market insiders with long contribution records (Szikra 2014). In this way, the Fidesz–KDNP government deviated from the insider-oriented pension policy supported by radical right parties in Continental European (Chapter 4) and Northern Europe (Chapter 5) in order to rein in public debt, as the *Széll Kálmán plan* made clear: '[W]e will not let those leave the world of work prematurely who are still capable. This will also increase employment, with all the benefit to the government debt included in the previous section' (ibid., 19).

The abolition of all forms of early retirement formed part of a broader workfare agenda targeting the unemployed and social assistance claimants. As a result, the government reduced the maximum duration of unemployment benefit receipt from nine to three months while making access to social assistance conditional on the participation in public works programmes (Szikra 2014). At the same time, the value of social assistance has declined each year since 2008, because the government reduced its level from 100 to 80 per cent of the minimum pension and suspended indexation to annual inflation rates (Scheiring 2020: 271). It must be noted that the previous left-liberal Gyurcsány cabinet (2006–2010) had already established mandatory participation in public works programmes for the unemployed, but the Orbán cabinet massively expanded the scheme and reduced the salaries of public workers from 100 to 60 per cent of the statutory minimum wage (Szikra 2018). Related to this, it redirected almost all social spending funds from active labour market policy to the expansion of the compulsory public works programme (ibid.). Between 2010 and 2016, the number of people employed in the public works programme increased from 70,000 to 200,000, thereby raising the employment rate of the low-skilled in particular, albeit that number decreased after 2017 (Scheiring 2020: 278). At the same time, social investment in education, research and development, and healthcare remained seriously underfunded, following a strategy of 'austerity by stealth' (Bohle and Greskovits 2019: 18).

While raising employment levels to reduce fiscal deficits may well have been a structural demand for Hungarian governments of any political orientation during the early 2010s, the Fidesz–KDNP government's workfare approach provides insights into the authoritarian deservingness perceptions of radical right parties. Rather than focusing on social investments in education or care facilities to enhance job opportunities for new social risk groups (i.e. the low-skilled, women, the young), Orbán has considered unemployment a moral issue requiring a punitive approach to reinforce work incentives:

It would be a big mistake to equate those who want to work but do not get a job, and those who could work, but who think that living on benefits or other state benefits is more convenient, and that money can also be made from this and that. If nothing else, from stealing hens.

(Orbán 2011)

I want to take this as far as possible, I want to tell every Hungarian citizen that they will not get any social assistance if they are capable of working.

(Orbán 2012 cited in Scheiring 2020: 273)

Whereas Orbán's so-called 'war of liberation' in the aftermath of the global financial crisis implied fiscal austerity in unemployment protection, social assistance, early retirement, disability benefits, sick leave, healthcare, and public education, his anti-liberal rule promoted an expansion of a pro-natalist and conservative family policy (Rat and Szikra 2018, Szikra 2019). The dual objective of expanding birth rates (nativism) and encouraging mothers to take over care work while discriminating against non-heterosexual relationships (authoritarianism) forms the ideological bedrock of Hungary's new familialism.

Familialism and the refugee crisis (2014–2019)

Despite its strong conservative traits, Orbán's family policy is different from the traditional 'male breadwinner' model found in the Continental and Southern European welfare states of the post-war era. As Fodor (2022) shows, Hungary's emerging 'carefare' regime imposes the domestic care load on women *and* expects them to seek paid employment in a highly gender segregated labour market: 'Most women end up combining an increased volume of unpaid care work with long hours of full-time paid work in an economy that is shamelessly slated against those with care responsibilities' (p. 3). Instead of expanding the provision of public childcare and enhancing gender equality through statutory legislation and collective bargaining at the workplace, Hungary's policy response to the problem of work–family reconciliation has been to expand financial support for (married) middle-class and upper-class couples in paid employment through a myriad of tax credits, loans, and grants. In effect, an increase in women's work burden seems to be the government's favoured solution to the apparent tension between reproductive work and paid employment in Hungary's segregated labour market.

Although Orbán's familialist project may be unique in many ways, it also draws on historical and institutional legacies that facilitated such a reform path. Haney (1997, 2002) finds that already in the communist past, the welfare entitlements of women rested mainly on motherhood, and not on material need. Her work shows how women protested against the reconceptualization of need based on material conditions rather than maternity in the 1990s (ibid.). Hence, the maternity-*cum*-welfare nexus established under the Orbán cabinet is not a completely new phenomenon. Moreover, women in Hungary, and the post-communist CEE states more broadly, were overwhelmingly in charge of domestic care work, although both men and women used to be in paid employment in the communist era. The socialization of child and elderly care helped to reconcile work–family life at first, but the expansion of in-kind benefits was too limited to ease women's domestic care burden, as time budget surveys and ethnographic accounts suggest (Ghodsee 2005). As Fodor (2022: 12–13) argues, the communist party gradually shifted the care burden further onto women in the household when intensive industrialization slowed down and multigenerational homes became less common in the wake of an urbanization trend from the mid-1960s. The introduction of lengthy maternity leaves was a widespread response to this situation across the region (ibid.). What added to the 'unfairness of this domestic division of labor' (Fodor 2022: 13) was the widespread disdain for feminism and Western women's movements in combination with the communist party's active ban of Western feminist literature (ibid.). It is thus hardly surprising that gender-mainstreaming initiatives and gender equality legislation from the EU lacked strong political support in the new member states of the former Soviet Union (Szelewa and Polakowski 2022).

In this context, Hungarians on average tend to have attitudes that are more conservative on gender roles compared to citizens from other EU countries (Pongracz 2005). According to ESS data (2018), for example, only 19 per cent of Hungarians 'approve' if a woman has a full-time job and a child under three years old, which is the second lowest score after Estonia with 17 per cent across thirty European countries, whereas this figure jumps to 87 per cent in Norway and 86 per cent in Denmark. At the same time, the Hungarian figures are remarkably similar to those found in conservative Continental European welfare states with male breadwinner legacies, with 26 per cent in Switzerland, 25 per cent in Austria, and 20 per cent in Germany (ibid.). It seems that, whereas public opinion in the Western European countries moved from a conservative legacy towards a more progressive direction—despite strong ongoing variation between Northern and Continental/Southern Europe—liberal EU-led initiatives for gender equality have been more contested in the Eastern European countries (Cook and Inglot 2021: 886–889).

Taken together, there are historical legacies and, for that matter, political support coalitions that have been conducive to Orbán's familialist project (Szelewa and Polakowski 2022). As I will outline below, the distributive design of this agenda implies greater inequalities in terms of gender (domestic care load), class (expansion of earnings-related tax credit system and non-indexation of universal benefits), and, albeit indirectly, ethnicity (Roma families are less likely to qualify for earnings-related family support). The initial steps towards a policy of familialist protection came immediately after the 2010 election despite the fiscal strains caused by the global financial crisis. First, the Fidesz–KDNP government undid cuts from previous

Socialist cabinets by restoring the durations of earnings-related parental leave back to two years and of flat-rate childcare allowance to three years. Second, and even more importantly, it introduced a generous tax-credit system, which provided increased financial support for better-off families at the expense of poorer (and Roma) families (Szikra 2014: 494). Third, in the area of pension reform, women with forty years of contributions—including durations of child-rearing—have become entitled to retire without cutbacks in order to reward motherhood. Beyond social policy reforms, the political ambitions to protect the 'traditional family' and reject LGBTQ+ rights have become enshrined in constitutional law.

Whereas the expansion of tax credits rewards higher-earning working couples disproportionally thanks to their higher levels of deductible income from paid employment, the universal parental leave (GYED) and family benefit schemes—which are accessible to non-working and poorer families—have remained non-indexed and gradually lost in value (Fodor 2022: 38–39). Specifically, the generosity of the universal parental leave benefit had stood at 41 per cent of the statutory minimum wage in 2008, but this amount decreased to 18 per cent by 2020 (ibid.). In fact, the Fidesz–KDNP government passed a legislation in 2021, which froze the nominal value of the parental leave benefit and the minimum pension by ruling out an indexation to price and wage developments. Similarly, the universal family benefit decreased in its value from 21 per cent of the average wage in 1989 to a mere 5 per cent in 2019 (ibid.). By contrast, the earned income tax credit system provides 33,000 HUF (about 100 euro) to working parents per child if their total family income reaches a certain threshold, which excludes parents when they both earn the minimum wage (40 per cent of employees) as well as divorced mothers in case their income alone is not enough (ibid., 40). By implication, most of the Roma ethnic minority is excluded from the tax credit system in indirect ways due to their lower employment rates, even though they are more likely to have children. Taken together, the reform caters to white, heterosexual, working families whose entitlement to financial support increases with the number of children and the level of income they have.

Although the role of the family and Christianity in preserving the Hungarian nation had played an important role in the government's rhetoric since 2010, the Orbán cabinet broadened and deepened its familialist project especially after its 2014 re-election. An important enabling factor behind the subsequent family policy expansion was the loosening of fiscal strains. Hungary was no longer subject to the EU's excessive deficit procedure and the IMF's bailout conditions whilst the annual budget deficits ceased to surpass the 3 per cent limit of the EU's Stability and Growth Pact from 2012. At the same time, Hungary's employment rate gradually increased from 57 per cent in 2010 to almost 72 per cent in 2020, and economic growth significantly outperformed EU averages since 2013. This economic success created fiscal leeway for his familialist project in particular and, according to Orbán (2014) himself, proved to be an important precondition for the entrenchment of his anti-liberal rule.

In addition to the improving fiscal situation, Europe's 2015 refugee crisis created opportunities for the Orbán cabinet to recast family policy in a demographic light. Although most refugees from the Middle East, who had arrived in Budapest, moved further to Western European countries, Hungary had close to 180,000 asylum applications in the early autumn of 2015, compared to an annual average of 2000 to 3000 in the years before (Fodor 2022: 35). In response, the Orbán cabinet defined refugees as threats to national security, built a wall to restrict entry on Hungary's southern border, and doubled down on an anti-immigration campaign that was pitted against the allegedly liberal immigration plans of the EU and the Hungarian-born businessperson and philanthropist George Soros (Fodor 2022: 36). While the number of asylum seekers declined to pre-2015 levels within three years, Orbán's campaigning seems to have had a strong impact on public opinion, given that many Hungarians seem to have developed a measurable fear of the person of the 'refugee' (ibid.). In this context, the slogan 'We want more children, not migrants' defined the government's re-election campaign in 2018. In his 2017 state of the nation speech, for example, Orbán connected his family policy to the demographic survival of the Hungarian nation:

I must confess, that it is not the tomorrow that worries me, but the day after tomorrow. What about the Hungarians? What will happen to Hungarian life in fifteen to twenty years? It is gratifying that the number of births is now the highest since 2010, the number of marriages is increasing, the decrease of the population has not been so slow for years, but the loss, even if it is slowing down, remains a loss. Who carries how many children is the most personal decision for everyone. And while personal, it is also the most important thing for our community. I also know that the time frame for change here is a decade, success depends on the predictability and perseverance of family policy, but I want you to know that there is no breakthrough on this crucial front yet, so the government will give all support if someone decides to have a child. They say there is usually no direct correlation between changes in living standards and demographics, but I think there is a correlation between a nation's desire to live, people's self-sufficiency, and demographic trends.

(Orbán 2017)

That Orbán's pro-natalist agenda rested on the assumption that women take over domestic care work clearly emerged in his national radio speech given after his 2018 election victory: 'I would like to make a deal with Hungarian women, Hungarian ladies, about the future and their role in it as well as the new opportunities the government could offer.' The lack of public childcare provision underpins the government's conservative discourse on gender roles. In 2020, only 10.5 per cent of children below the age of three years have been enrolled in formal childcare in Hungary, whereas this figure stands at 32.3 per cent in the EU average and 67.7 per cent in Denmark (Eurostat 2022). Still, the government's family policy expansion prioritized tax breaks, and not the provision of childcare or other measures to allow women to reconcile work–family life. Hence, women often drop out of paid employment for at least three years per child, before re-entering a labour market, which lacks equality legislation and workers' representation (Fodor 2022: 47). That Hungary nevertheless recorded the OECD's second highest public spending rates on family policy as a percentage of GDP in 2017 (OECD 2021) can therefore be attributed to the expansion of social expenditure on tax breaks rather than in-kind benefits.

The Fidesz–KDNP government expanded its pro-natalist and conservative family policy in many ways through the legislation of the 'Family Protection Action Plan' in 2018/2019. First, the reform introduced a lifetime exemption from personal income tax for women who bear and raise four or more children. Second, women under forty who marry for the first time and have worked for at least three years became eligible for a 31,700-euro 'childbearing' loan at a discounted rate, which is forgiven when they have more children. Third, for the second and every additional child, the reform expanded the state's financial support for the mortgage loans of families. Fourth, larger families can apply for a 7900-euro government grant toward the purchase of a seven-seat automobile. Finally, grandparents taking care of children were made eligible for benefits and leave from work, and the government announced the creation of 21,000 new subsidized childcare places. Further expansions came in the generosity of maternity leave (CSED) and with the introduction of a special subsidy for multigenerational homes in 2021. The 'Family Protection Action Plan' resembles Orbán's previous legislation in that access to monetary family support—i.e. tax exemptions, loans, and grants— is tied to marriage, paid employment, and the number of children born and raised within a household. In line with the previously introduced tax credit system, the winners of this policy are 'hard-working' and thus 'deserving families' rather than poorer families with precarious attachments to the labour market. However, the expansion of public childcare deviates from the previous reliance on mainly monetary family support for working couples. Table 6.1 provides a summary of the main family policy changes under the Fidesz–KDNP government from 2010 to 2020.

Table 6.1 Major changes in Hungarian family policy from 2010 to 2020.

Parental leave	• Duration of universal citizenship-based parental leave (GYES) reinstated to last three years (Act CLXXI of 2010), but its value remained unchanged due to non-indexation since 2008. • Allowing mothers to work full time while receiving insurance-based parental leave (GYED) after the child is six months old (Act CCXXIV of 2013) • Women who attended university become eligible for maternity leave after their studies (Act CCXXIV of 2013) • Extension of maternity leave payment for university students by one additional year (Act CLXXVIII of 2017) • Expansion of parental leave options to grandparents when parents are both in paid employment (Act XCVIII of 2019) • Replacement rate of baby care allowance (CSED) increased from 70 to 100 per cent of mother's previous gross wage (Act CXXXIV of 2020)
Family benefits and loans	• Introduction of financial support (interest rate subsidy and one-time cash benefit) for couples who want to have children for buying a new home (Statute of 16/2016. (II. 10.)) • Expansion of eligibility for 'life starter' support (1691/2017. (IX. 22.)), motherhood support (Act XLV. of 2017), and baby bond to Hungarians living abroad (Act CXCIII of 2017) • Reduction of the mortgage loans of large families (Statute of 337/2017. (XI. 14.)) • Introduction of interest-free loans for families who are expecting a baby in the amount of 10 million HUF (~26,000 euro) (Statute of 44/2019. (III. 12.))
Tax credits	• Loosening of eligibility criteria for family tax credit (Act CLVI of 2011) • Relief on social contribution requirements of families (Act CC of 2013) • Increase in the tax credits for families; tax reduction for couples after first marriage (Act LXXXI of 2015) • Exemption of women with four or more children from paying personal income tax (Act LXXIII of 2019)
Childcare	• Expansion of care facilities for toddlers from 2.5 years old (Act CCXXIII of 2015) • Introduction of free food in kindergartens for children if they are part of a large family, have a sickness, are in need or adopted (Act LXIII of 2015) • Commitment to develop nurseries from state budget (Act C of 2017) • Nursery school construction programme (2019) (mostly on EU funds)

Ruling by decree (2019–2022)

Although Orbán had already gained almost complete control of Hungary's 'illiberal' regime, he nevertheless responded to the onset of the Covid-19 pandemic by declaring a national state of emergency that allowed him to rule by decree. The government used its emergency powers primarily to squeeze opposition-led municipalities before the 2022 general election, but it acted less forcefully with respect to the pandemic: 'Rather than taking decisive actions through lockdowns or vaccine mandates, it has passed the buck to employers, saying that it is up to them to decide whether they require their employees to be vaccinated' (Bíró-Nagy et al. 2022: 18). Shortly before his emergency powers were about to expire, Orbán declared to rule by decree once again in order to handle the post-pandemic inflation crisis and the consequences of the war in Ukraine. Similar to previous policies of selective economic nationalism (Bohle and Greskovits 2019), the Fidesz–KDNP government imposed windfall taxes on foreign-owned banks, insurers, retail chains, energy and trading companies, telecommunications companies, and airlines in order to fund government subsidies of consumer utility prices and price controls (*The Economist*, 25.05.2022). It is interesting to observe how Orbán's 2022 State of the Nation speech, which he had given two weeks before Russia's invasion of Ukraine, emphasized that economic turmoil will not threaten the government's familialist project:

> The emergency required extraordinary decisions, so we did not look idly at the price cut, but introduced a policy of four stops: the utilities stop, a fuel price stop, an interest rate stop and a food price stop [...]. The interest rate stop protects families with home mortgages, and the food price stop helps everyone, but most of all, people with little money. So there will be money, because Hungary will continue to work in the future. We will maintain and even expand family benefits. We do not presume that having a child creates a favourable financial situation rather than financial difficulties. We will have children, we will have money, and we will protect families. That's the way to go!
>
> (Orbán 2022)

In addition to strained relations on the rule of law, Orbán criticized the EU's sanctions against Russia instead of blaming Putin for launching the war in Ukraine, which has also created a wedge with its closest ally, the Polish government led by the nationalist-conservative PiS (*Prawo i Sprawiedliwość*, Law and Justice). Whereas PiS had been quick to denounce Russia's aggressive war and call for solidarity with Ukraine, its Hungarian counterpart insisted on taking a 'neutral' position, which commentators attributed to the country's heavy dependence on gas and oil from Russia. Despite these geopolitical cracks in Hungarian–Polish relations, both governments have had a similar familialist approach in the area of welfare state reform. To show that the Hungarian experience analysed above is not simply an artefact of case selection, I will now briefly show that the Polish PiS government has had a similar familialist agenda in office since 2015, testifying to the crucial role played by the Visegrád region's welfare state context.

Shadow case study: Poland's PiS on a familialist path

PiS had had a conservative outlook from its beginnings, but it radicalized by co-opting many stances of the radical right (and staunchly Catholic) League of Polish Families party (LPR) during the mid-2000s (De Lange and Guerra 2009: 542). In terms of welfare state context, Poland is also a case of 'embedded neoliberalism' (Bohle and Greskovits 2012: Ch. 4), whereby political actors attracted FDI from Western countries through neoliberal reform while at the same time compensating the losers of its growth model with generous (insurance-based) welfare benefits. In both cases, welfare expansion often took the form of 'labour-shedding' through early retirement arrangements for workers being made redundant in the post-communist transition phase, but radical right parties have prioritized familialism and demographic concerns when entering government in the 2010s.

In the economic policy domain, the PiS government's economic nationalism—aimed to reduce dependence on foreign capital—resembles what we could observe in the Hungarian case under the Orbán cabinet (Toplišek 2020). While its measures are relatively similar in its nationalist policy direction, they are less radical in degree. In short, the PiS government also imposed a levy on the banking and insurance sectors as well as a turnover tax on the retail sector, increased state control of the domestic banking sector, and consolidated its state ownership in the energy sector (ibid.). While Hungary forced banks to convert foreign currency loans into domestic Forint, Poland imposed quarterly payments into a mortgage relief fund to help borrowers indebted in foreign currency mortgages to meet their financial obligations. In a similar vein, the PiS government only nationalized 25 per cent of the assets held by the second-pillar private pension funds, whereas the Fidesz–KDNP government confiscated them in total. At the same time, however, the PiS government has incentivized the attraction of FDI in the manufacturing sector to boost relatively well-paid employment tied to the

German production model (similar to Hungary again). Interestingly, we can once again observe a distinction made between 'good' FDI in manufacturing causing growth and employment on the one hand, and 'bad' FDI causing economic dependency on the other (e.g. banking, retail, insurance, energy).

We can also see similarities in the area of social policy. As Inglot (2020) shows, Polish family policy had started to take a more progressive turn for greater gender equality in the 2000s, but PiS has put an end to this policy with a more pro-natalist and conservative approach since entering government in 2015. At the same time, PiS connected its familialist turn with strong anti-immigrant and anti-LGBTQ+ campaigns in the wake of the refugee crisis. Introduced in 2016, PiS's hallmark social policy has been the '500+' child benefit programme, which represented an unprecedented welfare expansion by granting each family a monthly tax-free benefit of 500 Zloty (*c.*120 euro) for the second and subsequent children and the same amount for the first child in families with incomes below a certain threshold. In 2019, the benefit was made universal for all children aged 0–14, which benefited mainly middle- and higher-income earning families (Meardi and Guardiancich 2022: 141). The declared objective of the policy was to reduce child poverty on the one hand (ibid.), but it was also embedded in a broader narrative of demographic emergency.

According to Petrova and Inglot (2020: 887), Fidesz and PiS resemble each other in their 'distinctive success in placing such demographic nationalism at the center of their countries' policy and electoral competition'. In both ways, the policy was very successful, as it substantially reduced child poverty and helped to entrench PiS in power (Meardi and Guardiancich 2022: 141). According to opinion polls conducted in 2019, 62 per cent of adult Poles had a positive opinion of the government's family policy, which led the liberal opposition party PO to promise they would not cancel the 500+ programme, despite their initially harsh opposition to it (ibid.). In a similar familialist fashion, PiS reduced the statutory retirement age of women from sixty-five to sixty years on the grounds of their grandmotherly role.

While we can observe a familialist turn under both Fidesz–KDNP in Hungary and PiS in Poland, there are also two notable differences between the two cases. First, the PiS's 500+ programme is more redistributive than Fidesz's tax credit and loan system, because the former is a universal citizenship right for every family with children, whereas the latter is tied to paid employment and income levels. One important reason for this difference in distributive design seems to be Hungary's more sizeable Roma minority, which is excluded from Orbán's pro-natalist agenda of boosting the birth rates of the 'productive Magyar family' in paid employment (Lugosi 2018,

Petrova and Inglot 2020: 884). PiS could therefore embark on a more inclusive familialist reform path, as it was not concerned about ethnic minorities
considered 'non-deserving' of family benefits. Second, it is also important to
note that PiS lowered the retirement age of men from sixty-seven to sixty-five,
which will reduce labour supply among the sixty-plus generation (Meardi
and Guardiancich 2022: 141). At the same time, it compensated lower pension earners with an increase of the minimum pension and promised more
generous pension levels with a thirteenth and fourteenth monthly payment.
As Poland has had a fiscally more sustainable situation than Hungary, it
could inject further spending into its pension system without ever violat-
ing the Maastricht deficit rules (ibid.). Notably, Poland has been one of
the very few countries that underwent the global financial crisis without
experiencing a recession. Hence, the difference in austerity pressure is an
important factor behind this variation in pension expansion. Despite these
two contextual differences, it is clear that PiS's new benefit scheme followed
a similar strategy of strengthening familialist protection, which, tellingly, the
government had termed 'child-rearing benefit' (świadczenie wychowawcze)
(Inglot 2020: 904). By contrast, the expansion of childcare facilities, which
would foster greater gender equality in reconciling work–family life, has
played a less prominent role under the PiS government, similar to what we
could observe under Fidesz–KDNP in Hungary (Szelewa and Polakowski
2022).

Familialist reform agendas can also be observed in other Eastern European
countries once similar governments with nativist and authoritarian credentials take power (Cook and Inglot 2021: 885). As Bluhm and Varga (2020:
655) argue, there are striking similarities between Hungary and Poland on the
one hand, and Russia on the other: 'The focus lies on family policy that once
again subsumes the individual rights of women, children and sexual minorities under the agenda of a national "recovery," both in the demographic sense
as well as in terms of traditionalist values.' More recently, Serbian president
Vucic, who represents another case of democratic backsliding, announced
a family policy modelled on Poland's 500+ benefit to address population
decline and strengthen family values (Orenstein and Bugaric 2022: 188).
Similar to Hungary, pro-natalism and conservatism in the family domain
went hand in hand with a geopolitical reorientation away from the attraction
of Western FDI towards new sources of investment, especially from China,
Russia, and the United Arab Emirates (ibid.). It remains to be seen to what
extent other peripheral countries draw inspiration from Hungary's path of
familialist protection and selective economic nationalism.

Conclusion

The global financial crisis ended in problems for which Orbán claimed to have a nationalist solution that involved regaining economic sovereignty in Hungary's foreign-led capitalism. As disillusionment with the social outcomes of post-communist transition had already built up in the previous two decades, the post-2008 economic turmoil in combination with the left-liberal government's consent for IMF-mandated austerity created opportunities for Orbán to mobilize on an election campaign that pledged to regain national self-determination from external interference. While responding to the constraints posed by foreign public debt and foreign ownership in strategic sectors, the Fidesz–KDNP government also used its two-thirds majority to weaken the opposition and thereby silence the losers its agenda was about to create by redesigning the electoral system and media landscape. Hence, Orbán stayed true to his word when he remarked ominously that '[w]e have only to win once, but then properly' (*The Economist*, 02.04.2020). As Polanyi (1944 [2001]: 250) would have expected, the perceived subservience to international foreign powers—i.e. the EU and IMF—proved an asset to authoritarian forces in the small and naturally dependent economy of post-communist Hungary.

The Hungarian case is a clear reminder of Polanyi's fundamental insight that political counter-movements to the structural demands of capital accumulation do *not* have to take a left-wing form. While the radical left and right may well share the ambition to restore policymaking autonomy, they do so to achieve radically different ends, traditionally involving promises of equality and working-class solidarity on the left *versus* hierarchy and ethno-nationalist solidarity on the right. In fact, some outcomes of Fidesz–KDNP's policy performance appear fairly conventional for a right-wing government, given that cutbacks in social spending increased inequality even though employment increased substantially, whereas domestic business elites benefited from favourable tax deals and deregulatory measures. Important features of post-communist neoliberalism have remained in place, including an emphasis on credibility with financial markets, trade and financial openness, and external competitiveness (Scheiring 2022). At the same time, social investment in healthcare, education, and research and development have remained underfunded due to the dictates of sound public finances and low taxation (Bohle and Greskovits 2019). However, it is important to understand that the ideological objectives of the radical right defy the economic left–right cleavage on which contemporary debates about the rise and fall of neoliberalism are typically based. In other words, the radical right typically pursues economic policies to protect social groups it considers 'deserving' for largely non-economic ends.

In the Hungarian case, the Orbán cabinet unleashed its so-called 'war of liberation' in an effort to entrench pro-natalist and conservative principles after two decades of prevailing liberalization in Hungarian capitalism. Its economic agenda has protected and rewarded primarily the one social unit deemed essential for the nationalist cause of resisting demographic decline and upholding traditional gender norms, which is the 'productive Magyar family', defined as white, fertile, hard-working, and heterosexual. The President of the Hungarian Parliament László Kövér summarized this worldview succinctly when he asked his audience the following question: 'Who is a decent Hungarian citizen? Not someone who speaks Hungarian. It is someone who has three to four children, nine to twelve grandchildren, they all speak Hungarian and are committed to the Hungarian nation.' Orbán's policy of familialist protection reflects this notion of the 'decent Hungarian citizen' all too clearly by tying social rights to marriage, paid employment, and raising children, whereas those who do not conform to this ideal face heightened economic insecurities from the ongoing dictates of fiscal austerity and external competitiveness in a labour market hostile to workers' representation. In a similar vein, the renationalization of strategic sectors such as banking and energy was not only used to establish loyal support among the domestic business class; it also allowed the government to protect middle-class families from rising costs, for example by converting foreign currency mortgages into Hungarian Forint.

From a comparative perspective, the welfare state context of the Visegrád region played a crucial role in stimulating Orbán's policy of familialist protection. Unlike in Western Europe, the radical right's nativism does not translate into welfare chauvinist legislation due to the absence of high immigration rates and generous welfare benefits for non-citizens, whereas fiscal strains put constraints on the radical right's authoritarianism geared to protect labour market insiders for their 'hard work' across their lifetime in the form of early retirement arrangements. Hence, a policy of chauvinist insider protection, which we could observe in the Continental and Northern European context, appeared less feasible in the Visegrád context. The Hungarian radical right could instead capitalize on culturally conservative attitudes in the broader electorate, which helped to generate widespread support for a pro-natalist and conservative family policy that stands out from a comparative perspective (Fodor 2022).

The Polish case confirms the familialist orientation of the radical right in the Visegrád region, but it also qualifies my claim that pro-elderly and insider-oriented measures are less likely to take place in this welfare state context, given legacies of low employment and fiscal overspending during the post-communist transition phase. Thanks to an outstanding fiscal position, the PiS-led government was able to lower the retirement age and expand pension entitlements in ways that bear resemblance to the social policy demands of Western European radical right parties. Hence, the degree of austerity pressure is an important factor in shaping the extent to which Eastern European radical right parties connect their familialist stance with an expansion in pension entitlements. Notably, the lowering of the pension age for women was also justified on familialist grounds, in the sense that it may allow grandmothers to assume a greater role as caregivers.

In the USA, by contrast, the welfare state appears ill-suited to protect and reward the social groups considered 'deserving' of state support according to radical right parties, i.e. labour market insiders and their families. In the absence of a welfare regime that incorporates their social needs through generous public welfare arrangements, Trump has prioritized trade protection as a functional equivalent of social protection, a policy agenda to which we will turn in the next chapter.

7
The Trumpian Exception of Trade Protection in the USA

The radicalization of the Republican Party (GOP) has been long in the mak-ing before Trump's ascent to power. Captured by wealthy economic elites and party donors, the GOP abandoned economic policies that would address the material situation of electoral majorities and pursued instead neolib-eral reforms to an unprecedented degree from an international comparative perspective (Hacker and Pierson 2020, Thelen and Wiedemann 2021). To achieve majoritarian support despite this economic agenda, the party fell back on an increasingly open racist agenda in an effort to reconcile lower-income whites with high-income elites (Hacker and Pierson 2020, Skocpol 2020). In ideological terms, the GOP gradually resembled European radical right parties as it shifted towards a pronounced nativist anti-immigration and authoritarian law and order platform (Mudde 2018). As Minkenberg (2011) argues, the Tea Party in particular represented an American mirror image of the European radical right (see also Skocpol and Williamson 2011). It therefore comes as little surprise that the Republican Party has taken inspi-ration from Orbán's policy agenda, with political observers arguing that the 'American right fell in love with Hungary' (*The New York Times*, 19.10.2021).

To assess the electoral support base of Trump's victory in the 2016 presi-dential election, I follow the approach of the previous chapters and draw on Oesch's class scheme (2006) with data from the American National Election Studies (ANES) (see Figure 7.1).[1] On the one hand, Trump's class composi-tion in the 2016 election resembled those of a *Volkspartei* ('people's party') by attracting support from different social strata of the American electorate, similar to what we could observe in the Hungarian case (Chapter 6). On the other hand, Donald Trump received relatively high levels of support from production workers and relatively low levels from sociocultural professionals

---

[1] All retired people and people who are no longer active have been assigned a class position by former occupation, through coding V161282b. All inactive homemakers were assigned a class position through recoding V161301b, the occupation of their spouse. If someone had a past employment relationship as self-employed they were coded as part of the group for self-employed and big employers, through recoding V161284. There was no variable to establish a class for small business owners.

How the Radical Right Has Changed Capitalism and Welfare in Europe and the USA. Philip Rathgeb, Oxford University Press.
© Philip Rathgeb (2024). DOI: 10.1093/oso/9780192866332.003.0007

in comparison to Hillary Clinton, similar to the blue-collar-dominated electorates of the Austrian and Danish radical right parties (Chapters 4 and 5). This development resonates with previous longitudinal studies showing that since the 1990s the GOP has attracted growing majorities of white working-class voters (Carnes and Lupu 2021). Seen in this way, Trump's election victory was the culmination of a decades-long process of electoral realignment. Trump's tenure in power can thus be seen as a functional equivalent of the European radical right in mobilizing similar voters—white males with lower levels of education—through an American nativist-authoritarian platform, combined with a populist anti-establishment rhetoric (Mudde 2018, Wondreys and Mudde 2022). As Figure 7.1 shows, we should not, however, underestimate Trump's catch-all appeal as a presidential candidate in America's majoritarian election system.

Despite Trump's relatively strong electoral support among (white) working-class voters (Carnes and Lupu 2021), his administration focused much less on social policy expansions for the 'deserving' native core workforces compared to European radical right parties in power. Let us recall that in Continental and Northern Europe the radical right pushed for enhanced protections for labour market insiders with long contribution records—typically including early retirement arrangements and minimum pension benefits after forty years of paid employment—while cutting the entitlements of immigrants in social assistance (Chapters 4 and 5). In Eastern Europe

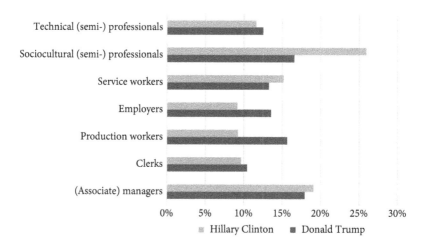

Figure 7.1 Electoral class composition of Donald Trump and Hillary Clinton in the 2016 presidential election.

Source: American National Election Study (2017).

and, to a smaller extent, Continental Europe, the radical right also expanded on a conservative family policy with pro-natalist traits (Chapters 4 and 6). Although Trump promised to leave the 'earned' benefit entitlements of the 'deserving' elderly population untouched (Social Security, Medicare), his 2021 budget proposed spending reductions even on those areas, whereas family policy played a minor role in his tenure. The Trump administration has also followed the GOP's long-term priority on tax cuts that further constrained fiscal resources for social policy. Much of his tax cuts went into the pockets of the top one per cent of income earners, whereas the repeal of the Affordable Care Act ('Obamacare')—which eventually lacked one vote in the Senate—would have deprived 16 million Americans of healthcare coverage (Hacker and Pierson 2020: Ch. 5).

However, Trump's social policy record does not mean he eschewed protectionist elements completely. In fact, his policy of trade protection has been widely considered the most distinctive economic agenda of Trump's presidency compared to previous Republican administrations. Whereas Europe's radical right parties focused on social policy to reward and attract 'hardworking' labour market insiders and their families, the Trump administration catered to similar groups of voters with a different policy, namely trade protection. His 'America First' economics implied a series of sweeping tariffs imposed on a number of imported goods aimed to protect America's remaining manufacturing base from international competition, especially vis-à-vis China. Trump's immigration policy was couched in similar protectionist terms, involving for example the construction of a wall on the border between the US and Mexico. The pro-welfare hypothesis (e.g. Afonso and Rennwald 2018) and the position-blurring hypothesis (e.g. Rovny 2013) are difficult to square with Trump's combination of tax cuts and trade protectionism.

This chapter argues that understanding Trump's policy priority on trade protection requires an appreciation of the welfare state context in which he assumed office. The American welfare state's insistence on 'deservingness' reflects the radical right's preferred logic of welfare provision, but any social policy expansion in this direction faces fiscal and political limits. The GOP's long-standing anti-tax agenda (Hacker and Pierson 2010, 2020) and the 'racialization' of American social policy (Spies 2018: Ch. 2), especially pronounced among Trump's Tea Party base, pose barriers to enhanced social protection. By contrast, the Trump administration faced fewer constraints in the area of trade protection, a policy which enjoyed high levels of support among GOP voters with lower levels of education, especially among deindustrializing regions and communities exposed to imports from China (Ferrara 2023). In this context, trade protection turns into a functional equivalent of social protection, because it aims to protect the radical right's key constituencies by other means than social transfers or services, namely limits to foreign economic competition.

This chapter proceeds as follows. I will first reconstruct the broad contours of America's welfare state development and the GOP's corresponding programmatic trajectory in order to provide background and context to Trump's subsequent policy approach. The second part discusses the reasons for why the Trump administration was more likely than European radical right parties to prioritize trade over social protection. The subsequent empirical section will show how the US welfare state context made the area of trade policy the preferred instrument for Trump's ambition to protect the deserving 'hard-working' Americans from economic insecurities, leading to a policy approach of *trade protectionism*.

Freer trade without stronger social protection

Both the centre-right Republican Party and the centre-left Democratic Party enhanced economic insecurities through freer trade and welfare retrenchment in the decades preceding Trump's 2016 election victory. Faced with the inflation crisis of the late 1970s, American governments across the partisan divide set in motion the gradual stages of the neoliberal era, involving the rise of monetarism (late 1970s), the state's withdrawal from full employment policies (1980s), fiscal austerity and the deregulation of capital markets (1990s), and bank bailouts coupled with quantitative easing (post-2008) (Streeck 2011). Importantly, the turn away from classic Keynesianism, which had aimed to provide for full employment through aggregate demand management, ushered in a new logic Crouch (2009) called 'privatized Keynesianism'. Rather than maintaining public demand through deficit spending as in classic Keynesianism, its privatized form incentivized citizens themselves to take on greater debt through bank loans and credit cards. In other words, the idea behind financial deregulation was to substitute public benefit entitlements with easier access to private financial instruments as a way of allowing, or in fact compelling, lower-income citizens to take out loans at their own risk with which to pay for their education or housing as potential sources of future prosperity. All of these developments had in common a state-led expansion of market mechanisms in the allocation of material resources and life chances, leading to what Hacker (2006) called the 'Great Risk Shift' in which the risks and uncertainties previously covered by firm-based benefits and government policies are shifted onto citizens themselves.

Hence, the removal of barriers on foreign trade was more consequential in the USA than in Europe. Whereas European welfare states cushioned the effects of heightened international competition through job security regulations, social safety nets, and social investment measures, America's welfare state lacked the institutional legacies and political support coalitions to perform such a protective function. As a result, social policy has underpinned a 'winner takes all economy' (Hacker and Pierson 2010) that reinforces the detrimental impact of deindustrialization and globalization on the economic prospects of (manufacturing) workers with low or obsolete skills (Häusermann 2020, Kurer 2020). In this context, trade protection may become a functional equivalent of social protection for radical right movements aiming to attract 'hard-working' and thus 'deserving' workers who have faced increased risks from a rapidly transforming employment structure. This section will show how American governments failed to compensate enhanced economic uncertainties in order to contextualize Trump's subsequent policy of trade protectionism.

The neoliberal trajectory of reducing collective risk protection while liberating market mechanisms started with the so-called 'Volcker shock' in December 1979. By raising interest rates to unprecedented heights under the Democratic Carter administration (1977–1981), the Federal Reserve under Paul Volcker caused the steepest increase in unemployment since the Great Depression, from below 6 to almost 11 per cent in the early 1980s. While inflation rates fell thanks to Volcker's monetarist turn, the Republican Reagan administration (1981–1989) compounded the problem of rising public debt, which emerged from the end of full employment, by aggressively cutting federal income taxes. In 1981, Congress passed the Economic Recovery Tax Act, which reduced federal income taxes by an average of 23 per cent and cut the highest marginal rate from 70 to 50 per cent. Within five years, Reagan and his congressional allies managed to slash the tax burden on America's highest income earners by 60 per cent (Gerstle 2022: 122). At the same time, the Reagan administration shaped a discourse that pitted 'taxpayers' against 'tax recipients', arguing that the country's tax burden 'penalizes successful achievement' (Waddan 2014: 99). Although Reagan's assault on America's high tax regime meant a decline in state revenues, his administration stepped up state spending on the military in competition with the Soviet Union and the prison system to ensure 'law and order' at home (ibid., 129).

Reagan's efforts to cut federal taxes while expanding the prison system is important for our context, because carceral state-building was mobilized on the back of racial resentments that helped to cut off public support for 'welfare' (i.e. social assistance). Unemployment rates reached new heights among minority communities in the 1980s, reaching levels above 50 per cent among young black males (Gerstle 2022: 130). Whereas the GOP rejected welfare for the poor as a failed policy, it embarked on a tough-on-crime approach that paved the way for America to have the largest incarcerated population in the world since the 1990s. A crucial term developed in that context was that of the 'underclass', a racially charged concept referring to high levels of intergenerational poverty, chronic unemployment, out-of-wedlock births, crime, drugs, and 'welfare dependency as a way of life' (Gilens 1999: 129). Although black Americans indeed composed a large proportion of this so-called 'underclass', news coverage portrayed it to be 100 per cent black, which ultimately reduced public support for welfare arrangements (ibid.). In the words of Gerstle (2022: 132), the 'underclass' debate represented a 'powerfully racist connotation of urban black as less than human and unfit for inclusion in any "normal" community of men and women', resulting in mass incarceration as an accompanying feature of Reagan's free market agenda. While the impact of the Republican administrations under Ronald Reagan and then George H. Bush (1989–1993) on actual welfare spending remained muted (Pierson 1996), their taxation agenda did cause enduring austerity pressures and strengthened the belief that the capacity of government to protect against social risks was fading.

In this post-New Deal context of low taxation, the Democratic Clinton administration (1993–2001) assumed office with the goal to reduce the 'two deficits', the fiscal deficit and the trade deficit. While Clinton's ambitious national health insurance plan failed, his administration was successful in imposing tougher work requirements and lifetime limits on benefit receipt, which was part of Clinton's declaration to 'end welfare as we know it'. The ensuing 'Aid to Families With Dependent Children' (AFDC, originally ADC) and the 'Personal Responsibility and Work Reconciliation Act' (PRWORA) alongside various other welfare-to-work programmes meant that after the dismantling of the high tax regime inherited from the New Deal era, Clinton also nullified social assistance commitments introduced by Franklin D. Roosevelt (1933–1941) and expanded by Lyndon B. Johnson (1963–1969). In return, the Clinton administration broadened eligibility to the Earned Income Tax Credit (EITC), i.e. a negative income tax targeting working families with children, excluding those out of work (Rieger and Leibfried 2003: 177). Hence, America's welfare state seemed to consist of a much-retrenched and punitive component of benefits for children and the working-age population on the one hand, and a more generous social insurance component for the 'deserving' elderly in the form of Social Security and Medicare on the other (Waddan 2014: 182).

Yet, as Hacker (2004) shows, policy inaction in America's core social insurance programmes has made them less effective in protecting against new social risks, a process he termed 'policy drift'. Although benefit schemes for the elderly may look unchanged (Social Security, Medicare), 'their ability to achieve the goals embodied in them has noticeably weakened' due to a changed risk structure (ibid., 256). This argument relates to the emerging mismatch between post-industrial labour market change and social policy arrangements rooted in the industrial logic of the male breadwinner and his 'family wage' (Thelen 2014). To compensate for this declining scope and generosity of America's social insurance, *private* social expenditure increased and eventually surpassed all OECD countries, whereas *public* social expenditure remained below the OECD average, especially for younger and poorer citizens.

According to the Clinton administration, successful fiscal consolidation not only required welfare-to-work activation, but also further reassurance of Wall Street through the widespread deregulation of capital markets (Gerstle 2022: 173). Indeed, the USA did record budget surpluses in the late 1990s for the first time in decades. However, the financialization of American capitalism and the related turn towards 'privatized Keynesianism' paved the way for an enormous increase in *private* debt as opposed to *public* debt. At first, the new financial instruments promised a much-needed substitute for those social goods (e.g. housing, education, old-age benefits) a deregulated labour market with enhanced employer discretion and a government committed to 'permanent austerity' (Pierson 1998) would no longer provide. In hindsight, of course, all of this ended when in 2008 the international credit system on which America's prosperity of the late 1990s and early 2000s had rested suddenly collapsed.

At the same time, the Clinton administration removed barriers on international economic competition through free trade agreements, including most prominently the North American Free Trade Agreement (NAFTA) in 1994 and America's consent for China's accession to the WTO in 2001. When signing NAFTA, Clinton remarked that there was no alternative to borderless trade in light of communism's collapse: 'We cannot repeal the economic competition that is everywhere. We can only harness the energy to our benefit. [...] [T]he cold war is over. The grim certitude of the contest with communism has been replaced by the exuberant uncertainty of international economic competition.' The role of government, according to Clinton, was now to direct and improve markets, rather than constrain them. In the end, Clinton may have done more to free markets from regulation than even Reagan himself had done (Gerstle 2022: 157).

Taken together, instead of adapting the welfare state to the economic insecurities unleashed by deindustrialization and globalization, American governments have reinforced these by cutting taxes and social rights while expanding access to private credits as a substitute for public goods ('privatized Keynesianism'). Lynch (2014: 151) therefore concludes that 'it seems fair to portray the American welfare state, in general terms and on the basis of its social insurance programs, as less generous and less comprehensive than almost any other welfare state in the community of democratic, industrialized nations'. Given the resulting lack of job security and social protection, working people with lower or obsolete skill levels have received clear incentives to hold on to their current jobs in a context of heightened international competition, massive deindustrialization, and compressed social mobility (Iversen and Soskice 2019: Ch. 5).

The GOP since Clinton: From mainstream right to radical right

The Republican Party developed its own approach to the post–New Deal context described above, involving a mix of renewed ethno-nationalism for white lower-income voters and radical neoliberal reform for higher-income elites. Clinton's social policy, at least the PRWORA, signalled a triumph of conservative ideas in American welfare politics (Béland and Waddan 2012: Ch. 1). The GOP's battle against the social democratic legacies of the New Deal era seemed to come into fruition in the area of social policy. However, the GOP further radicalized towards an uncompromising tax-cutting agenda tied to the interests of their wealthy donors. Hacker and Pierson (2010: 199) summarized the economic agenda of the GOP since the 1990s in the following terms: '[T]he new GOP bore little resemblance to the go-slow fiscal conservatism of its predecessor. Everywhere and always, the modern GOP called for the retreat of government from regulation and the provision of public goods. Everywhere and always, the modern GOP saw high-end tax cuts as the solution to any problem.'

Despite this neoliberal radicalization, it is interesting to observe that free trade had been controversial within the GOP long before Trump came to power, as we can see in the case of NAFTA during the early 1990s. Both the Republican Bush senior administration and Democratic Clinton administration worked hard to turn the North American continent into a single common market by eliminating tariffs on most goods passing across the borders of Mexico, the US, and Canada, thereby resembling the EU's single market constructed around the same time. While the deal resonated with the free market ideology of governing elites, it failed to grasp fears that the economic hardship emerging in American manufacturing would be aggravated when Mexico could undercut the wages and working standards of American workers.

The challenger of Bush senior in the 1992 Republican primaries, Patrick Buchanan, gave voice to these concerns over the continental free trade zone of NAFTA (Gerstle 2022: 151). Buchanan referred to a paper mill worker in New Hampshire, whom he had met on the campaign trail pleading him to 'save our jobs', when asked about his motives behind this position (ibid.). Notably, Buchanan's campaign was not only protectionist with respect to trade, on the putative grounds that it caused unemployment risks for 'tough hearty [white] men', who would lose their pride and ability to support their families (ibid.). He connected his anti-NAFTA position with an ethno-nationalist position against Mexican immigrants of 'inferior racial character', who would be able to cross the border more freely with the construction of a free trade zone (ibid.). At the same time, Ross Perot, a right-wing third-party candidate independent of the Republicans and Democrats, entered the 1992 election campaign with a highly resourceful campaign against NAFTA for similar protectionist reasons, which eventually cost Bush senior his presidential re-election, paving the way for Clinton to complete the North American free trade zone.

In addition to anti-NAFTA sentiments, growing parts of the GOP took issue with the cultural openness and cosmopolitan nature in which Clinton pursued his neoliberal agenda. Whereas both parties came to support the free movement of trade and capital, the GOP had been less comfortable with the free movement and mixing of people. In other words, 'identity politics' proved to be the new point of contention. Clinton celebrated ethnic diversity and multiculturalism as the cultural essence of Americanism, but also as a source of economic prosperity in the new so-called 'knowledge economy'. The 1990s was thus the decade in which the neoliberal revolution and its claims to personal freedom provided global cities and corporate conglomerates with strong economic growth and job opportunities, whereas outside the metropolitan borders the 'old' middle and working classes observed a dramatic erosion in living standards and spread of low-paid jobs (Iversen and Soskice 2019: Ch. 5). In light of this uneven development, the highly educated 'new' middle class came to consider borderless trade and capital mobility as sources of cultural liberation, and not just of capital liberalization as originally conceived—a sentiment perfectly captured by Clinton's rhetoric.

The 9/11 attacks heightened the public salience of immigration control under the newly elected Republican Bush junior administration (2001–2009). Although the GOP restricted immigration laws under the banner of 'securitization', Chebel d'Appollonia (2012: Ch. 3) argues that these changes did not yet mark a dramatic departure from America's prior stance on the immigration–terrorism nexus. Bush's commitment to religious pluralism and cosmopolitanism prevented the resurgence of ethno-nationalist politics under the new GOP administration, which contributed to his popularity among Latino voters (Gerstle 2022: 208–209). In a similar vein, his economic policies remained within the confines of traditional GOP policy, pushing for neoliberal reform abroad as much as at home, including for example the 2001 tax cut that benefited high-income earners. More controversially, his administration also aimed to restructure Social Security through a partial privatization in line with Bush's vision of the 'ownership society', but his plan eventually failed in Congress (Waddan 2014: 102–103).

It took the first presidency held by a black American to stoke an ethno-nationalist grass-roots campaign that would soon join forces with the established GOP elites. Independent of the GOP and its donors, the so-called 'Tea Party' emerged within six weeks of the new president's inauguration as a white nativist grass-roots movement that mobilized street protests in 542 counties across the country (Madestam et al. 2013). The GOP establishment eventually integrated the Tea Party's base of support by combining its traditional reliance on neoliberal reform with an emphasis on white nativism and selective protectionism for the 'deserving' core workforces in America's remaining manufacturing industries. The policy outlook of the Trump administration reflected this synthesis all too clearly.

Why Trump prioritized trade protection over social protection

The basic story of Trump's 2016 election victory is by now well rehearsed, involving his grass-roots support from the Tea Party, media support from Fox News, transactional bargains with the National Rifle Association (NRA) and the evangelical right, and his strong appeal to white males with lower levels of education, mostly in rural and suburban places that lost out in the post-industrial knowledge economy. It is less known, however, why Trump combined the radical right's typical anti-immigration and law and order agenda with a focus on trade protection. As we could see in the previous chapters, Europe's radical right parties have also attracted disproportionate support among production workers. They have also developed ideological claims to the core male workforce 'deserving' of state support thanks to the 'hard work' they have displayed through long and uninterrupted employment biographies. Yet, European radical right parties have focused more on social protection than trade protection to attract this group of voters, involving insider-oriented welfare benefits and monetary family support. So, what explains this Trumpian exception of trade protection? The following section will address that question from a comparative international perspective.

As we could see above, Trump's reign in power must be placed in a comparative welfare state context of high levels of (1) labour market risk on the one hand, and low levels of (2) social policy coverage on the other, which means that American workers have greater cause for concern over job losses than European workers (Thelen and Wiedemann 2021). America's low levels of employment protection enhance the risk of unemployment, because it makes it easier for employers to hire and fire workers. At the same time, the event of unemployment is more threatening for workers because important benefits (e.g. occupational pensions, healthcare) are tied to employment, while the unemployment insurance provides one of the lowest unemployment benefit payments across the advanced capitalist economies (Lynch 2014). These two features are important in light of heightened economic competition (NAFTA, China) and the decline in America's employment levels since the late 1990s. Whereas the labour force participation rate stood at 67.2 per cent in 1997, it gradually decreased to less than 62 per cent in 2020. This means that the 'anxiety of precarity' (Thelen and Wiedemann 2021) is more widespread than America's typically low unemployment rates would suggest.

In theory, there are at least three social policy options available to protect workers with low or obsolete skills against declining economic prospects and unemployment risks: (1) facilitating transitions to growing sectors through human capital development (social investment); (2) enhancing the generosity and coverage of welfare benefits (social protection); (3) protecting the job security of workers through import restrictions (trade protection). The first option—social investment—is a policy ruled out by radical right parties more or less across the board. The main target group of social investment policies has been the new middle class with its values of social mobility and lifelong learning, whereas the old middle and working classes typically prefer status protection and security within their *current* job rather than the prospect of a *new* job elsewhere thanks to retraining (Williams 2017: Ch. 11). At the same time, it is questionable whether retraining instruments are effective for the re-employment of older and handicapped job seekers in America's context of low social mobility (Iversen and Soskice 2019: 221). In other words, the idea to provide employment security through lifelong learning has its limits on a highly volatile labour market characterized by high levels of earnings inequality and low levels of upward mobility.

The second option—social protection—is a policy ruled out by the GOP's reliance on low taxation and the Tea Party's racially charged emphasis on 'deservingness'. It is well known that middle-class voters are more likely to support the right than the left in majoritarian party systems as a way of avoiding high levels of taxation and redistribution towards the poor (Iversen and Soskice 2006). Indeed, Tea Party members oppose tax hikes as much as the average Republican voter (Skocpol and Williamson 2011: 31). Whereas the lack of public support for taxation puts fiscal constraints on welfare state expansion more generally (Campbell and Sances 2014), the GOP's long-standing *raison d'être* to cut rather than raise taxes makes a policy of welfare state expansion even under an anti-establishment candidate like Donald Trump highly unlikely. In addition, the racial coding of 'welfare' has traditionally undermined redistributive state intervention in American welfare politics (Gilens 1999). For example, as Spies (2018: Ch. 2) shows, US whites are more likely to support spending cuts for working-age bene-fits when they hold negative attitudes about African Americans and Latino immigrants. His evidence at the micro level resonates with a broader histor-ical trajectory of 'racialization' in American welfare politics, whereby white workers benefited from their integration into social insurance (Lieberman 2001) and homeownership programmes (Thurston 2018), whereas black Americans—then as now disproportionately poor—relied on decentralized, often racially charged, social assistance programmes (Michener 2018). In this context, Trump ran on a platform to defend Social Security and Medicare for the 'deserving' (mostly white) elderly with long contribution records, but he eschewed a policy of social protection for the working-age population. Trump's approach therefore contrasts with the policies adopted by European radical right parties. Unlike in the USA, European welfare states create oppor-tunities for radical right parties to defend and expand institutional legacies of insider-oriented social protection, job security relations, vocational training, and family support (Beramendi et al. 2015, Manow et al. 2018, Hassel and Palier 2020).

The third option—trade protection—is in many ways more likely to occur in the USA than in European countries. First, the USA's hegemonic economic position has traditionally provided American governments with great lee-way in altering the international trading system (VanGrasstek 2019). At the same time, its large domestic market made the USA less reliant on foreign trade compared to their smaller European competitors. America's absence of a European-style welfare state has traditionally reduced political support for high levels of foreign trade (Rieger and Leibfried 2003: Ch. 3), which has made the country more susceptible to the globalization backlash embodied by Trump's presidency. Figure 7.2 shows the divergence between the USA and the EU average in the levels of foreign trade from 1980 until 2020, measured as the sum of exports and imports of goods and services as a share of GDP. Given their smaller size, the EU member states have had on average much higher levels of foreign trade than the USA. Whereas the share of foreign trade in the EU average increased from 50 per cent in 1980 to more than 90 per cent in the late 2010s, this figure has stayed below 30 per cent in the USA throughout. Unlike in the USA, Europe's comprehensive welfare states made foreign trade less contentious in political terms, especially in the export-surplus countries of Northern and Continental Europe (see e.g. Katzenstein 1985, Rieger and Leibfried 2003).

America's chronic trade deficits, especially vis-à-vis rivalling China, created opportunities for a protectionist approach in trade policy, a position that was not without precedents in the GOP. As VanGrasstek (2019: Ch. 2) shows, the Republican Party held protectionist positions from the 1860s well into the 1960s. More recently, imports from China have gained salience in American trade politics, as they have affected the job security of domestic manufacturing workers. Low levels of industry- and firm-specific investment

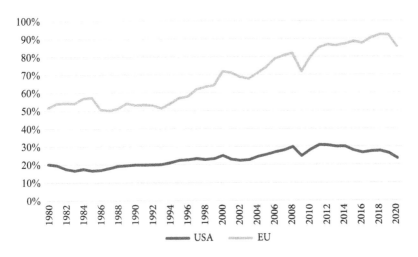

Figure 7.2 Foreign trade of GDP in the USA and EU-27 average, 1980–2020 (percentages).

Notes: Trade is the sum of exports and imports of goods and services measured as a share of gross domestic product. The aggregation method for the EU uses a weighted average of its member states.
Source: World Bank (2023b)

in vocational training and active labour market policy made US manufacturing vulnerable to low-cost competitors from emerging economies (Iversen and Stephens 2008).

While the level of foreign trade remained well below the EU average, Figure 7.3 shows the increased international exposure of America's economy since the Clinton era. Until the early 2000s, imports started to grow much more than exports as a share of GDP. Since then, the share of exports and imports has increased pretty much in tandem, at least until the 2008 financial crash. Foreign trade recovered by the early 2010s, but both exports and imports declined since the mid-2010s. The long-term erosion of America's manufacturing base was thus not only linked to secular technological change, but also to enhanced import competition from China, a factor that accounts for around one quarter of aggregate decline in US manufacturing employment from 1990 to 2007 (Autor et al. 2013). Hence, America's trade deficit with China is certainly not solely (or even mainly) responsible for the decline in manufacturing jobs, but it is the cause most visible to the public. Trade Adjustment Assistance programmes (TAA) provided benefits to workers displaced by trade shocks, but they accounted for a negligible part of trade-induced increases in federal transfers (ibid.).

Trump's trade policy tapped into a protectionist sentiment among a sizeable group of voters with lower levels of income and education. Quite unexpectedly for a GOP candidate, Trump appealed to what he called the

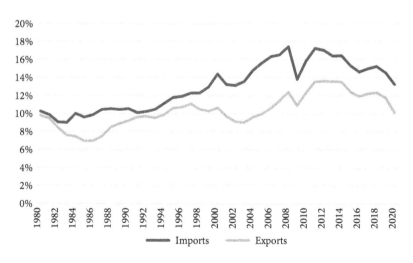

Figure 7.3 US exports and imports of goods and services, 1980–2020 (percentage of GDP).

Source: World Bank (2023c, 2023d)

'forgotten men and women' in order to win the Republican nomination before the 2016 general election (VanGrasstek 2019: 152). Public opinion data suggest that this electoral calculus was not unfounded. As Figure 7.4 shows, only every second Republican voter considered foreign trade 'mainly as an opportunity for economic growth through US exports rather than a threat to the economy from foreign imports' in the run-up to the 2016 election. It is interesting to observe that Democratic voters have become more positive about trade over time, whereas the opposite can be said about Republican voters. Since 2011, Democratic voters are more likely to support foreign trade than Republican voters, resonating with previous findings on the long-term electoral realignment of American politics (Carnes and Lupu 2021).

The same opinion polls show that the most educated Americans are most likely to view foreign trade as an economic opportunity for the US, while those with some college or a high school diploma are less likely to see foreign trade the same way. As Figure 7.5 shows, less than every second respondent with high school degree or lower favoured foreign trade, albeit that figure increased in the early 2010s. In 2019, Gallup asked respondents about the reasons for why they believe trade is either beneficial or detrimental to the American economy (Gallup 2019). Those who see trade mainly as an opportunity cite innovation and economic growth as key aspects of foreign trade,

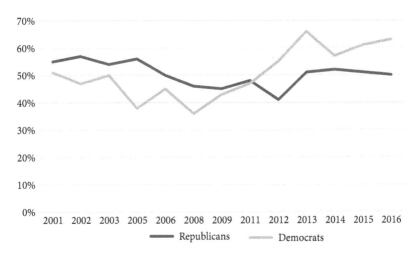

Figure 7.4 Percentage of respondents who see foreign trade mainly as an opportunity rather than a threat, by party identification, 2001–2016.

Notes: No data available for 2004, 2007, and 2010.
Source: Gallup poll (2016)

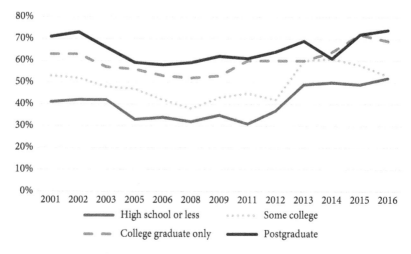

Figure 7.5 Percentage of respondents who see foreign trade mainly as an opportunity rather than a threat, by education in the USA, 2001–2016.

Notes: No data available for 2004, 2007, and 2010.
Source: Gallup poll (2016)

but respondents are least positive about the effects of trade on the availability of jobs, with 42 per cent stating that foreign trade had a negative impact on the employment situation of American workers (ibid.).

Taken together, we can see that Trump's trade protectionism has had a popular basis, at least among Republican voters and those with lower levels of education. From a comparative perspective, this should not come as a surprise, given that America's high-risk and low-mobility environment gives workers with lower levels of education strong stakes in holding on to their current jobs, whereas the reliance on low taxation and the racial coding of social protection makes a policy of welfare state expansion an unfeasible instrument for risk protection.

In order to understand the electoral appeal of trade protectionism as described above, it is also important to realize that the socially corrosive effects of America's deindustrialization could not only be counted in jobs and wages. As Pierce and Schott (2020) find, trade liberalization contributed to a relative increase in 'deaths of despair' (fatal drug overdoses and suicides), which have been concentrated among white working-age Americans living in areas haunted by sudden declines in employment. These findings resonate with the analysis by Baccini and Weymouth (2021: 564), which argues that 'deindustrialization appears to be central to the white voter backlash that culminated in the election of Donald Trump', by producing status anxieties and racial 'in-group solidarity and out-group negativity' among white voters in localities exposed to manufacturing job losses. By politicizing trade policy in the way he did, Trump reached displaced voters who had not voted in the 2012 election, which helps explain why opinion polls were so misleading for the 2016 election outcome (VanGrasstek 2019: 155). In this context, 'China' became one of Trump's famous buzzwords for the ills of 'Red America' (Grumbach et al. 2021), as we will see in the subsequent empirical analysis of the Trump administration's social and economic policy impact.

Trump in power: Neoliberal continuity and protectionist change

Trump may have been in many ways erratic and impulsive in his leadership style, but his administration pushed in fact for two projects that reflected the GOP's new political coalition: tax cuts and deregulatory reform on the one hand, and trade protectionism and white nativism on the other. As Skocpol (2020) shows, the policy preferences of Tea Party protestors differed from the GOP establishment affiliated with the 'Koch network', a set of tightly coordinated organizations united around an agenda of tax cuts and deregulatory reform. Unlike the Koch network's aggressive neoliberal ideology, the Tea Party has placed heavy emphasis on 'deservingness', meaning that those who 'work hard' over their lifetime should be entitled to generous benefit entitlements through Social Security and Medicare. In other words, whereas the Koch network has had an anti-welfare agenda more generally, the Tea Party was pro-welfare for the 'deserving' Americans whom they considered 'hard-working' thanks to long employment records, which typically excludes welfare programmes for the poor (Skocpol and Williamson 2011: 59–68). Trump's agenda attempted to reconcile these two bases of support through a combination of the GOP's traditional reliance on tax cuts (Koch Network) with white nativism and trade protectionism (Tea Party).

In the area of social policy, the GOP was united in its opposition to ACA—also known as 'Obamacare'—as it contributed to socialize healthcare (Koch network) and provide benefits to 'non-deserving' 'free-loaders' and minorities (Tea Party). Although the racialization of 'Obamacare' helped to unite the neoliberal and white-nativist wings of the party, the ensuing American Healthcare Act (AHCA) lacked one vote in the senate, which would have brought long-term cuts to Medicaid (federal health programme for the poor) and the exclusion of 16 million Americans from healthcare coverage (Hacker and Pierson 2020: 147–148). However, the Koch network's reliance on neoliberal reform and the Tea Party's selective deservingness perceptions created tensions between Trump's promise to keep the 'earned' benefit entitlements of 'hard-working' Americans untouched (Social Security and Medicare) with the Koch network's insistence to retrench tax levels and social safety nets (Waddan 2019). In fact, Trump's commitment to defend social insurance programmes rested on the recognition of previous Republican administrations that these schemes are too popular to privatize and retrench ('touch it and die'), but it also responded to popular demands from the Tea Party, his most passionate base of support. Hence, Trump's promise was to *defend* existing levels of social insurance generosity, but there was little, if any, fiscal room for manoeuvre to *expand* on these areas, given that the GOP's overriding concern remained cutting back on taxes.

Proof of Trump's tax-cutting agenda came in his first year in government with the 'Tax Cuts and Jobs Act of 2017'. With this bill, the Trump administration reduced the corporate tax rate from 35 to 21 per cent and the income tax rate for all individuals except those earning less than $38,000 a year, with the largest cuts accrued to those with very high incomes. Policy evaluations show that the winners of the reform are large corporations and wealthy individuals. According to the non-partisan Tax Policy Center (2017), more than 20 per cent of the tax reform's benefits over the first ten years, and more than 80 per cent of its benefits that last beyond the first ten years, go into the pockets of the top one per cent of income earners. Public opinion polls suggest that it is one of the most unpopular bills ever signed into law in America's post-war history (Hacker and Pierson 2020: 151). At the same time, Trump signed executive orders that made it (1) more difficult to organize trade unions, but (2) easier to fire employees while (3) protecting the financial industry in suspending enhanced consumer protection and anti-bailout laws introduced after the 2008 financial crash (Mizruchi and Galan 2023). In his 2018 State of the Union address, Trump (2018) nevertheless framed his tax cut as a policy benefiting the middle-class and small businesses, thereby deflecting from the influence the Koch network and the GOP establishment had had on the distributive design of his reform.

The 2017 tax cut created fiscal strains which the Trump administration compensated for by reducing social spending, with a particular focus on healthcare, food stamps, student loans, and disability payments. Within a decade, the 2018 budget implied cuts in $800 billion from Medicaid, $192 billion from nutritional assistance, and $272 billion from 'welfare' for poorer families (e.g. TANF) (*The New York Times*, 22.05.2017). At this point, the Trump administration kept its promise to leave Social Security and Medicare for the 'deserving' elderly untouched, but the 2018 budget hit the entitlements of the poor in many ways. Notably, however, Trump's 2021 budget proposal did include 'savings' from Medicare and the disability (SSDI) and supplemental income (SSI) components of Social Security, but his election defeat implied that this budget did not come into fruition.

Against the backdrop of these fiscal and political limits in the area of social policy, Trump directed his protectionist stance against the cross-border movement of foreign goods (trade policy) and foreign people (immigration policy). His 2015 presidential announcement speech set the tone for this agenda:

> And our real unemployment rate is anywhere from 18 to 20 per cent. Don't believe the 5.6. That's right. A lot of people up there can't get jobs. They can't get jobs, because there are no jobs, because China has our jobs and Mexico has our jobs. They all have jobs. But the real number, the real number is anywhere from 18 to 19 and maybe even 21 per cent, and nobody talks about it, because it's a statistic that's full of nonsense. [...] I'll bring back our jobs from China, from Mexico, from Japan, from so many places. I'll bring back our jobs, and I'll bring back our money.
>
> **Trump (2015)**

Creating a link between unemployment on the one hand, and immigration and international trade on the other, was a strategy devised by Stephen Miller and Steve Bannon to attract white working-class voters with lower turnout rates, thereby abandoning George W. Bush's previous pro-immigration stance catered to Latino voters (Ngai 2022: 149). While immigration is the radical right's key policy issue across countries, the Trump presidency diverged from its European counterparts by prioritizing trade over social protection. The GOP's reliance on low taxation and the 'racialization' of welfare cut off political support for social protection, but China's growing exports to the USA turned trade policy into a potential source of protection for the 'hard-working' native core workforces that radical right parties typically consider 'deserving' of state support. According to Autor et al. (2013), the USA lost 2.4 million manufacturing jobs to Chinese competition between 1999 and 2011, especially in the politically important states of the 'Rust Belt'. Hence, institutional legacies and their repercussions on voters' attitudes may explain the limits of social policy expansion, but Trump also responded to structural problem pressures experienced in the manufacturing-dominated states. While trade protection mainly enhances the job security of a shrinking groups of manufacturing workers (i.e. the traditional labour market insiders), Trump catered to a broader sense of nostalgia with his policy. For example, in Ohio, a state that was key to his success in the 2016 election, Trump pledged to reverse the trend of regional economic decline in favour of former manufacturing towns:

> I'll tell you what, I rode through your beautiful roads coming up from the airport, and I was looking at some of those big once incredible job-producing factories, and my wife, Melania, said what happened? I said, those jobs have left Ohio. They're all coming back. They're all coming back. [...] Let me tell you folks in Ohio and in this area, don't sell your house. Don't sell your house. Do not sell it. We're going to get those values up. We're going to get those jobs coming back, and we're going to fill up those factories or rip them down and build brand new ones. It's going to happen.
>
> **Trump (2017a)**

In his inaugural address, Trump (2017b) reaffirmed this position by connecting the prospect of job creation to a policy of trade protectionism: 'We must protect our borders from the ravages of other countries making our products, stealing our companies, and destroying our jobs. Protection will lead to great prosperity and strength.' Beyond trade protectionism and the related policy to 'buy American and hire American', Trump promised to restore manufacturing employment by deregulating environmental standards, especially with regard to air and water pollution. Shortly after taking office, the Trump administration reversed Obama's halting of the Keystone and Dakota Access oil pipelines and repealed regulations for coalmine operators, which explains Trump's overwhelming support among coal-mining regions.

Trump's 'America First' economics implied the most sweeping use of tariffs since the 'Smoot-Hawley tariffs' in the 1930s on a number of imported goods—including e.g. solar panels and washing machines (30–50 per cent), steel (25 per cent), and aluminium (10 per cent)—with the declared objective to reduce America's trade deficit and thereby restore domestic manufacturing employment and wage levels. These measures aimed at reducing the trade imbalance with China and bringing back manufacturing jobs to the USA. In this context, Trump established the US's Office of Trade and Manufacturing Policy with the declared objectives 'to defend and serve American workers and domestic manufacturers while advising the President on policies to increase economic growth, decrease the trade deficit, and strengthen the United States manufacturing and defense industrial bases' (Conley 2020: 290). At one point, Trump even threatened to completely decouple the American and Chinese economies, as he declared on Twitter that 'American companies are hereby ordered to immediately start looking for an alternative to China, including bringing your companies HOME and making your products in the USA' (Mann 2022: 268).

However, Trump's confrontational stance and trade protectionism had little effect on China's industrial policies. On the contrary, China retaliated Trump's trade protectionism by placing tariffs on hundreds of American-made goods and agricultural crops at the expense of American workers and farmers. Moreover, Chinese officials made clear in negotiations with the Trump administration that the Communist Party had no intention to change course on state subsidies, technology transfers, and theft of intellectual property (Mann 2022: 269). In December 2019, the two sides eventually reached a deal, according to which China purchased an additional $200 billion in American exports, including at least $40–50 billion in agricultural products. In return, the USA made modest cuts in tariffs, but most of them remained in place. Nevertheless, America's trade deficit with China remained almost unchanged between 2016 and 2019, only slightly decreasing from $310 to $308 billion. It took the Covid-19 pandemic to decrease the deficit from $308 billion in 2019 to $285.5 billion in 2020, as the virus disrupted global supply chains, first in China and then across the world. It is ironic that although Trump made frequent references to American manufacturing workers in connection to his trade policy, it was America's high-tech industries that stood to gain most from the government's approach by imposing stricter limits and regulations on China's key telecommunication firm *Huawei* and ZTE (ibid., 270). In other words, the economic decoupling between America and China went furthest in high-tech industries with national security implications, but had little impact on production levels in America's manufacturing sector.

As the Trump administration failed to produce tangible results for manufacturing workers (or ex-workers), it doubled down on its protectionist claims through immigration policy. Trump's 2017 presidential announcement speech associated Mexican migrants with drugs, crime, and rape in a nativist 'law and order' fashion, but his 2019 State of the Union address attempted to justify his immigration policy on more economic grounds:

No issue better illustrates the divide between America's working class and America's political class than illegal immigration. Wealthy politicians and donors push for open borders while living their lives behind walls and gates and guards. Meanwhile, working class Americans are left to pay the price for mass illegal migration—reduced jobs, lower wages, overburdened schools and hospitals, increased crime, and a depleted social safety net.

Trump (2019)

Following this line of reasoning, the Trump administration adopted the so-called 'public charge rule' in 2018, which created a wealth test for immigrants seeking permanent residency as a way of preventing access to applicants deemed likely to use social safety net programmes. However, a federal judge overturned this policy for constitutional reasons (Administrative Procedure Act). Trump's key project was to construct a border wall to Mexico at an estimated cost of $15 billion—the most expensive public works project ever built in America's history. To overcome environmental regulations in the construction of the wall, the Trump administration declared a state of emergency resulting from 'an invasion of drugs and criminals coming into our country' (*The New York Times*, 15.02.2019). Faced with opposition from California leaders, Trump called undocumented migrants 'animals' that need to be stopped from crossing the border. To bypass the veto from Congress against funding the border wall, the Trump administration declared another state of emergency and repurposed various pools of federal resources. During the second half of his tenure, Trump made good progress on the construction along the 1952-mile-long border to Mexico, leading to 453 miles of new primary and secondary wall, a further 211 miles of new primary and secondary wall were under construction, and approximately 74 miles of border wall were at the pre-construction stage (Smith 2022: 170). Whereas investments in infrastructure was one of Trump's most important appeals during the campaign, his most important policy legacy in this regard was the construction of the border wall, which was one of the few projects that received consistent focus and funding throughout his period in office.

The construction of the wall was part of a broader white nativist agenda that involved a travel ban against citizens of largely Muslim countries ('Muslim ban'), increased efforts to deport illegal migrants outside the country, and the separation of parents and children found to cross the US–Mexican border (for an overview of Trump's executive orders on immigration policy, see Waslin 2020). Beyond the area of immigration policy, Tump's rhetoric fuelled what Belew (2022) calls 'militant whiteness', a set of activist groups and practices openly proclaiming racism and violence. For example, Trump endorsed police brutality in response to street protests emerging after the murder of George Floyd ('When the looting starts, the shooting starts') and declined to condemn white supremacist groups in the first 2020 presidential debate with Joe Biden ('Proud boys, stand back and stand by'). After his general election defeat, Trump mobilized militant groups through his 'Stop the Seal' campaign and invited his crowd near the White House to march to the Capitol, leading to the 1/6 insurrection ('If you don't fight like hell, you won't have a country anymore'). Hence, Trump's reign in power not only called into question the liberal-constitutional component of America's democracy ('checks and balances' and minority protection) but also its popular component by refusing to accept the outcome of the 2020 general election.

In his final year in government, Trump at first downplayed the risk of Covid-19 and delayed travel and entry restrictions, but as the pandemic progressed and state governments began issuing social distancing measures and workplace hazard controls, his administration mobilized the National Guard in favour of the most affected areas. Moreover, the Trump administration implemented two stimulus packages to cushion the economic impact of the pandemic, given the absence of strong automatic stabilizers in America's welfare state context (CARES Act and the Consolidated Appropriations Act). Overall, Trump received heavy criticism from the medical scientific community, as it deflected responsibility to China and rejected evidence and expertise in handling the fallout of the pandemic.

Conclusion

The observed absence of welfare state expansion under Trump's reign in power appears puzzling in light of America's high social risk and low social mobility context. From a comparative perspective, the USA case clearly stands out in terms of high levels of labour market risk coupled with low levels of collective risk coverage, which exposes lower-skilled individuals to the heightened economic insecurities of skill-biased technological change and globalized economic competition (Iversen and Soskice 2019: Ch. 5; Thelen and Wiedemann 2021). However, the GOP's traditional reliance on tax cuts and the renewed white nativism embodied by Trump's presidency precluded a policy of social protection and instead paved the way for another round of pro-rich tax cuts and deregulatory reform. By leaving Social Security and Medicare in large parts untouched, the Trump administration upheld social insurance benefits for the 'deserving'—at least until the 2021 budget proposal—while cutting back benefits for poorer families considered 'non-deserving'.

At the same time, however, the Trump administration fell back on a protectionist trade policy to target exactly the groups of voters European radical right parties attracted through insider-oriented welfare rights and familialist benefits, i.e. white males without college education. Similar to the social protection offered by European radical right parties, Trump's trade protection revolved around a particularistic conception of social solidarity as it appealed to the native male core workforces whose social and economic status had come under pressure from structural economic change. Meanwhile, social investment measures in education or skill formation as well as the new social risks of women (i.e. lone parenthood and work–family reconciliation) or the young (i.e. temporary employment) played a negligible role in the Trump administration's policy outlook. The racially charged framing of Trump's anti-immigration policy and his support from white supremacist groups underpinned the particularistic nature of his protectionist promise by excluding (non-white) immigrants and people of colour.

Trump's policy of trade protection must be seen as a functional equivalent to European-style social protection, because it aimed to protect threatened labour market insiders from losses of income by other means than social transfers or services, namely limits to economic competition. Whereas the European radical right focused on the benefit entitlements of 'hard-working' people by expanding insider-oriented and/or familialist social policies, the GOP under Trump targeted a similar group of voters by abandoning free trade agreements and imposing tariffs on foreign goods. From a comparative political economy perspective, Trump's prioritizing of trade over social protection should not come as a surprise, given that he assumed office in an institutional and political environment characterized by harsh deservingness conceptions that pit 'lazy' benefit recipients against 'hard-working' people (Larsen 2008). American production workers—who overwhelmingly voted for Trump—are therefore much less supportive of public welfare arrangements than their counterparts in Western Europe (Williams 2017: Ch. 12), in line with a traditionally welfare-hostile media discourse (Gilens 1999). However, growing shares of voters with lower levels of education considered foreign trade as a threat rather than as an opportunity. As a result, China's competitive advantage in industrial mass production turned into Trump's scapegoat for America's unequal development at the expense of rural and suburban 'Red America' (Grumbach et al. 2021).

8
Conclusions

This book has exposed the diverse ways in which the radical right has left behind its neoliberal post-war origins and gradually assumed a more protectionist role geared to previously dominant groups of voters whose social status has come under pressure in the post-industrial knowledge economy. We have seen how the radical right's nativist and authoritarian deservingness conceptions favour primarily threatened labour market insiders and male breadwinners while disadvantaging the unemployed, the poor, immigrants, ethnic minorities, and new social risk groups such as labour market outsiders and working women. However, the diverse welfare state contexts in which radical right parties operate has created different opportunities and constraints in legislating an agenda of selective protectionism that caters to the 'losers' of globalization and technological change. The types of policies observed can be roughly summarized as follows: the selective protection of labour market insiders in Continental and Northern Europe; the creation of new social divides between citizens and non-citizens through welfare chauvinism in Continental and Northern Europe; the attempted re-traditionalization of gender relations through familialist policies in Eastern and (to a lesser extent) Continental Europe; and a backlash against globalization through trade protectionism in the USA and economic nationalism in Eastern Europe.

The radical right's social and economic policies cannot be understood without recognizing the historically evolved and regionally distinct welfare state contexts in which these parties rose to power. The *authoritarian* preference for protecting only 'hard-working' and thus 'deserving' labour market insiders could be primarily realized in countries with mature social insurance regimes (Continental and Northern Europe), whereas the authoritarian preference for familialist policies relied on conservative institutional legacies or attitudes in the broader electorate (Eastern and Continental Europe). The *nativist* preference for 'putting our own people first' responded to the diverse exposures of domestic societies to globalization. It took the form of welfare chauvinism in generous welfare states with high levels of immigration (Continental and Northern Europe), economic nationalism in FDI-dependent

How the Radical Right Has Changed Capitalism and Welfare in Europe and the USA. Philip Rathgeb, Oxford University Press.
© Philip Rathgeb (2024). DOI: 10.1093/oso/9780192866332.003.0008

growth models in response to the fallout of the global financial crisis (Eastern Europe), and trade protectionism in a context of chronic current account deficits in the USA.

The degree and scope of the radical right's policy impact since the turn of the millennium is striking given that many observers have seen these parties primarily as agents of immigration control. In this view, we would have expected radical right parties to 'blur' their social and economic policies in return for tighter restrictions on immigration (Rovny 2013, Rovny and Polk 2020). To be sure, the rejection of immigration and multiculturalism is at the heart of the radical right across the board, with severe policy implications for the rights of non-citizens (Lutz 2019), but it would be wrong to conclude from this finding that the radical right has no bearing on distributive politics. At the same time, it would be misleading to contend that radical right parties have turned into 'pro-welfare parties' that moved to the left on the socio-economic dimension. From that point of view, we would have expected a redistributive state intervention from radical right parties, in line with their growing working-class support (e.g. Afonso 2015, Eger and Valdez 2015, Ivaldi 2015, Harteveld 2016, Lefkofridi and Michel 2017, Afonso and Rennwald 2018). This expectation has not been borne out by the evidence either.

The findings of this book diverge from previous studies as they rest on a comparative investigation of the radical right's policy choices in office. The last two decades have seen enormous advances in the study of individual-level attitudes and party manifesto positions that improved our understanding of the radical right and party politics under fundamentally changing (and increasingly complex) patterns of voting behaviour and party competition. However, the predominant focus of political scientists on what citizens *think* (based on survey analyses) or what parties *say* (based on manifesto analyses) entails the risk of missing what governments actually *do* in power (based on policy-focused analyses). The institutional architecture of welfare states and national models of capitalism is not a static feature, but constantly shaped by gradual institutional change, with transformative implications over time— and the role of the radical right is much more central to these processes than previously assumed. I will therefore use this last chapter to reflect and expand on five broad analytical conclusions derived from the preceding empirical chapters and embed them in the literatures of comparative politics, party politics, comparative political economy, and welfare state research.

(1) *Sociocultural values shape the socio-economic policies of the radical right.*

Much of today's political science is characterized by a rigid distinction between 'economy' versus 'culture', 'class' versus 'identity', 'redistribution' versus 'recognition' when theorizing and analysing political conflict. Inspired by spatial models of party competition, the assumption is that the traditional economic cleavage along the labour vs capital divide can be separated from the cultural cleavage along the liberalism vs authoritarianism divide. Seen in this way, political parties can take more or less four different strategies: right-authoritarian, right-liberal, left-authoritarian, and left-liberal. While such models of politics are useful as a heuristic device for statistical analysis, they obscure the deep interrelations between these two dimensions. Using a conventional textbook definition, it could be argued that the welfare state is an economic institution with purely distributive implications; it ensures economic redistribution ('Robin Hood' function), risk protection ('piggy bank' function), and social mobility ('stepping stones' function).

But the welfare state has always been an economic *and* cultural institution in its origins, trajectories, and outcomes. Let us take the Fordist family wage of the post-war era as an example. In economic terms, it rested on large-scale industrial production and trade unions powerful enough to translate productivity gains into wage levels sufficient to sustain single-earner households. The underlying balance of class power between labour and capital was underpinned by Keynesian state-management, but also by ongoing (post-)colonial and environmental exploitation. In cultural terms, it relied on the ideal of the male breadwinner model, which was made possible by racial and sexual exclusions at the expense of 'guest workers' in Western Europe, black Americans in the USA, and dependent housewives in both contexts. The welfare state was crucial in providing the economic means—i.e. full employment and generous social protection—to uphold the cultural ideal of the male breadwinner model that ensured broadly shared middle-class and working-class prosperity while entrenching sexual and racial hierarchies at the same time. While it might seem like the welfare state responds only to material needs, it also reflects and underpins the sociocultural norms of the day.

Leaving aside important cross-national variation for the moment, the post-Fordist dual-earner model replaced the Fordist family wage in the late twentieth and twenty-first century. In economic terms, the neoliberal counteroffensive led to falling wage shares and growing profit shares, which called into question the financial viability of single-earner households. The demise of industrial relations institutions at the expense of organized labour rewarded financial rentiers and owners of productive capital while creating new social divisions within the labour force. In cultural terms, the 'silent revolution' of the post-1968 generation connected the recruitment of female labour with the ambition to end horizontal inequalities between men and women. As the new social movements failed to realize their transformative potential in the face of neoliberal economics, the feminist ideals of emancipation and liberation were reduced to calls for equal opportunities on deregulated and precarious labour markets increasingly slated against (migrant) working-class women. Instead of adapting the demands of *economic* production to the needs of *social* reproduction, the dual-earner model has relied on individual responsibility in what came to be known as reconciling 'work-family life' (Fraser 2016). In the process, the role of the welfare state has been to adjudicate between traditionalist notions of familialism inherited from the male breadwinner model on the one hand, and liberal notions of defamilialism originating from feminist claims of the post-1968 generation. By expanding public care services, the welfare state would reduce family dependencies in the provision of welfare, whereas the opposite occurs when the welfare state prioritizes cash benefits and tax breaks to allow families—and thus women in practice—to assume a greater role as caregivers. Similar connections between economic and cultural politics can be found beyond the domain of gender and family relations when analysing the role of the welfare state in defining the boundaries of national citizenship and moral deservingness. In other words, welfare states reflect and promote cultural ideals and values of belonging, care, race, and gender.

In light of these connections, the radical right has clearly recognized that it *needs* socio-economic policies to realize its sociocultural objectives. Let us recall how the radical right's sociocultural ideologies of nativism and authoritarianism stimulate socio-economic policy impacts on capitalism and welfare. First, nativism promotes a preference for selective cutbacks in the welfare entitlements of immigrants (welfare chauvinism) while increasing the fertility rates of the native population without relying on immigration at the same time (pro-natalism). The economic mirror image of welfare chauvinism can be a sort of 'business chauvinism' that aims to reward and expand domestic businesses by imposing special taxes and other regulations on multinational and foreign-owned companies. Of course, the radical right is selective when discriminating against non-domestic businesses as to avoid large-scale 'capital flight' (business exodus) or 'capital strike' (withdrawal of investment), but they face no such capitalist constraints when discriminating against foreign welfare claimants. Second, authoritarianism stimulates a preference for protecting only those considered 'deserving' thanks to long contribution records (labour market insiders) and a compliance with traditional values and gender hierarchies (male breadwinner families). By contrast, it implies a more punitive approach to the unemployed and the poor through benefit cuts and workfare measures as well as little support for a progressive welfare recalibration that would cover new social risk groups outside the native (male) core workforce.

Its economic policies thus provide a *particularistic* protectionist promise designed to attract a group of voters that used to represent the socially dominant groups of the twentieth century. Hence, the radical right's policies do not cater to those 'left behind' by unemployment or precarious employment; they mainly respond to the *fear* rather than the *outcome* of economic decline. However, the radical right's policy of status protection is defensive and regressive in its orientation because it typically connects selective protections with deteriorations for the unemployed, the poor, and non-standard workers. By expanding and deepening precarious employment and welfare standards, the radical right promotes a low-wage competition that may hurt their own voters in the long run. As radical right voters are typically more likely to face labour market risks from technological change, they are more vulnerable to the pressures on wages and working conditions that are unleashed by the radical right's promotion of a racialized and gendered precariat. This book therefore opens a frontier for future research on the distributive outcomes and implications of radical right parties in power. The hypothesis emerging from this study is clear, which is that the radical right does not address inequality, precarity, and poverty despite growing support among voters with declining economic prospects. In fact, its selective status protection may achieve the opposite by creating pressures on wages and working conditions among the precarious margins of labour force while undermining trade unions as counterveiling forces at the same time (Rathgeb and Klitgaard 2022). This leads us to the second conclusion of our findings.

(2) *Working-class support does not turn the radical right against inequality.*

Let us recall that although radical right parties tend to be *Volksparteien* ('people's parties') deriving support from different social strata, we have seen from survey data in the preceding empirical chapters that they have achieved disproportionate support especially from production workers (see also Afonso and Rennwald 2018). In Austria, Denmark, and Hungary, more than every second voter of the radical right has had a working-class background in most elections of the past two decades, whereas production workers have been the most overrepresented social class in Trump's 2016 election victory.

To understand why the radical right does not legislate inequality-reducing policies despite strong working-class support requires a historical contextualization of *how* it achieved electoral success among blue-collar voters in particular. Abou-Chadi et al. (2021) show that in the 2000s and 2010s the overwhelming majority of the radical right's voters did *not* previously vote for social democratic parties. As the radical right's working-class base lacks a long-standing attachment to social democratic parties, they may well be difficult to mobilize for a left-wing project dedicated to reducing inequality, precarity, and poverty. How did this come about? Simplifying greatly, there are two main explanations on the socio-economic transformation of Social democracy and its declining appeal among production workers. The first one is electoral in nature: As centre-left parties realized that the 'old' manual working-class shrinks in numbers, it pursued a market-conforming agenda geared to attract the growing share of 'new' middle-class voters in the post-industrial knowledge economy (e.g. Häusermann 2018). The other narrative is economic in nature: as business associations went on the offensive when Keynesian policies failed to overcome the stagflation crisis of the late 1970s, centre-left parties embraced supply-side economics as a way of restoring economic growth and adapting to the new realities of globalization (e.g. Mudge 2018). In both interpretations, the result is the same neoliberal consensus.

Yet, the unintended consequence of mainstream support for neoliberalism was the depoliticization of the economy in favour of sociocultural issues on which the radical right could mobilize its voters across the advanced capitalist democracies (Kitschelt and McGann 1995, Kriesi et al. 2008, Spies and Franzmann 2011, Rennwald and Evans 2014). This is the economic policy background that paved the way for the 'cultural backlash' of the twenty-first century (Norris and Inglehart 2019). The evidence that radical right voters prioritize immigration and law and order is indeed overwhelming (for recent overviews, see e.g. Mudde 2019, Art 2022), but it is important to realize how social democratic austerity created opportunities for the radical right to mobilize working-class voters on their favoured grounds. We have seen how the Austrian FPÖ attracted working-class voters in the 1990s and came to power in the 2000 election after the SPÖ had joined the ÖVP in prioritizing fiscal consolidation to meet the Maastricht convergence criteria; the Danish DF made its biggest win among production workers after the social democratic prime minister had broken his 2001 election promise to leave early retirement untouched; the Hungarian Fidesz–KDNP gained a two-thirds majority in the 2010 election after the ex-communist left had signed a bailout package with the International Monetary Fund (IMF); the Trump admin-istration assumed office after previous governments of the right and left enhanced freer trade without compensating the losers of deindustrialization and globalization.[1]

In these variegated processes of neoliberal convergence, blue-collar work-ers with weaker attachments to class-based projects of the political left found their political home among ethno-nationalist projects of the radical right. The perverse outcome is that the radical right turned into the political rep-resentative of the 'losers of globalization' (Kriesi et al. 2008, Steiner et al. 2023) even though it rejects a redistributive agenda that would respond to the material and symbolic devaluations experienced by many of its voters in the predominantly rural and suburban areas that lost out in the post-industrial knowledge economy. We can understand this paradox by recognizing how the radical right's exclusionary ideology cuts off an agenda of redistributive state intervention. In other words, nativism and authoritarianism cannot be squared with an inclusive economic agenda that incorporates the economic demands of the less well-off, regardless of race, ethnicity, and gender.

It should be noted, however, that working-class voters who are orga-nized in trade unions are still significantly less likely to vote for the radical right (Mosimann et al. 2020). This may simply be a self-selection effect in the sense that working people with a left-wing ideology are more likely to join a trade union. However, there is also evidence suggesting that trade unions socialize their members in ways that make them more immune to the nativist-authoritarian appeals of the radical right (Mosimann and Pontus-son 2017, Rennwald and Pontusson 2021, Mosimann and Pontusson 2022). Previous research shows that union members are more likely to participate in elections, to vote for the political left, and have stronger preferences for redistribution (Rathgeb 2021b). The implication of these findings is that the radical right's fortunes are linked to decades of working-class demobiliza-tion. Future research should thus take the role of class organization seriously in relation to the radical right. Such a research agenda may start from the premise that when working people no longer consider themselves in class terms, they are more likely to delegate their interests to authoritarian strong-men who at least claim to represent their interests by devaluing those below them in the social (and ethnic) hierarchy (for a similar argument, see Marx 1852 [2016]). The absence of an egalitarian redistributive agenda does not, however, mean that the radical right has no protectionist platform at all. On

---

[1] I am indebted to Josef Hien for making me aware of this pattern.

the contrary, the radical right has understood how its nativist appeals may cater to discontents caused by mainstream support for neoliberal globalization. However, as national societies are exposed to globalization in diverse ways, these policies have also taken different forms in different countries.

(3) *The radical right's nativism promotes variations of welfare chauvinism, economic nationalism, and trade protectionism in response to globalization.*

'Laissez-faire was planned, planning was not' (Polanyi 1944 [2001]: 147). With this statement, Polanyi summarized one of his key claims in his seminal *Great Transformation* where he traces the rise and fall of economic liberalism from the Middle Ages until the early twentieth century. His argument is that the utopia of 'self-regulating markets' required ideological and political power meticulously planned to enforce the price mechanism. By contrast, the subsequent counter-movements to the commodification of man and nature were not planned as such; they developed instead spontaneously in response to the problems inflicted by the laissez-faire principle of liberal economics. In a similar vein, the neoliberal era was not a secular trend of weakening government vis-à-vis the market; it required a strong government dedicated to remove constraints on capital (Baccaro and Howell 2017, Rathgeb 2018), involving the liberalization of capital flows, free trade, fiscal discipline, labour market flexibility, privatization, and the abstention from counter-cyclical policies as well as industrial policies.

The radical right can be considered a counter-movement to the laissez-faire principle of the neoliberal era as it offers a (white) nativist sense of solidarity in reaction to the discontents caused by what Rodrik (2011) called the 'hyper-globalization' of capitalism. To be sure, historical analogies always need to be taken with a pinch of salt, but Polanyi's work is instructive insofar as it helps us to see how the radical right's ideology of nativism connects to diverse policy responses to the cross-border movement of goods, services, capital, and people. Whereas globalization required meticulous planning in numerous multilateral deals around trade and capital account liberalization, the radical right's principle of 'natives first' stimulated improvised ad hoc responses that range from tariffs on foreign goods and the abandonment of free trade deals (e.g. TPP, TTIP) to the renationalizations of key sectors/companies and welfare cutbacks for immigrants.

The radical right is of course heavily opposed to immigration in all countries, but in the generous welfare states of Continental and Northern Europe, the inflow of foreign newcomers can be politicized more heavily along welfare chauvinist lines. In this context, the cross-border movement of people is the contentious feature of globalization, as it creates opportunities for the radical right to racialize and culturalize distributive conflicts. By contrast, the cross-border movement of capital appears less consequential in these economies, thanks to export surpluses that sustain their growth models. Hence, nativist actors have mobilized on the perceived injustice that while protections for the 'hard-working' native core workforces have come under pressure from the dictates of competitiveness and austerity, immigrants and refugees can gain access to relatively generous social assistance and health-care arrangements without having previously contributed to the funding of the welfare state. At the same time, of course, the radical right ignores that large-scale immigration has been crucial in rescuing the fiscal viability of those mature social insurance systems its voters hold dear. The pension systems from which labour market insiders—i.e. the radical right's electoral stronghold—benefit most heavily may have collapsed long ago under the impact of demographic ageing. A similar story applies to migrant care workers from which the ageing populations of Western Europe have relied heavily to uphold their production systems (Fraser 2016). More generally, it could be argued that immigration towards the global North may itself be an escape from what Rosa Luxemburg called *Landnahme* ('land-grabbing') in a more than literal sense to describe capitalist and imperialist predation in the global South (Harvey 2018: Ch. 12).

In effect, the radical right's welfare chauvinism has promoted racialized intra-labour divides that resemble the insider–outsider divides governments of the mainstream left and right previously created by liberalizing labour markets and welfare systems at the margins of the labour force in the interest of job creation (Rueda 2007, Palier and Thelen 2010, Emmenegger et al. 2012, Rathgeb 2018). As the political left gave up on maximalist solutions in the representation of working people, its policies followed a logic of trade-offs whereby either core workers (labour market insiders) or non-standard workers (labour market outsiders) have had to face greater costs of economic adjustment (Häusermann 2018). The radical right has emerged in this context as the forceful defender of threatened labour market insiders that blocks a welfare recalibration at the expense of migrant workers as well as new social risk groups such as working women in (part-time) employment, the low-skilled (long-term) unemployed, and the young struggling to find a permanent contract.

By contrast, the contentious feature of globalization in the FDI–led growth models of Eastern Europe has been the cross-border movement of capital. Unlike in Western Europe, these countries have experienced emigration rather than immigration while lacking the generous welfare states that could promote a legislative agenda focused on welfare chauvinism. Selective welfare cutbacks for non-citizens are therefore much less prominent in this welfare state context. However, the post-communist transition process required these countries to 'build capitalism without capitalists' (Eyal et al. 2002), which essentially meant the attraction of Western capital by following the neoliberal devices of the Washington Consensus (1990s) and the EU accession process (2000s), before the global financial crisis (post-2008) led to sudden stops in investment and reverse capital flows. The resulting (selective) economic nationalism embodied by Orbán's reign in power was a way to regain domestic control over strategic sectors of the economy in a context of high levels of foreign ownership and foreign public debt. Therefore, nativism has had very different economic policy implication in these welfare state contexts, leading to renationalizations and discriminatory taxes and regulations imposed on foreign companies. Such a policy of economic nationalism appears unthinkable under radical right parties in Western Europe.

Finally, the nativist reaction to globalization took a different form in the global hegemon haunted by chronic current account deficits. In the USA, welfare chauvinism took the form of the 2019 public charge rule that aimed to prevent poorer immigrants from achieving permanent residence status, but the absence of a generous publicly funded welfare state made selective welfare cuts for non-citizens much less salient compared to Western Europe. Unlike in Eastern Europe, its hegemonic status made the USA a rule-maker rather than a rule-taker in the international investment and trading system. However, America's economic openness proved contentious when it manifested itself in chronic current account deficits at the expense of pronounced manufacturing decline. Trump's most distinctive economic policy was therefore to pull out of free trade deals (TPP, TTIP) and impose the most sweeping tariffs on foreign goods since the 1930s. However, America's trade imbalances are unlikely to be resolved without addressing how its financial system absorbs the world's excess savings at the cost of domestic production. For a time, growing private debt helped American working people to afford persistent current account deficits, but the fallout of the global financial crisis exposed how America's defence of a strong currency in tandem with economic openness came at the expense of lower employment rates at home and higher spending rates on imports.

Despite the diversity of these nativist counter-movements, they have in common that they do not address how the world's rich used deepening globalization to reinforce domestic inequality at the expense of working people. As Klein and Pettis (2020) summarized so cogently, 'trade wars are class wars' rather than national competitions between countries. Their work shows how the interest of American financial elites to attract savings and goods from Europe's export surplus countries has been complementary to the interest of European (mostly German) industrialists to sell their excess production to the USA in return for providing Americans with access to cheap credits. Meanwhile, working people have faced rising indebtedness and job losses in the USA, and aggressive wage restraint in the Eurozone (Rathgeb and Tassinari 2022). Perhaps unsurprisingly, the radical right responded to these manifold displacements and losses with policies of nationalist scapegoating while obscuring the transnational class struggle at the heart of neoliberal globalization. After all, the radical right may be anti-globalist, but it remains pro-capitalist.

The implication for future research is to take seriously comparative political economy when addressing the causes and consequences of radical right parties in power. Nativism takes different forms in different places because the discontents caused by globalization vary according to the political-economic profiles of a given country. We have seen welfare chauvinism in generous welfare states, economic nationalism in foreign-led capitalisms, and trade protectionism in America's current account deficit context, but this list of nativist counter-movements is certainly not exhaustive in light of the particular vulnerabilities displayed by different countries, regions, and localities in relation to international economic competition. It may well be that the radical right's nativist economics gains greater relevance as the world's leading superpowers—China and the USA—have become more interventionist and protectionist at the expense of the EU's traditional insistence on upholding the World Trade Organization's (WTO's) rules on free trade.

(4) *The radical right's authoritarianism undermines the social investment welfare state through variations of familialism and insider protection in response to liberal value change.*

In 2002, leading scholars in social policy published the volume *Why We Need a New Welfare State* (Esping-Andersen et al. 2002) to show how changing family forms and skill demands produced a set of 'new social risks' that remained unaddressed by the welfare state arrangements inherited from the industrial era. Chief among them was the risk of reconciling work–family life in light of growing female employment; the risk of having low or obsolete skills in the wake of deindustrialization; and the risk of having insufficient benefit entitlements when out of work due to the proliferation of non-standard part-time employment careers. Whereas the industrial welfare state produced relatively high levels of economic growth and social solidarity by protecting primarily the male industrial worker and his families, the post-industrial welfare state, so the logic went, had to focus more on the social demands of working women, the young, and (precarious) non-standard workers.

The social investment welfare state is typically conceived as a set of policies that caters to new social risk groups (Hemerijck 2018). In this conceptualization, the welfare state aims to provide high-quality education across the life course to raise human capital to account for the greater unemployment risks experienced by those with low or obsolete skills (lifelong human capital stocks). Second, public child and elderly care arrangements aim to reconcile work and family life and thereby sustain enhanced labour productivity in the interest of working women (work–life balance flows). Third, access to and the level of benefit entitlements should become less dependent on social insurance contributions to prevent out-of-work poverty for those without steady and secure employment trajectories (inclusive buffers). Taken together, the social investment paradigm implies that the welfare state should no longer primarily *correct* markets by imposing obligations on capital; the task is much more to *enhance* markets through human capital formation. Whereas the logic of the industrial welfare state came to be associated with a 'politics against markets' (Esping-Andersen 1985), the post-industrial welfare state was deemed to follow a 'politics for markets' (Iversen and Soskice 2015) as governments would redefine social policies as means to provide national economies with the skills needed to excel on global markets. In other words, the new paradigm of the social investment welfare state has aimed to reconcile social democratic concerns for inclusivity with the neoliberal insistence on supply-side adaptation.

The radical right's welfare state agenda has clashed with the social investment welfare state in two ways. First, authoritarianism emphasizes 'deservingness' based on long employment records, which display a commitment to be 'hard-working' in principle. Whereas the social investment paradigm aims to incorporate labour market outsiders, the radical right aims to defend the social insurance rights and job security of threatened labour market insiders. Second, the radical right's preference for traditional family values and gender hierarchies is difficult, if not impossible, to square with the social investment's emphasis on facilitating gender equality through work–family policies (e.g. childcare). The radical right's valorization of (manual) 'hard work' and authority implies less emphasis on upward mobility through higher education and lifelong learning. It is thus of little surprise that social investment has received high levels of electoral support from the new middle class

(Häusermann et al. 2013, Beramendi et al. 2015), whereas the opposite is the case for the radical right's electorate, as it typically prefers status protection to human capital development, gender equality, and social mobility (Busemeyer et al. 2022).

Similar to the nativist counter-movements to globalization described above, the authoritarian opposition to the social investment paradigm has been mediated by the diversity of welfare state contexts. Most clearly, the Northern European welfare state has precluded radical right support for familialist policies, because the dual-earner model has been too entrenched in public opinion to be politicized along conservative lines. Hence, the radical right's role has been confined to the defence of public pension and early retirement rights while emphasizing the deservingness of the elderly more generally.

In the Continental European welfare state context, the radical right could draw on stronger institutional and political legacies in favour of the male breadwinner model, which helps explain why the radical right has connected insider protection with familialist policies such as expanded child benefits and tax breaks for families. The comparison between Austria and Germany has been instructive to identify the radical right's partisan policy impact in this regard. Whereas Austria has been overall more successful in combining relatively high levels of economic growth with low levels of social inequality (Obinger et al. 2012, Rathgeb 2018), it has lagged behind Germany in expanding childcare facilities as the FPÖ blocked such reforms and expanded familialist policies with the ÖVP instead (Leitner 2011). Without a radical right party close to power, German governments opted instead for a more de-familializing reform path that reduced gender inequalities in employment and welfare. The German case thus provided a sound factual scenario from which we could derive a counterfactual claim about the familialist impact of the radical right, at the expense of working women and in favour of traditional gender relations.

In the Eastern European welfare state context, the rejection of liberal values has been most pronounced, which helps explain the marked turn towards conservative and pro-natalist family policy expansion. The communist legacy of 'authoritarian egalitarianism' (Offe 1991) has stimulated conservative rather than universalist welfare state attitudes so that the EU's gender mainstreaming initiatives have found little support in this context (Kulin and Meulemann 2015, Szelewa and Polakowski 2022). At the same time, the Orbán cabinet and similar nationalist-conservative movements managed to recast the refugee crisis in a demographic light by connecting the authoritarian principle to reinvigorate conservative gender roles with the nativist principle to have 'more babies, not immigrants'. The familialist policy impact of the radical right in this welfare state context makes the prospects of social investment look rather bleak. In the USA, by contrast, the reliance on low taxation and the 'racialization' of welfare, especially pronounced among Trump's Tea Party base, in a context of employer- and market-based social policy made any sort of social investment unlikely. Hence, trade protection has been a functional equivalent of social protection by aiming to stabilize and increase employment (and thus welfare) security in declining manufacturing industries outside the metropolitan knowledge economy.

These anti-social investment policies resonate with previous studies identifying a sort of 'nostalgia' for the 'golden age' of the welfare state among voters and politicians of the radical right (Betz and Johnson 2004, Gest et al. 2018, Fenger 2018, Schreurs 2020). In other words, whereas the social investment paradigm aims to address horizontal inequalities in gender and ethnicity, the radical right's nostalgic frames and policies pull in the opposite direction of restoring the 'good old days' where state support catered to native male breadwinner families. In Eastern Europe, of course, welfare nostalgia has remained more ambiguous. On the one hand, the communist legacy of foreign rule promoted a desire for national self-determination (Verovsek 2021). On the other hand, dissatisfaction with the shock therapies of the post-communist transition process has stimulated nostalgia for the social stability of the communist era, at least among older-age cohorts (Ekman and Linde 2005). Seen in this way, the Eastern European radical right has carved out a platform that diverges from the 'authoritarian egalitarianism' of the communist post-war era as well as from the liberal values of the post-communist transition era. Taken together, radical right parties seem to be the strongest opponents to the spread of the social investment approach, which helps explain why political attempts to promote it often resemble a 'political uphill battle' (Hemerijck 2018). However, as described above, the challenges posed by the radical right for social investment policies differ according to welfare state contexts, with the strongest opposition in Eastern Europe in contrast to Northern Europe.

(5) *The radical right uses the welfare state to facilitate democratic backsliding.*

The welfare state has always been an integral part of authoritarian rule. While often couched in progressive terms around poverty reduction and economic redistribution, social policy has also been used as an instrument to facilitate the suppression of democratic rights. A good example in this regard is the one of Bismarck in late nineteenth-century Germany. Faced with growing working-class mobilization, Bismarck used the introduction of the first social insurances as the 'carrot' on the one hand, and the anti-socialist laws as the 'stick' on the other, to create loyalty for his regime (see e.g. Manow 2020: Ch. 2). Bismarck spoke quite candidly about how social policy enhanced the viability of his authoritarian regime, famously saying that '[w]hoever has a pension for his old age is far more content and far easier to handle than one who has no such prospect'. The Continental European welfare regime is a historical product of conservative-authoritarian elites developing occupationally fragmented social policies and contributory social insurance arrangements to legitimize paternalist nation states in a 'divide and rule' fashion. A defining characteristic of authoritarianism now and then is the suggestion that a benevolent strongman is enough to protect working people from the vagaries of the market, whereas trade unions are undesirable as they threaten 'national unity'.

The relationship between welfare and democracy may also work the other way around. Whereas Bismarck used social policy *expansion* to enhance support for authoritarian rule in the late nineteenth century, the hollowing out of popular democracy has helped to legislate social policy *retrenchment* in the late twentieth century. It is no coincidence that declining voter turnout, increasing voter volatility, and declining party membership went in hand in hand with the withdrawal of elites from democratic accountability to 'non-majoritarian institutions' (e.g. WTO, European Central Bank, IMF) in the neoliberal era (Mair 2013). As governments felt compelled to display increased 'responsibility' towards market demands, they had less room for 'responsiveness' towards voter demands (ibid.). In other words, neoliberal rule has led to 'undemocratic liberalism' (Berman 2017) and could survive best when it relied on the long-term weakening of democratic institutions (Madariaga 2020). This hollowing out of the popular component of democracy at the expense of civil society and class-based organizations has provided fertile ground for radical right parties to challenge the liberal-constitutional component of democracy as a way of giving voice to 'our own people' at the expense of minority protection and checks and balances systems.

Social protection remains a crucial instrument for authoritarian strongmen to entrench themselves in power. In Hungary, for example, the Orbán cabinet capitalized on the economic uncertainties caused by IMF- and EU-mandated austerity in Hungary's foreign-led capitalism. The so-called 'war of liberation' directed against further external interference did not only have a nationalist appeal of self-sufficiency; Orbán's measures also shielded majoritarian middle-class families from the aftermath of the global financial crisis, involving generous bailouts for mortgage loan holders and the incremental expansion of familialist policies. This way, the Fidesz–KDNP government reached out to key electoral groups while undermining liberal-democratic institutions and norms at the same time (Scheiring 2020, 2022). In Austria, the FPÖ's rebranding as a 'social homeland party' (*Soziale Heimatpartei*) has not changed much the party's distributive priorities on the protection of threatened labour market insiders and male breadwinners. However, it did signal an abandonment of the fiscal austerity agenda that caused internal turmoil in its first coalition government with the centre-right ÖVP in the early 2000s. When re-entering government in 2017, the FPÖ concentrated welfare cuts among non-citizens, which proved highly popular in opinion polls. At the height of the government's popularity, the Ibiza affair revealed how Strache's claim to put 'Austrians first' went hand in hand with a desire to centralize control over Austria's media system along the lines of Hungary under Orbán. After its 2019 election defeat, the FPÖ has recovered remarkably fast and is leading the polls at the time of writing, which may well pose new challenges to the viability of Austria's liberal democracy.

In the USA, Trump's deviation from the GOP's long-standing positions on trade and immigration policy tapped into a protectionist sentiment that helped him win the Republican nomination before the 2016 general election (VanGrasstek 2019: 152). While Trump's subsequent presidency posed in many ways a stress test for America's checks and balances systems, it is remarkable how Trump motivated his supporters to march to the Capitol in his January 6 speech by arguing that his competitor would put an end to his 'America First' policy: 'Did you see the other day where Joe Biden said, I want to get rid of the America First policy? What's that all about? Get rid of. How do you say I want to get rid of America First? Even if you're going to do it, don't talk about it, right? Unbelievable what we have to go through. What we have to go through. You have to get your people to fight' (NPR, 10.02.2021). By contrast, it seems that in Denmark, party system fragmentation and regular power-sharing through minority governments cut off significant threats of democratic backsliding, although various human rights violations have been reported in the wake of Denmark's sharp tightening of immigration and asylum policies.

Taken together, the welfare state may well help to *safeguard* liberal democracy against the illiberal challenge posed by the radical right, as suggested by previous research (Berman and Snegovaya 2019, Nässtrom 2021, Vlandas and Halikiopoulou 2022). But once in office, the radical right's own promise of protection may also *enable* democratic backsliding by generating the political support necessary to capture the state and undermine fair party competition contexts. An important frontier this book opens up for future research is therefore on the causal role played by the radical right's socio-economic agenda in facilitating democratic backsliding processes. While there is little research on the contemporary nexus between welfare and authoritarianism, we know that dissatisfaction with democracy is often tied to declining economic conditions (Pew Research Center 2019), especially among the radical right's electoral strongholds who have experienced a *relative* economic decline (Oesch 2008, Bornschier and Kriesi 2013, Häusermann 2020). Throughout this book, the radical right has connected attacks on liberal-democratic rules with a nativist-authoritarian version of what Berman (2006) calls the 'primacy of politics' against the seemingly inexorable march of neoliberal globalization. This repoliticization after decades of TINA politics ('there is no alternative') has caused confrontations with powerful transnational actors, including the European Court of Justice (welfare chauvinism), the WTO (trade protectionism), the European Commission (anti-gender mainstreaming), and the IMF (economic nationalism).

However, the radical right has never called into question the economic inequalities and environmental degradations produced by the neoliberal paradigm that informed the era of 'hyper-globalization' (Rodrik 2011). Its strategy has instead been to manufacture consent for authoritarianism through a 'divide and rule' approach that valorizes and protects the deserving and hard-working 'makers', as opposed to the undeserving and lazy 'takers' who supposedly fail to contribute to the national community in a hostile environment of international competition. As a result, the radical right's policy impact has overall reinforced horizontal inequalities in terms of gender and ethnicity without addressing vertical inequalities between the rich and the poor.

The distributive outcomes of the radical right in power might teach us a great deal about the main purposes behind its authoritarian rule, which is to protect itself against a democratic backlash from the many losers it creates. By abandoning liberal-democratic institutions—or even denying election outcomes—the radical right has little to fear from electoral majorities. Whereas the new middle classes with high levels of education typically remain out of reach for the radical right, its political fortunes rely on the enduring exclusion of the poor, the unemployed, and other new social risk groups outside the native (male) core workforce and domestic business elite. Neoliberalism not only caused growing inequalities by protecting capitalism from democracy (Slobodian 2018, Madariaga 2020); it also enabled authoritarian strongmen to exploit the hollowing out of popular democracy with a protectionist agenda the political mainstream no longer seemed to offer. Status anxieties and disappointed expectations are likely to take new forms in the face of digitalization, artificial intelligence, and the transition to a carbon-neutral economy in the decades to come. There ought to be better ways than the neoliberal consensus of the past or the radical right's policy of selective status protection for working-class and lower middle-class voters struggling to catch up with the ever-changing demands of capitalist market expansion.

References

Abou-Chadi, T., R. Mitteregger, and C. Mudde. 2021. 'Left Behind by the Working Class? Social Democracy's Electoral Crisis and the Rise of the Radical Right'. Berlin: Friedrich Ebert Stiftung. Last accessed 18 July 2023. Retrieved from: https://library.fes.de/pdf-files/a-p-b/18074.pdf.

Abou-Chadi, T. and M. Wagner. 2020. 'Electoral Fortunes of Social Democratic Parties: Do Second Dimension Positions Matter?' *Journal of European Public Policy* 27(2): pp. 246–272.

Abts, K., E., Dalle Mulle, S. Van Kessel, and E. Michel. 2021. 'The Welfare Agenda of the Populist Radical Right in Western Europe: Combining Welfare Chauvinism, Producerism and Populism'. *Swiss Political Science Review* 27(1): pp. 21–40.

Adorno, T. W., E. Frenkel-Brunswik, D. J. Levinson, and R. N. Sanford. 1950. *The Authoritarian Personality*. New York, NY: Harpers.

Afonso, A. 2013. *Social Concertation in Times of Austerity. European Integration and the Politics of Labour Market Reforms in Austria and Switzerland*. Amsterdam: Amsterdam University Press.

Afonso, A. 2015. 'Choosing Whom to Betray: Populist Right-Wing Parties, Welfare State Reforms and the Trade-Off between Office and Votes'. *European Political Science Review* 7(2): pp. 271–292.

Afonso, A. 2018. 'Migrant Workers or Working Women? Comparing Labour Supply Policies in Post-War Europe'. *Journal of Comparative Policy Analysis: Research and Practice* 21(3): pp. 251–269.

Afonso, A. and Y. Papadopoulos. 2015. 'How the Populist Radical Right Transformed Swiss Welfare Politics: From Compromises to Polarization'. *Swiss Political Science Review* 21(4): pp. 617–635.

Afonso, A. and L. Rennwald. 2017. *The Far-Right's Leftist Mask*. Jacobin Magazine, 3 July. Last accessed 18 July 2023. Retrieved from: https://www.jacobinmag.com/2017/03/far-right-ukip-fn-welfare-immigration-working-class-voters.

Afonso, A. and L. Rennwald. 2018. 'Social Class and the Changing Welfare State Agenda of Radical Right Parties'. In *Welfare Democracies and Party Politics. Explaining Electoral Dynamics in Times of Changing Welfare Capitalism*, edited by Philip Manow, Bruno Palier, and Hanna Schwander, pp. 171–194. Oxford: Oxford University Press.

Afonso, A. and F. Bulfone. 2019. 'Electoral Coalitions and Policy Reversals in Portugal and Italy in the Aftermath of the Eurozone Crisis'. *South European Society and Politics* 24(2): pp. 233–257.

Aftenposten. 2021. 'Siv Jensen går av som partileder i Frp', 18 February. Last accessed 18 July 2023. Retrieved from: https://www.aftenposten.no/norge/politikk/i/oA7zBj/siv-jensen-gaar-av-som-partileder-i-frp-peker-paa-sylvi-listhaug-som-ny-leder.

Aichholzer, J., S. Kritzinger, M. Wagner, and E. Zeglovits. 2014. 'How has Radical Right Support Transformed Established Political Conflicts? The Case of Austria'. *West European Politics* 37(1): pp. 113–137.

Aichholzer, J., S. Kritzinger, M. Wagner, N. Berk, H. Boomgaarden, and W. C. Müller. 2018. *AUTNES Comparative Study of Electoral Systems Post-Election Survey 2017*. Vienna: AUSSDA.

Aichholzer, J. and M. Zandonella. 2016. 'Psychological Bases of Support for Radical Right Parties'. *Personality and Individual Differences* 96: pp. 185–190.

Altemeyer, R. A. 1981. *Right-Wing Authoritarianism*. Winnipeg: University of Manitoba Press.

Alternative für Deutschland. 2020. 'Konzept zur Sozialpolitik des 11. Bundesparteitages der AfD in Kalkar vom 28./29. September 2020'. AfD: Berlin. Last accessed 18 July 2023. Retrieved from: https://www.afd.de/wp-content/uploads/sites/111/2021/04/20210326_Konzept_zur_Sozialpolitik_ohne_Programm.pdf.

Akkerman, T. 2015. 'Gender and the Radical Right in Western Europe: A Comparative Analysis of Policy Agendas'. *Patterns of Prejudice* 49(1–2): pp. 37–60.

American National Election Studies. 2017. 'ANES 2016 Time Series Study' (ICPSR36824.v2). Data file and codebook. University of Michigan and Stanford University. https://doi.org/10.3886/ICPSR36824.v2.

Andersen, J. G. 2003. 'The General Election in Denmark, November 2001'. *Electoral Studies* 1(22): pp. 186–193.

Andersen, J. G. 2012. 'Universalization and De-universalization of Unemployment Protection in Denmark and Sweden'. In *Welfare State, Universalism and Diversity*, edited by Anneli Anttonen, Liisa Häikiö, and Kolbeinn Stefánsson, pp. 162–186. Cheltenham and Northampton: Edward Elgar.

Andersen, J. G. 2019. 'The Welfare State as a Victim of Neoliberal Economic Failure?' In *Welfare and the Great Recession*, edited by Stefán Ólafsson, Mary Daly, Olli Kangas, and Joakim Palme, pp. 192–209. Oxford: Oxford University Press.

Andersen, J. G. and T. Bjørklund. 1990. 'Structural Changes and New Cleavages: The Progress Parties in Denmark and Norway'. *Acta Sociologica* 33(3): pp. 195–217.

Anker, J., J. Linden, M. H. Wagner, and J. A. Holch. 2009. *Overview and Analysis of Minimum Income Schemes in Denmark*. A Study of National Policies on Behalf of the European Commission, DG Employment, Social Affairs and Equal Opportunities.

Appel, H. and M. A. Orenstein. 2018. *From Triumph to Crisis. Neoliberal Economic Reform in Postcommunist Countries*. Cambridge: Cambridge University Press.

Arndt, C. 2013. 'The Electoral Consequences of Welfare State Reforms for the Danish Social Democrats'. *World Political Science* 9(1): pp. 319–335.

Arndt, C. 2014. 'Beating Social Democracy on Its Own Turf: Issue Convergence as Winning Formula for the Centre-Right in Universal Welfare States'. *Scandinavian Political Studies* 37(2): pp. 149–170.

Art, D. 2022. 'The Myth of Global Populism'. *Perspectives on Politics* 20(3): pp. 999–1011.

Arzheimer, K. 2012. 'Working Class Parties 2.0? Competition Between Centre Left and Extreme Right Parties'. In *Class Politics and the Radical Right*, edited by Jens Rydgren, pp. 75–90. New York: Routledge.

Aspalter, C., K. Jinsoon, and P. Sojeung. 2009. 'Analysing the Welfare State in Poland, the Czech Republic, Hungary and Slovenia: An Ideal-Typical Perspective'. *Social Policy & Administration* 43(2): pp. 170–185.

Attewell, D. 2021. 'Deservingness Perceptions, Welfare State Support and Vote Choice in Western Europe'. *West European Politics* 44(3): pp. 611–634.

Autor, D. H., D. Dorn, and G. H. Hanson. 2013. 'The China Syndrome: Local Labor Market Effects of Import Competition in the United States'. *American Economic Review* 103(6): pp. 2121–2168.

Avisen, D. K. 2011. 'DF lovede ikke ved efterlønnen', 13 May. Last accessed 18 July 2023. Retrieved from: https://www.avisen.dk/df-lovede-ikke-at-roere-ved-efterloennen_146418.aspx.

Baccaro, L., M. Blyth, and J. Pontusson. 2022. 'Rethinking Comparative Capitalism'. In *Diminishing Returns. The New Politics of Growth and Stagnation*, edited by Lucio Baccaro, Mark Blyth, and Jonas Pontusson, pp. 1–52. Oxford/New York: Oxford University Press.

Baccaro, L. and M. Höpner. 2022. 'The Political-Economic Foundations of Export-Led Growth: An Analysis of the German Case'. In *Diminishing Returns. The New Politics of Growth and Stagnation*, edited by Lucio Baccaro, Mark Blyth, and Jonas Pontusson, pp. 238–267. Oxford/New York. Oxford University Press.

Baccaro, L. and C. Howell. 2017. *Trajectories of Neoliberal Transformation. European Industrial Relations Since the 1970s*. Cambridge/New York: Cambridge University Press.

Baccaro, L. and J. Pontusson. 2016. 'Rethinking Comparative Political Economy: The Growth Model Perspective'. *Politics & Society* 44(2): pp. 175–207.

Baccini, L. and S. Weymouth. 2021. 'Gone for Good: Deindustrialization, White Voter Backlash, and US Presidential Voting'. *American Political Science Review* 115(2): pp. 550–567.

Bahle, T. and C. Wendt. 2021. 'Social Assistance'. In *The Oxford Handbook of the Welfare State*, edited by Daniel Béland, Kimberly J. Morgan, Herbert Obinger, and Christopher Pierson, pp. 624–640. Oxford/New York: Oxford University Press.

Ban, C. and D. Adascalitei. 2022. 'The FDI-Led Growth Models of the East-Central and South-Eastern European Periphery'. In *Diminishing Returns. The New Politics of Growth and Stagnation*, edited by Lucio Baccaro, Mark Blyth, and Jonas Pontusson, pp. 189–212. Oxford/New York: Oxford University Press.

Barker, D. C. and J. D. Tinnick. 2006. 'Competing Visions of Parental Roles and Ideological Constraint'. *American Political Science Review* 100(2): pp. 249–263.

Bartolini, S. 2000. *The Political Mobilization of the European Left, 1860–1980: The Class Cleavage*. Cambridge: Cambridge University Press.

Bech, E. C., K. Borevi, and P. Mouritsen. 2017. 'A "Civic Turn" in Scandinavian Family Migration Policies? Comparing Denmark, Norway and Sweden'. *Comparative Migration Studies* 5(1): pp. 1–24.

Béland, D. and A. Waddan. 2012. *The Politics of Policy Change: Welfare, Medicare, and Social Security Reform in the United States*. Washington DC: Georgetown University Press.

Belew, K. 2022. 'Militant Whiteness in the Age of Trump'. In *The Presidency of Donald J. Trump*, edited by Julian E. Zelizer, pp. 83–102. Princeton/Oxford: Princeton University Press.

Beramendi, P., S. Häusermann, H. Kitschelt, and H. Kriesi 2015. 'Introduction: The Politics of Advanced Capitalism'. In *The Politics of Advanced Capitalism*, edited by Pablo Beramendi, Silja Häusermann, Herbert Kitschelt, and Hanspeter Kriesi, pp. 1–64. Cambridge: Cambridge University Press.

Berezin, M. 2009. *Illiberal Politics in Neoliberal Times: Culture, Security and Populism in the New Europe*. Cambridge: Cambridge University Press.

Berman, S. 2006. *The Primacy of Politics: Social Democracy and the Making of Europe's Twentieth Century*. New York: Cambridge University Press.

Berman, S. 2017. 'The Pipe Dream of Undemocratic Liberalism'. *Journal of Democracy* 28(3): pp. 29–38.

Berman, S. and M. Snegovaya. 2019. 'Populism and the Decline of Social Democracy'. *Journal of Democracy* 30(3): pp. 5–19.

Beskæftigelsesministeriet. 2020. 'Pensionsaftale: Folk med lange og hårde arbejdsliv får ret til tidlig pension'. Press statement. Copenhagen: Beskæftigelsesministeriet. Last accessed 18 July 2023. Retrieved from: https://bm.dk/nyheder-presse/pressemeddelelser/2020/10/pensionsaftale-folk-med-lange-og-haarde-arbejdsliv-faar-ret-til-tidlig-pension/

Betz, H.-G. 1993. 'The Two Faces of Radical Right-Wing Populism in Western Europe'. *The Review of Politics* 55(4): pp. 663–685.

Betz, H.-G. and C. Johnson. 2004. 'Against the Current—Stemming the Tide: The Nostalgic Ideology of the Contemporary Radical Populist Right'. *Journal of Political Ideologies* 9(3): pp. 311–327.

Betz, H.-G. and S. Meret 2012. 'Right-Wing Populist Parties and the Working Class Vote: What Have You Done for Us Lately?' In *Class Politics and the Radical Right*, edited by Jens Rydgren, pp. 107–121. Abingdon: Routledge.

Bíró-Nagy, A., G. Scheiring, and Á. Szászi. 2022. *Hungarian Politics in 2021*. Budapest: Policy Solutions.

Bjerkem, J. 2016. 'The Norwegian Progress Party: An Established Populist Party'. *European View* 15(2): pp. 233–243.

Bjugan, K. 1999. 'The 1998 Danish Parliamentary Election: Social Democrats Muddle through to Victory'. *West European Politics* 22(1): pp. 172–178.

Blanchet, A. and N. Landry. 2021. 'Authoritarianism and Attitudes Toward Welfare Recipients under Covid-19 Shock'. *Frontiers in Political Science* 3: pp. 1–12.

Bluhm, K. and M. Varga. 2020. 'Conservative Developmental Statism in East Central Europe and Russia'. *New Political Economy* 25(4): pp. 642–659.

Bohle, D. 2014. 'Post-socialist Housing Meets Transnational Finance: Foreign Banks, Mortgage Lending, and the Privatization of Welfare in Hungary and Estonia'. *Review of International Political Economy* 21(4): pp. 913–948.

Bohle, D. 2017. 'Baltische Wege aus der Finanzkrise. Musterbeispiele für erfolgreiche Austeritätspolitik?' *Aus Politik und Zeitgeschichte* 67(8): pp. 40–45.

Bohle, D. and B. Greskovits. 2012. *Capitalist Diversity on Europe's Periphery*. Ithaca, NY: Cornell University Press.

Bohle, D. and B. Greskovits. 2019. 'Politicising Embedded Neoliberalism: Continuity and Change in Hungary's Development Model'. *West European Politics* 42(5): pp. 1069–1093.

Bohle, D., B. Greskovits, and M. Naczyk. 2023. 'The Gramscian Politics of Europe's Rule of Law Crisis'. *Journal of European Public Policy*, https://doi.org/10.1080/13501763.2023.2182342.

Bonoli, G. 2007. 'Time Matters: Postindustrialization, New Social Risks, and Welfare State Adaptation in Advanced Industrial Democracies'. *Comparative Political Studies* 40(5): pp. 495–520.

Bonoli, G. 2010. 'The Political Economy of Active Labor-Market Policy'. *Politics & Society* 38(4): pp. 435–457.

Boräng, F. 2018. *National Institutions—International Migration: Labour Markets, Welfare States and Immigration Policy*. London: ECPR Press.

Bornschier S. and H. Kriesi. 2013. 'The Populist Right, the Working Class, and the Changing Face of Class Politics'. In *Class Politics and the Radical Right*, edited by Jens Rydgren, pp. 10–29. New York: Routledge.

Braun, B. 2022. 'Exit, Control, and Politics: Structural Power and Corporate Governance under Asset Manager Capitalism'. *Politics & Society* 50(4): pp. 630–654.

Bremer, B. and S. McDaniel. 2020. 'The ideational foundations of social democratic austerity in the context of the Great Recession'. *Socio-Economic Review* 18(2): pp. 439–463.

Bull, A. C. and M. Gilbert. 2001. *The Lega Nord and the Politics of Secession in Italy*. Basingstoke: Palgrave Macmillan.

Bundesministerium für Inneres. 2023. 'Nationalratswahlen'. Last accessed 19 July 2023. Retrieved from: https://www.bmi.gv.at/412/Nationalratswahlen/Historischer_Rueckblick.aspx.

Burgoon, B. and M. Rooduijn 2021. '"Immigrationization" of Welfare Politics? Anti-immigration and Welfare Attitudes in Context'. *West European Politics* 44(2): pp. 177–203.

Burgoon, B., S. van Noort, M. Rooduijn, and G. Underhill. 2019. 'Positional Deprivation and Support for Radical Right and Radical Left Parties'. *Economic Policy* 34(97): pp. 49–93.

Busemeyer, M., P. Rathgeb, and A. Sahm 2022. 'Authoritarian Values and the Welfare State: The Social Policy Preferences of Radical Right Voters'. *West European Politics* 45(1): pp. 77–101.

Bustikova, L. 2019. *Extreme Reactions: Radical Right Mobilization in Eastern Europe*. Cambridge: Cambridge University Press.

Campbell, A. L. and M. W. Sances. 2014. 'Constituencies and Public Opinion'. In *The Oxford Handbook of U.S. Social Policy*, edited by Daniel Béland, Christopher Howard, and Kimberly J. Morgan, pp. 206–221. Oxford/New York: Oxford University Press.

Careja, R., C. Elmelund-Praestekaer, M. Baggesen Klitgaard, and E. Larsen. 2016. 'Direct and Indirect Welfare Chauvinism as Party Strategies: An Analysis of the Danish People's Party'. *Scandinavian Political Studies* 39(4): pp. 435–457.

Careja, R. and E. Harris. 2022. 'Thirty Years of Welfare Chauvinism Research: Findings and Challenges'. *Journal of European Social Policy* 32(2): pp. 212–224.

Carnes, N. and N. Lupu. 2021. 'The White Working Class and the 2016 Election'. *Perspectives on Politics* 19(1): pp. 55–72.

Carreras, M., Y. I. Carrera, and S. Bowler. 2019. 'Long-Term Economic Distress, Cultural Backlash, and Support for Brexit'. *Comparative Political Studies* 52(9): pp. 1396–1424.

Cerami, A. and P. Vanhuysse. 2009. 'Introduction: Social Policy Pathways, Twenty Years after the Fall of the Berlin Wall'. In *Post-Communist Welfare Pathways: Theorizing Social Policy Transformations in Central and Eastern Europe*, edited by Alfio Cerami and Pieter Vanhuysse, pp. 1–14. London: Palgrave Macmillan.

Chebel d'Appollonia, A. 2012. *Frontiers of Fear. Immigration and Insecurity in the United States*. Ithaca, NY: Cornell University Press.

Conley, R. S. 2020. *Donald Trump and American Populism*. Edinburgh: Edinburgh University Press.

Cook, L. J. and T. Inglot. 2021. 'Central and Eastern European Countries'. In *The Oxford Handbook of the Welfare State*, edited by Daniel Béland, Kimberly J. Morgan, Herbert Obinger, and Christopher Pierson, pp. 881–898. Oxford/New York: Oxford University Press.

Christensen, J. 2017. *The Power of Economists within the State*. Stanford: Stanford University Press.

Christiansen, F. J. 2016. 'The Danish People's Party: Combining Cooperation and Radical Positions'. In *Radical Right-Wing Populist Parties in Western Europe: Into the Mainstream?* edited by Tjitske Akkerman, Sarah L. de Lange, and Matthijs Rooduijn, pp. 94–112. New York: Routledge.

Chueri, J. 2022. 'An Emerging Populist Welfare Paradigm? How Populist Radical Right-Wing Parties Are Reshaping the Welfare State'. *Scandinavian Political Studies* 45(4): pp. 383–409.

Crouch, C. 2009. 'Privatised Keynesianism: An Unacknowledged Policy Regime'. *British Journal of Politics & International Relations* 11(3): pp. 382–399.

Crouch, C. 2011. *The Strange Non-Death of Neoliberalism*. Cambridge: Polity Press.

Csaba, L. 2022. 'Unorthodoxy in Hungary: An Illiberal Success Story?' *Post-Communist Economies* 34(1): pp. 1–14.

Emmenegger, P., S. Häusermann, B. Palier, and M. Seeleib-Kaiser. 2012. *The Age of Dualization. The Changing Face of Inequality*. Oxford/New York: Oxford University Press.

Dansk Folkeparti. 1997. 'Principprogram'. 1997 Party Manifesto of the Danish People's Party. Last accessed 18 July 2023. Retrieved from: http://www5.kb.dk/pamphlets/dasmaa/2008/feb/partiprogrammer/object41242/da/.

Dansk Folkeparti. 2001. 'Fælles værdier—fælles ansvar: Arbejdsprogram for Dansk Folkeparti—som vedtaget af Dansk Folkepartis folketingsgruppe september 2001'. 2001 Working programme of the Danish People's Party's parliamentary group. Last accessed 18 July 2023. Retrieved from: http://www5.kb.dk/pamphlets/dasmaa/2008/feb/partiprogrammer/object45536/da/.

Dansk Folkeparti. 2009. Dansk Folkepartis Arbejdsprogram. 2009 working programme of the Danish People's Party's parliamentary group. Last accessed 18 July 2023. Retrieved from: http://www5.kb.dk/pamphlets/dasmaa/2008/feb/partiprogrammer/object92133/da/.

De Koster, W., P. Achterberg, and J. Van der Waal. 2013. 'The New Right and the Welfare State: The Electoral Relevance of Welfare Chauvinism and Welfare Populism in the Netherlands'. *International Political Science Review* 34(1): pp. 3–20.

De Lange, S. 2007. 'A New Winning Formula? The Programmatic Appeal of the Radical Right'. *Party Politics* 13(4): pp 411–435.

De Lange, S. and S. Guerra. 2009. 'The League of Polish Families between East and West, Past and Present'. *Communist and Post-Communist Studies* 42(4): pp. 527–549.

De Vries, C. E. and S. B. Hobolt. 2020. *Political Entrepreneurs: The Rise of Challenger Parties in Europe*. Princeton: Princeton University Press.

Dehdari, S. H. 2022. 'Economic Distress and Support for Radical Right Parties—Evidence from Sweden'. *Comparative Political Studies* 55(2): pp. 191–221.

Denmark Government. 2016. 'Denmark's National Reform Programme 2016'. Last accessed 18 July 2023. Retrieved from: https://en.fm.dk/media/15635/DenmarksNationalReformProgramme2016.pdf.

Ebbinghaus, B. 2006. *Reforming Early Retirement in Europe, Japan and the USA*. Oxford: Oxford University Press.

Economist. 2020. 'How Hungary's leader, Viktor Orban, gets away with it', 2 April. Last accessed 18 July 2023. Retrieved from: https://www.economist.com/europe/2020/04/02/how-hungarys-leader-viktor-orban-gets-away-with-it.

Economist. 2022. 'Hungary ends its covid emergency—and declares one over Ukraine', 25 May. Last accessed 18 July 2023. Retrieved from: https://www.economist.com/europe/2022/05/25/hungary-ends-its-covid-emergency-anddeclares-one-over-ukraine.

Eger, M. A. and S. Valdez. 2015. 'Neo-nationalism in Western Europe'. *European Sociological Review* 31(1): pp. 115–130.

Ekman, J. and J. Linde. 2005. 'Communist Nostalgia and the Consolidation of Democracy in Central and Eastern Europe'. *Journal of Communist Studies and Transition Politics* 21(3): pp. 354–374.

Enggist, M. and M. Pinggera. 2022. 'Radical Right Parties and Their Welfare State Stances—Not So Blurry after All?' *West European Politics* 45(1): pp. 102–128.

Engler, S. and D. Weisstanner 2021. 'The Threat of Social Decline: Income Inequality and Radical Right Support'. *Journal of European Public Policy* 28(2): pp. 153–173.

Ennser-Jedenastik, L. 2016. 'A Welfare State for Whom? A Group-Based Account of the Austrian Freedom Party's Social Policy Profile'. *Swiss Political Science Review* 22(3): pp. 409–427.

Ennser-Jedenastik, L. 2018. 'Welfare Chauvinism in Populist Radical Right Platforms: The Role of Redistributive Justice Principles'. *Social Policy & Administration* 52(1): pp. 293–314.

Ennser-Jedenastik, L. 2019. 'Von der Fundamentalopposition auf die Regierungsbank: Die FPÖ unter Heinz-Christian Strache'. In *Die schwarz-blaue Wende in Österreich. Eine Bilanz*, edited by Emmerich Tálos, pp. 29–48. Vienna: LIT-Verlag.

Ennser-Jedenastik, L. 2022. 'The Impact of Radical Right Parties on Family Benefits'. *West European Politics* 45(1): pp. 77–101.

Enyedi, Z. 2016. 'Populist Polarization and Party System Institutionalization'. *Problems of Post-Communism* 63(4): pp. 210–220.

Esping-Andersen, G. 1985. *Politics against Markets: The Social Democratic Road to Power*. Princeton: Princeton University Press.

Esping-Andersen, G. 1990. *The Three Worlds of Welfare Capitalism*. New Jersey: Princeton University Press.

Esping-Andersen, G., D. Gallie, A. Hemerijck, and J. Myles. 2002. *Why We Need a New Welfare State*. Oxford/New York: Oxford University Press.

ESS Round 1: European Social Survey Round 1 Data. 2002. Data file edition 6.6. NSD—Norwegian Centre for Research Data, Norway—Data Archive and distributor of ESS data for ESS ERIC.

ESS Round 3: European Social Survey Round 3 Data. 2006. Data file edition 3.7. NSD—Norwegian Centre for Research Data, Norway—Data Archive and distributor of ESS data for ESS ERIC.

ESS Round 4: European Social Survey Round 4 Data. 2008. Data file edition 4.5. NSD—Norwegian Centre for Research Data, Norway—Data Archive and distributor of ESS data for ESS ERIC.

ESS Round 5: European Social Survey Round 5 Data. 2010. Data file edition 3.4. NSD—Norwegian Centre for Research Data, Norway—Data archive and distributor of ESS data for ESS ERIC.

ESS Round 6: European Social Survey Round 6 Data. 2012. Data file edition 2.4. NSD—Norwegian Centre for Research Data, Norway—Data Archive and distributor of ESS data for ESS ERIC.

ESS Round 8: European Social Survey Round 8 Data. 2016. Data file edition 2.2. NSD—Norwegian Centre for Research Data, Norway—Data Archive and distributor of ESS data for ESS.

ESS Round 9: European Social Survey Round 9 Data. 2018. Data file edition 3.1. NSD—Norwegian Centre for Research Data, Norway—Data Archive and distributor of ESS data for ESS ERIC.

ESS Round 10: European Social Survey Round 10 Data. 2020. Data file edition 1.2. Sikt—Norwegian Agency for Shared Services in Education and Research, Norway—Data Archive and distributor of ESS data for ESS ERIC.

Estevez-Abe, M. 2008. *Welfare and Capitalism in Postwar Japan: Party, Bureaucracy, and Business*. Cambridge: Cambridge University Press.

Eurostat. 2022. 'Formal Childcare, by Age of Child and Duration of Care in 2020'. Last accessed 18 July 2023. Retrieved from: https://ec.europa.eu/eurostat/statistics-explained/index.php?title=File:Tab_1._Formal_childcare,_by_age_of_child_and_duration_of_care,_2020_(%25).png.

Eurostat. 2023. 'Population on 1 January by Age Group, Sex and Citizenship'. Last accessed 19 July 2023. Retrieved from: https://ec.europa.eu/eurostat/databrowser/view/MIGR_POP1CTZ__custom_2721580/bookmark/table?lang=en&bookmarkId=d5fc9575-36aa-49fc-857f-5a1461299202.

Evans, G. and J. Tilley. 2011. 'How Parties Shape Class Politics: Explaining the Decline of the Class Basis of Party Support'. *British Journal of Political Science* 41(1): pp. 137–161.

Eyal, G., I. Szelenyi, and E. R. Townsley. 2002. *Making Capitalism without Capitalists. The New Ruling Elites in Eastern Europe*. London: Verso.

Feather, N. T. 1999. 'Judgments of Deservingness: Studies in the Psychology of Justice and Achievement'. *Personality and Social Psychology Review* 3(2): pp. 86–107.

Feldman, S. 2003. 'Enforcing Social Conformity: A Theory of Authoritarianism'. *Political Psychology* 24(1): pp. 41–74.

Fenger, M. 2018. 'The Social Policy Agendas of Populist Radical Right Parties in Comparative Perspective'. *Journal of International and Comparative Social Policy* 34(3): pp. 188–209.

Ferrara, F. M. 2023. 'Why Does Import Competition Favor Republicans? Localized Trade Shocks and Cultural Backlash in the US'. *Review of International Political Economy* 30(2): pp. 678–701.

Ferrera, M. 1996. 'The "Southern Model" of Welfare in Social Europe'. *Journal of European Social Policy* 6(1): pp. 17–37.

Fodor, E. 2022. *The Gender Regime of Anti-Liberal Hungary*. Cham: Palgrave Pivot.

Folketingets Oplysning. 2023. 'Folketingsvalgene 1953–2022'. Last accessed 18 July 2023. Retrieved from: https://www.ft.dk/-/media/sites/ft/pdf/folkestyret/valg-og-afstemninger/folketingsvalg-fra-1953.ashx.

FPÖ-Parlamentsklub. 2018. 'FPÖ-Belakowitsch: "Strukturreform der Sozialversicherungsträager ist der erste Schritt zu einer gerechten Gesundheitsversorgung"', 26 October. Last accessed 18 July 2023. Retrieved from: https://www.ots.at/presseaussendung/OTS_20181024_OTS0130/fpoe-belakowitsch-strukturreform-der-sozialversicherungstraeger-ist-der-erste-schritt-zu-einer-gerechten-gesundheitsversorgung.

Fraser, N. 2016. 'Contradictions of Capital and Care'. *New Left Review* 100(July/August): pp. 71–97.

Fraser, N. 2019. *The Old Is Dying and the New Cannot Be Born: From Progressive Neoliberalism to Trump and Beyond*. London: Verso.

Freiheitliche Partei Österreichs. 2017. *Das Freiheitliche Wirtschaftsprogramm: Fairness. Freiheit, Fortschritt*. Wien: FPÖ-Bildungsinstitut. Last accessed 18 July 2023. Retrieved from: https://www.fw.at/wp-content/uploads/sites/10/2017/08/Wirtschaftsprogramm-PDF-Beilage.pdf.

Gallup. 2019. 'Trade under Trump'. Policy Briefing. Washington DC: Gallup World Headquarters. Last accessed 4 October 2022. Retrieved from: https://news.gallup.com/reports/267386/trade-under-trump-gallup-briefing.aspx.

Gallup. 2016. 'Americans remain upbeat about foreign trade'. Washington DC: Gallup World Headquarters. Last accessed 4 October 2022. Retrieved from: https://news.gallup.com/poll/189620/americans-remain-upbeat-foreign-trade.aspx.

Garvik, M. and M. Valenta. 2021. 'Seeking Asylum in Scandinavia: A Comparative Analysis of Recent Restrictive Policy Responses Towards Unaccompanied Afghan Minors in Denmark, Sweden and Norway'. *Comparative Migration Studies* 9(1): pp. 1–22.

Gilens, M. 1999. *Why Americans Hate Welfare. Race, Media, and the Politics of Antipoverty Policy*. Chicago: University of Chicago Press.

Gerstle, G. 2022. *The Rise and Fall of the Neoliberal Order. America and the World in the Free Market Era*. New York: Oxford University Press.

Gest, J. 2016. *The New Minority: White Working Class Politics in an Age of Immigration and Inequality*. Oxford: Oxford University Press.

Gest, J., T. Reny, and J. Mayer. 2018. 'Roots of the Radical Right: Nostalgic Deprivation in the United States and Britain'. *Comparative Political Studies* 51(13): pp. 1694–1719.

Ghodsee, K. 2005. *The Red Riviera: Gender, Tourism, and Postsocialism on the Black Sea*. Durham, NC: Duke University Press.

Giddens, A. 1999. *The Third Way: The Renewal of Social Democracy*. Cambridge: Polity Press.

Gidron, N. and P. A. Hall. 2017. 'The Politics of Social Status: Economic and Cultural Roots of the Populist Right'. *British Journal of Sociology* 68(1): pp. 57–84.

Gidron, N. and P. A. Hall. 2020. 'Populism as a Problem of Social Integration'. *Comparative Political Studies* 53(7): pp. 1027–1059.

Glyn, A. 2007. *Capitalism Unleashed: Finance Globalisation and Welfare*. Oxford: Oxford University Press.

Goul Andersen, J. and T. Bjørklund. 1990. 'Structural Changes and New Cleavages: The Progress Parties in Denmark and Norway'. *Acta Sociologica* 33(3): pp. 195–217.

Government of Hungary. 2011. *Széll Kálmán Terv*. Budapest. Last accessed 18 July 2023. Retrieved from: https://2010-2014.kormany.hu/download/4/d1/20000/Sz%C3%A9ll%20K%C3%A1lm%C3%A1n%20Terv.pdf.

Goul Andersen, J. and K. Møller Hansen. 2013. 'Vælgernes krisebevidsthed'. In *Krisevalg - Økonomien og folketingsvalget 2011*, edited by Rune Stubager, Kasper Møller Hansen and Jørgen Goul Andersen, pp. 137–162. København: Djøf Forlag.

Green-Pedersen, C. 2002. *The Politics of Justification: Party Competition and Welfare State Retrenchment in Denmark and the Netherlands from 1982 to 1998*. Amsterdam: Amsterdam University Press.

Greskovits, B. 2020. 'Rebuilding the Hungarian Right through Conquering Civil Society: The Civic Circles Movement'. *East European Politics* 36(2): pp. 247–266.

Greve, B. 2020. 'Denmark: A Universal Welfare System with Restricted Austerity'. In *Routledge Handbook of European Welfare Systems*, edited by Sonja Blum, Johanna Kuhlmann, and Klaus Schubert, pp. 129–144. Oxon: Routledge.

Grillmayer, D. 2006. *National und Liberal: Die Geschichte der Dritten Kraft in Österreich*. Vienna: Edition Genius.

Grumbach, J. M., S. Hacker, and P. Pierson. 2021. 'The Political Economies of Red States'. In *The American Political Economy. Politics, Markets, and Power*, edited by Jacob S. Hacker, Alexander Hertel-Fernandez, Paul Pierson, and Kathleen Thelen, pp. 209–244. New York: Cambridge University Press.

Guillén, A., M. Jessoula, M. Matsaganis, R. Branco, and E. Pavolini. 2022. 'Southern European Welfare Systems in Transition'. In *Mediterranean Capitalism Revisited*, edited by Ana M. Guillén, Matteo Jessoula, Manos Matsaganis, Rui Branco, and Emmanuele Pavolini, pp. 149–171. Ithaca, NY: Cornell University Press.

Hacker, J. 2004. 'Privatizing Risk without Privatizing the Welfare State: The Hidden Politics of Social Policy Retrenchment in the United States'. *American Political Science Review* 98(2): pp. 243–260.

Hacker, J. 2006. *The Great Risk Shift: The New Economic Insecurity and the Decline of the American Dream*. Oxford/New York: Oxford University Press.

Hacker, J. and P. Pierson. 2010. *Winner-Take-All Politics: How Washington Made the Rich Richer–and Turned Its Back on the Middle Class*. New York: Simon & Schuster.

Hacker, J. and P. Pierson. 2020. *Let Them Eat Tweets: How the Right Rules in Age of Extreme Inequality*. New York, NY: Liveright, a division of W. W. Norton & Company.

Haider, J. 1993. *Die Freiheit, die ich meine*. Frankfurt am Main: Ullstein.

Halikiopoulou, D. and T. Vlandas. 2020. 'When Economic and Cultural Interests Align: The Anti-immigration Voter Coalitions Driving Far Right Party Success in Europe'. *European Political Science Review* 12(4): pp. 427–448.

Hall, P. A. 1989. *The Political Power of Economic Ideas: Keynesianism across Nations*. Princeton: Princeton University Press.

Hall, P. A. 2022. 'The Shifting Relationship between Post-War Capitalism and Democracy'. *Government and Opposition* 57(1): pp. 1–30.

Haney, L. 1997. '"But We Are Still Mothers": Gender and the Construction of Need in Post-Socialist Hungary'. *Social Politics* 4(2): pp. 208–244.

Haney, L. 2002. *Inventing the Needy: Gender and the Politics of Welfare in Hungary*. Oakland, CA: University of California Press.

Harteveld, E. 2016. 'Winning the "Losers" but Losing the "Winners"? The Electoral Consequences of the Radical Right Moving to the Economic Left'. *Electoral Studies* 44: pp. 225–234.

Harvey, D. 2010. *A Brief History of Neoliberalism*. Oxford: Oxford University Press.

Harvey, D. 2018. *The Limits to Capital*. London: Verso.

Hassel, A. and B. Palier. 2020. 'Tracking the Transformation of Growth Regimes in Advanced Capitalist Economies'. In *Growth and Welfare in Advanced Capitalist Economies. How Have Growth Regimes Evolved?* edited by Anke Hassel and Bruno Palier, pp. 3–56. Oxford: Oxford University Press.

Höbelt, L. 2003. *Defiant populist: Jörg Haider and the politics of Austria*. West Lafayette, Indiana: Purdue University Press.

Hochschild, A. R. 2016. *Strangers in Their Own Land: Anger and Mourning on the American Right*. New York: The New Press.

Häusermann, S. 2012. 'The Politics of Old and New Social Policies'. In *The Politics of the New Welfare State*, edited by Giuliano Bonoli and David Natali, pp. 111–132. Oxford: Oxford University Press.

Häusermann, S. 2018. 'Social Democracy and the Welfare State in Context: The Conditioning Effect of Institutional Legacies and Party Competition'. In *Welfare Democracies and Party Politics. Explaining Electoral Dynamics in Times of Changing Welfare Capitalism*, edited by Philip Manow, Bruno Palier, and Hanna Schwander. Oxford: Oxford University Press, pp. 150–170.

Häusermann, S. 2020. 'Dualization and Electoral Realignment'. *Political Science Research and Methods* 8(2): pp. 380–385.

Häusermann, S., G. Picot, and D. Geering. 2013. 'Partisan Politics and the Welfare State. Recent Advances in the Literature'. *British Journal of Political Science* 43(1): pp. 221–240.

Häusermann, S. and H. Kriesi. 2015. 'What Do Voters Want? Dimensions and Configurations in Individual-Level Preferences and Party Choice'. In *The Politics of Advanced Capitalism* edited by Pablo Beramendi, Silja Häusermann, Herbert Kitschelt, and Hanspeter Kriesi. New York: Cambridge University Press, pp. 202–230.

Häusermann, S., M. Pinggera, M. Ares, and M. Enggist. 2022. 'Class and Social Policy in the Knowledge Economy'. *European Journal of Political Research* 61(2): pp. 462–484.

Heinisch, R. 2003. 'Success in Opposition—Failure in Government: Explaining the Performance of Right-Wing Populist Parties in Public Office'. *West European Politics* 26(3): pp. 91–130.

Heinisch, R. 2004. 'Die FPÖ—Ein Phänomen im Internationalen Vergleich. Erfolg und Misserfolg des Identitären Rechtspopulismus'. *Austrian Journal of Political Science* 33(3): pp. 247–261.

Heinisch, R. and A. Werner. 2021. 'The Kurz affair has uncovered the Trumpian dimension of Austrian politics'. *LSE European Politics and Policy Blog* (EUROPP), 8 November. Last accessed 9 November 2023. Retrieved from: https://blogs.lse.ac.uk/europpblog/2021/11/08/the-kurz-affair-has-uncovered-the-trumpian-dimension-of-austrian-politics/

Hemerijck, A. 2018. 'Social Investment as a Policy Paradigm'. *Journal of European Public Policy* 25(6): pp. 810–827.

Höbelt, L. 1999. *Von der vierten Partei zur dritten Kraft. Die Geschichte des VdU*. Graz: Leopold Stocker Verlag.

Hopkin, J. 2020. *Anti-System Politics. The Crisis of Market Liberalism in Rich Democracies*. Oxford/New York: Oxford University Press.

Hopkin, J. and M. Blyth. 2019. 'The Global Economics of European Populism: Growth Regimes and Party System Change in Europe'. *Government & Opposition* 54(2): pp. 193–225.

Huber, E. and J. D. Stephens. 2001. *Development and Crisis of the Welfare State. Parties and Policies in Global Markets*. Chicago: University of Chicago Press.

Hugrée, C., E. Penissat, and A. Spire. 2020. *Social Class in Europe. New Inequalities in the Old World*. London/New York: Verso.

Ignazi, P. 1992. 'The Silent Counter-Revolution: Hypotheses on the Emergence of Extreme Right-Wing Parties in Europe'. *European Journal of Political Research* 22(1): pp. 3–34.

Inglehart, R. F. 1990. *Culture Shift*. Princeton: Princeton University Press.

Inglot, T. 2008. *Welfare States in East Central Europe, 1919–2004*. Cambridge: Cambridge University Press.

Inglot, T. 2020. 'The Triumph of Novelty over Experience? Social Policy Responses to Demographic Crises in Hungary and Poland since EU Enlargement'. *East European Politics and Societies and Cultures* 34(4): pp. 984–1004.

Inglot, T., D. Szikra, and C. Raţ. 2022. *Mothers, Families or Children? Family Policy in Poland, Hungary, and Romania, 1945-2020*. Pittsburgh: University of Pittsburgh Press.

ISSP Research Group. 2016. 'International Social Survey Programme: Family and Changing Gender Roles IV—ISSP 2012'. GESIS Data Archive, Cologne. ZA5900 Data file Version 4.0.0.

ISSP Research Group. 2017. 'International Social Survey Programme: Work Orientations IV—ISSP 2015'. GESIS Data Archive, Cologne. ZA6770 Data file Version 2.1.0.

ISSP Research Group. 2022. 'International Social Survey Programme: Environment IV—ISSP 2020'. GESIS Data Archive, Cologne. ZA7650 Data file Version 1.0.0.

Ivaldi, G. 2015. 'Towards the Median Economic Crisis Voter? The New Leftist Economic Agenda of the Front National in France'. *French Politics* 13(4): pp. 346–369.

Ivarsflaten, E. 2005. 'The Vulnerable Populist Right Parties: No Economic Realignment Fuelling Their Electoral Success'. *European Journal of Political Research* 44(3): pp. 465–492.

Iversen, T. and T. Cusack. 2000. 'The Causes of Welfare State Expansion: Deindustrialization or Globalization?' *World Politics* 52(3): pp. 313–349.

Iversen, T. and D. Soskice. 2006. 'Electoral Institutions and the Politics of Coalitions: Why Some Democracies Redistribute More than Others'. *American Political Science Review* 100(2): pp. 165–181.

Iversen, T. and D. Soskice. 2015. 'Politics for Markets'. *Journal of European Social Policy* 25(1): pp. 76–93.

Iversen, T. and D. Soskice. 2019. *Democracy and Prosperity: Reinventing Capitalism through a Turbulent Century*. Princeton: Princeton University Press.

Iversen, T. and J. D. Stephens. 2008. 'Partisan Politics, the Welfare State, and Three Worlds of Human Capital Formation'. *Comparative Political Studies* 41(4–5): pp. 600–637.

Johnston, J. and A. Barnes. 2015. 'Financial Nationalism and Its International Enablers: The Hungarian Experience'. *Review of International Political Economy* 22(3): pp. 535–569.

Jupskås, A. R. 2015. 'Institutionalised Right-Wing Populism in Times of Economic Crisis: A Comparative Study of the Norwegian Progress Party and the Danish People's Party'. In *European Populism in the Shadow of the Great Recession*, edited by Hanspeter Kriesi and Takis S. Pappas, pp. 23–40. Colchester: ECPR Press.

Jylhä, K. M., J. Rydgren, and P. Strimling. 2019. 'Radical Right-Wing Voters from Right and Left: Comparing Sweden Democrat Voters Who Previously Voted for the Conservative Party or the Social Democratic Party'. *Scandinavian Political Studies* 42(3–4): pp. 220–244.

Karlhofer, F. 2010. 'The Politics of Asymmetry: (Non-)Corporatist Policy Making, 2000–2006'. In *The Schüssel Era in Austria: Contemporary Austrian Studies, XVIII*, edited by Günter Bischof and Fritz Plasser, pp. 104–118. New Orleans: Uno Press.

Katzenstein, P. J. 1985. *Small States in World Markets*. Ithaca, NY: Cornell University Press.

Kazin, M. 1995. *The Populist Persuasion: An American History*. Ithaca, NY: Cornell University Press.

Kitschelt, H. and A. J. McGann. 1995. *The Radical Right in Western Europe: A Comparative Analysis*. Ann Arbor: University of Michigan Press.

Kjærsgaard, P. 1997. 'Pia Kjærsgaards tale ved Dansk Folkepartis årsmøde 1997'. Speech. Last accessed 18 July 2023. Retrieved from: https://dansketaler.dk/tale/pia-kjaersgaards-tale-ved-dansk-folkepartis-aarsmoede-1997/.

Kjærsgaard, P. 1998. 'Pia Kjærsgaards tale ved Dansk Folkepartis årsmøde 1998'. Speech. Last accessed 18 July 2023. Retrieved from: https://dansketaler.dk/tale/pia-kjaersgaards-tale-ved-dansk-folkepartis-aarsmoede-1998/.

Kjærsgaard, P. 2001. 'Pia Kjærsgaards tale ved Dansk Folkepartis årsmøde 2001'. Speech. Last accessed 18 July 2023. Retrieved from: https://dansketaler.dk/tale/pia-kjaersgaards-tale-ved-dansk-folkepartis-aarsmoede-2001/.

Kjærsgaard, P. 2006a. 'Pia Kjærsgaards grundlovstale 2006'. Speech. Last accessed 18 July 2023. Retrieved from: https://dansketaler.dk/tale/pia-kjaersgaards-grundlovstale-2006/.

Kjærsgaard, P. 2006b. 'Pia Kjærsgaards tale ved Dansk Folkepartis årsmøde 2006'. Speech. Last accessed 18 July 2023. Retrieved from: https://dansketaler.dk/tale/pia-kjaersgaards-tale-ved-dansk-folkepartis-aarsmoede-2006/.

Kjærsgaard, P. 2011. 'Pia Kjærsgaards tale ved Dansk Folkepartis årsmøde 2011'. Speech. Last accessed 19 July 2023. Retrieved from: https://dansketaler.dk/tale/pia-kjaersgaards-tale-ved-dansk-folkepartis-aarsmoede-2011/.

Klein, M. C. and M. Pettis. 2020. *Trade Wars Are Class Wars: How Rising Inequality Distorts the Global Economy and Threatens International Peace*. New Haven, CT: Yale University Press

Kleine Zeitung. 2017. 'Kammerzwang bleibt, Kammerumlage wird deutlich gesenkt', 12 December. Last accessed 18 July 2023. Retrieved from: https://www.kleinezeitung.at/politik/innenpolitik/5336873/OeVPFPOe-einig_Kammerzwang-bleibt-Kammerumlage-wird-deutlich-gesenkt.

Klitgaard, M. B. 2007. 'Why Are They Doing It? Social Democracy and Market-Oriented Welfare State Reforms'. *West European Politics* 30(1): pp. 172–194.

Klitgaard, M. B. and C. Elmelund-Praestekaer. 2013. 'Partisan Effects on Welfare State Retrenchment: Empirical Evidence from a Measurement of Government Intentions'. *Social Policy & Administration* 47(1): pp. 50–71.

Klitgaard, M. B. and A. S. Nørgaard. 2009. 'Arbejdsmarkedsreformer med og uden kommis-sioner'. In *De store kommissioner: Vise mænd, smagsdommere eller nyttige idioter*, edited by Jørgen Grønnegaard Christensen, Poul Erik Mouritzen, and Asbjørn Sonne Nørgaard, pp. 91–116. Odense: Syddansk Universitetsforlag.

Klos, M. 2014. *33.900 har mistet deres dagpengeret i 2013, Status for hele 2013*. Copenhagen: AK-Samvirke.

Korpi, W. 2006. 'Power Resources and Employer-Centered Approaches in Explanations of Welfare States and Varieties of Capitalism: Protagonists, Consenters, and Antagonists'. *World Politics* 58(2): pp. 167–206.

Kosiara-Pedersen, K. 2020a. 'Danish Peoples Party: Centre Oriented Populists?' In *The Oxford Handbook of Danish Politics*, edited by Peter Munk Christiansen, Jørgen Elklit and Peter Nedergaard, pp. 313–328. Oxford: Oxford University Press.

Kosiara-Pedersen, K. 2020b. 'Stronger Core, Weaker Fringes: The Danish General Election 2019'. *West European Politics* 43(4): pp. 1011–1022.

Krastev, I. 2017. *After Europe*. Philadelphia: University of Pennsylvania Press.

Krekó, P. and G. Mayer. 2015. 'Transforming Hungary—Together? An Analysis of the Fidesz-Jobbik Relationship'. In *Transforming the Transformation? The East European Radical Right in the Political Process*, edited by Michael Minkenberg, pp. 183–205. London/New York: Routledge.

Kriesi, H. 1998. 'The Transformation of Cleavage Politics'. *European Journal of Political Research* 33(2): pp. 165–185.

Kriesi, H. 2018. 'Revisiting the Populist Challenge'. *Czech Journal of Political Science* 25(1): pp. 5–27.

Kriesi H., E. Grande, R. Lachat, M. Dolezal, S. Bornschier, and T. Frey. 2008. *West European Politics in the Age of Globalization*. Cambridge: Cambridge University Press.

Kronen Zeitung. 2018. 'Abrechnung mit Schuldenpolitik'. 21 March. Last accessed 18 July 2023. Retrieved from: https://www.pressreader.com/austria/kronen-zeitung-9gf1/20180321/283296048117139.

Kulin, J. and B. Meulemann. 2015. 'Human Values and Welfare State Support in Europe: An East–West Divide?' *European Sociological Review* 31(4): pp. 418–432.

Kurer, T. 2020. 'The Declining Middle: Occupational Change, Social Status, and the Populist Right'. *Comparative Political Studies* 53(10–11): pp. 1798–1835.

Kurer, T. and B. Palier. 2019. 'Shrinking and Shouting: The Political Revolt of the Declining Middle in Times of Employment Polarization'. *Research & Politics* 6(1). https://doi.org/10.1080/13501763.2023.2182342

Kurer, T. and B. Van Staalduinen. 2022. 'Disappointed Expectations: Downward Mobility and Electoral Change'. *American Political Science Review* 116(4): pp. 1340–1356.

Landini, I. 2022. *Welfare Chauvinism and Social Policy: How Politicians Justify Migrants' Exclusion from Social Programs in Western Europe*. PhD dissertation, Rome: LUISS Rome.

Larsen, C. A. 2008. 'The Institutional Logic of Welfare Attitudes: How Welfare Regimes Influence Public Support'. *Comparative Political Studies* 41(2): pp. 145–168.

Larsen, C. A. and J. G. Andersen. 2009. 'How New Economic Ideas Changed the Danish Welfare State: The Case of Neoliberal Ideas and Highly Organized Social Democratic Interests'. *Governance* 22(2): pp. 239–261.

Lefkofridi, Z. and E. Michel. 2017. 'The Electoral Politics of Solidarity'. In *The Strains of Commitment: The Political Sources of Solidarity in Diverse Societies*, edited by Keith Banting and Will Kymlicka, pp. 233–267. Oxford: Oxford University Press.

Leitner, S. 2003. 'Varieties of Familialism: The Caring Function of the Family in Comparative Perspective'. *European societies* 5(4): pp. 353–375.

Leitner, S. 2011. 'Germany Outpaces Austria in Childcare Policy: The Historical Contingencies of "Conservative" Childcare Policy'. *Journal of European Social Policy* 20(5): pp. 456–467.

Lendvai, P. 2010. *Mein verspieltes Land. Ungarn im Umbruch*. Salzburg: Ecowin Verlag.

Levitsky, S. and D. Ziblatt 2018. *How Democracies Die*. New York: Crown Publisher.

Lieberman, R. C. 2001. *Shifting the Color Line. Race and the American Welfare State*. Cambridge, MA: Harvard University Press.

Lindvall, J. 2010. *Mass Unemployment and the State*. Oxford: Oxford University Press.

Lipset, S. 1959. 'Democracy and Working-Class Authoritarianism'. *American Sociological Review* 24(4): pp. 482–501.

Lipset, S. and S. Rokkan. 1990. 'Cleavage Structures, Party Systems, and Voter Alignments'. In *The West European Party System*, edited by Peter Mair, pp. 91–138. Oxford: Oxford University Press.

Lugosi, N. V. T. 2018. 'Radical Right Framing of Social Policy in Hungary: Between Nationalism and Populism'. *Journal of International and Comparative Social Policy* 34(3): pp. 210–233.

Luther, K. R. 2008. 'Electoral Strategies and Performance of Austrian Right-Wing Populism, 1986-2006'. In *The Changing Austrian Voter*, edited by Günter Bischof and Fritz Plasser, pp. 104–122. New York: Routledge.

Lutz, P. 2019. 'Variation in Policy Success: Radical Right Populism and Migration Policy'. *West European Politics* 42(3): pp. 517–544.Lynch, J. 2014. 'A Cross-National Perspective on the American Welfare State'. In *The Oxford Handbook of U.S. Social Policy*, edited by Daniel Béland, Christopher Howard, and Kimberly J. Morgan, pp. 112–130. New York: Oxford University Press.

Madariaga, A. 2020. *Neoliberal Resilience. Lessons in Democracy and Development from Latin America and Eastern Europe*. Princeton: Princeton University Press.

Madestam, A., D. Shoag, S. Veuger, and D. Yanagizawa-Drott. 2013. 'Do Political Protests Matter? Evidence from the Tea Party Movement'. *The Quarterly Journal of Economics* 128(4): pp. 1633–1685.

Magyar, B. 2016. *Post-Communist Mafia State*. Budapest: Central European University Press.

Mair, P. 2013. *Ruling the Void. The Hollowing of Western Democracy*. London: Verso.

Mann, J. 2022. 'Trump's China Policy: The Chaotic End to the Era of Engagement'. In *The Presidency of Donald J. Trump*, edited by Julian E. Zelizer, pp. 259–278. Princeton/Oxford: Princeton University Press.

Manow, P. 2018. *Die Politische Ökonomie des Populismus*. Berlin: Suhrkamp.

Manow, P. and H. Schwander. 2017. '"Modernize *and* Die"? German Social Democracy and the Electoral Consequences of the Agenda 2010'. *Socio-Economic Review* 15(1): pp. 117–134.

Manow, P., B. Palier, and H. Schwander. 2018. 'Welfare Democracies and Party Politics: Explaining Electoral Dynamics in Times of Changing Welfare: Introduction'. In *Welfare Democracies and Party Politics. Explaining Electoral Dynamics in Times of Changing Welfare Capitalism*, edited by Philip Manow, Bruno Palier, and Hanna Schwander, pp. 1–26. Oxford: Oxford University Press.

Manow, P. 2020. *Social Protection, Capitalist Production. The Bismarckian Welfare State in the German Political Economy, 1880–2015*. Oxford: Oxford University Press.

Manwaring, R. and J. Holloway. 2022. 'A New Wave of Social Democracy? Policy Change across the Social Democratic Party Family, 1970s–2010s'. *Government and Opposition* 57(1): pp. 171–191.

Mares, I., and L. E. Young. 2019. *Conditionality & Coercion. Electoral Clientelism in Eastern Europe*. Oxford: Oxford University Press.

Marx, K. 1852 [2016]. 'Der achtzehnte Brumaire des Louis Bonaparte'. In *Karl Marx/Friedrich Engels. Gesammelte Werke*, edited by Kurt Lhotzky, pp. 327–448. Bonn: Anaconda Verlag.

Marx, P. and E. Naumann. 2018. 'Do Right-Wing Parties Foster Welfare Chauvinistic Attitudes? A Longitudinal Study of the 2015 "Refugee Crisis" in Germany'. *Electoral Studies* 52: pp. 111–116.

Meardi, G. and I. Guardiancich. 2022. 'Back to the Familialist Future: The Rise of Social Policy for Ruling Populist Radical Right Parties in Italy and Poland'. *West European Politics* 45(1): pp. 129–153.

Michener, J. 2018. *Fragmented Democracy: Medicaid, Federalism, and Unequal Politics*. Cambridge: Cambridge University Press.

Milanovic, B. 2016. *Global Inequality. A New Approach for the Age of Globalization*. Cambridge, MA: Harvard University Press.

Minkenberg, M. 2011. 'The Tea Party and American Populism Today: Between Protest, Patriotism and Paranoia'. *Der Moderne Staat* 4(2): pp. 283–296.

Minkenberg, M. 2013. 'From Pariah to Policy-Maker? The Radical Right in Europe, West and East: Between Margin and Mainstream'. *Journal of Contemporary European Studies* 21(1): pp. 5–24.

Mizruchi, M. S. and R. Galan. 2023. 'The Trump Phenomenon and Right-Wing Extremism: Is Donald Trump a Populist?' In *Business Elites and Populism: The Odd Couple?* edited by Glenn Morgan and Magnus Feldmann, pp. 39–58. Oxford: Oxford University Press.

Mosimann, N. and J. Pontusson. 2017. 'Solidaristic Unionism and Support for Redistribution in Contemporary Europe'. *World Politics* 69(3): pp. 448–492.

Mosimann, N. and J. Pontusson. 2022. 'Varieties of Trade Unions and Support for Redistribution'. *West European Politics* 45(6). pp. 1310–1333.

Mosimann, N., L. Rennwald, and A. Zimmerman. 2020. 'The Radical Right, the Labour Movement and the Competition for the Workers' Vote'. *Economic and Industrial Democracy* 40 (1): pp. 65–90.

Mounk, Y. 2018. *The People vs. Democracy. Why Our Freedom Is in Danger and How to Save It*. Cambridge, MA: Harvard University Press.

Mudde, C. 2004. 'The populist Zeitgeist'. *Government and Opposition* 39(4): pp. 541–563.

Mudde, C. 2007. *Populist Radical Right Parties in Europe*. Cambridge: Cambridge University Press.

Mudde, C. 2016. 'The Study of Populist Radical Right Parties: Towards a Fourth Wave'. C-REX Working Paper Series no. 1.

Mudde, C. 2018. *The Far Right in America*. London/New York: Routledge.

Mudde, C. 2019. *The Far Right Today*. Cambridge: Polity Press.

Mudde, C. and R. Kaltwasser. 2012. 'Exclusionary vs. Inclusionary Populism: Comparing Contemporary Europe and Latin America'. *Government & Opposition* 48(2): pp. 147–174.

Mudge, S. 2018. *Leftism Reinvented. Western Parties from Socialism to Neoliberalism*. Cambridge, MA: Harvard University Press.

Mühlbradt, M. 2014. 'New government paves way for labour reforms'. *Eurofound*, 27 January. Last accessed 18 July 2023. Retrieved from: https://www.eurofound.europa.eu/publications/article/2014/new-government-paves-way-for-labour-reforms.

Müller, W. C. 2000a. 'The Austrian General Elections of 1999—A Shift to the Right'. *West European Politics* 23(2): pp. 191–200.

Müller, W. C. 2000b. 'Wahlen und die Dynamik des österreichischen Parteiensystems seit 1986'. In *Das österreichische Wahlverhalten*, edited by Fritz Plasser, Peter A. Ulram and Franz Sommer, pp. 13–54. Wien: Signum.

Müller, W. C. and F. Fallend. 2004. 'Changing Patterns of Party Competition in Austria: From Multipolar to Bipolar System'. *West European Politics* 27(5): pp. 801–835.

Naumann, I. 2012. 'Childcare Politics in the "New" Welfare State: Class, Religion and Gender in the Shaping of Political Agendas'. In *The Politics of the New Welfare State*, edited by Giuliano Bonoli and David Natali, pp. 158–181. Oxford: Oxford University Press.

Näsström, S. 2021. 'Democrtic Self-Defense: Bringing the Social Model Back In'. *Distinktion: Journal of Social Theory* 22(3): pp. 376–396.

Nemzeti Választási Iroda. 2023. 'Elections and Referendums'. Last accessed 19 July 2023. Retrieved from: https://www.valasztas.hu/web/national-election-office/elections.

Ngai, M. 2022. 'Immigration Policy and Politics under Trump'. In *The Presidency of Donald J. Trump*, edited by Julian E. Zelizer, pp. 144–161. Princeton/Oxford: Princeton University Press.

Nölke, A. and A. Vliegenthart. 2009. 'Enlarging the Varieties of Capitalism: The Emergence of Dependent Market Economies in East Central Europe'. *World Politics* 61(4): pp. 670–702.

Norocel, O. C. 2016. 'Populist Radical Right Protectors of the Folkhem: Welfare Chauvinism in Sweden'. *Critical Social Policy* 36(3): pp. 371–390.

Norris, P. and A. Inglehart. 2019. *Cultural Backlash. Trump, Brexit, and Authoritarian Populism*. Cambridge: Cambridge University Press.

NPR. 2021. 'Read Trump's Jan. 6 speech, a key part of impeachment trial', 10 February. Last accessed 18 July 2023. Retrieved from: https://www.npr.org/2021/02/10/966396848/read-trumps-jan-6-speech-a-key-part-of-impeachment-trial.

NYT. 2017. 'Trump's budget cuts deeply into Medicaid and anti-poverty efforts', 22 May. Last accessed 18 July 2023. Retrieved from: https://www.nytimes.com/2017/05/22/us/politics/trump-budget-cuts.html.

NYT. 2019. 'Trump declares a national emergency, and provokes a constitutional clash', 15 February. Last accessed 18 July 2023. Retrieved from: https://www.nytimes.com/2019/02/15/us/politics/national-emergency-trump.html.

NYT. 2021. 'How the American right fell in love with Hungary', 19 October. Last accessed 18 July 2023. Retrieved from: https://www.nytimes.com/2021/10/19/magazine/viktor-orban-rod-dreher.html.

Obinger, H. and E. Tálos. 2006. *Sozialstaat Österreich zwischen Kontinuität und Umbau. Eine Bilanz der ÖVP/FPÖ/BZÖ-Regierung.* Wiesbaden: Verlag für Sozialwissenschaften.

Obinger, H., P. Starke, and A. Kaasch. 2012. 'Responses to Labor Market Divides in Small States since the 1990s'. In *The Age of Dualization. The Changing Face of Inequality in Deindustrializing Countries*, edited by Patrick Emmenegger, Silja Häusermann, Bruno Palier, and Martin Seeleib-Kaiser, pp. 176–200. New York: Oxford University Press.

OECD. 2021. 'PF1.1: Public Spending on Family Benefits', Updated January 2021. Last accessed 18 July 2023. Retrieved from: https://www.oecd.org/els/soc/PF1_1_Public_spending_on_family_benefits.pdf.

OECD. 2023. 'PF3.2: Enrolment in childcare and pre-school', Updated January 2023. Last accessed 25 October 2023. Retrieved from: https://www.oecd.org/els/soc/PF3_2_Enrolment_childcare_preschool.pdf

Oesch, D. 2006. 'Coming to Grips with a Changing Class Structure: An Analysis of Employment Stratification in Britain, Germany, Sweden and Switzerland'. *International Sociology* 21(1): pp. 263–288.

Oesch, D. 2008. 'Explaining Workers' Support for Right-Wing Populist Parties in Western Europe: Evidence from Austria, Belgium, France, Norway, and Switzerland'. *International Political Science Review* 29(3): pp. 349–373.

Oesch, D. and L. Rennwald. 2018. 'Electoral Competition in Europe's New Tripolar Political Space: Class Voting for the Left, Centre-Right and Radical Right'. *European Journal of Political Research* 57(4): pp. 783–807.

Offe C. 1991. 'Capitalism by Democratic Design? Democratic Theory Facing the Triple Transition in East Central Europe'. *Social Research* 58(4): pp. 865–892.

Orbán, V. 2011. 'Orbán Viktor országértékelő beszéde' (Annual State of the Nation Speech), 7 February. Last accessed 18 July 2023. Retrieved from: https://2010-2014.kormany.hu/hu/miniszterelnokseg/miniszterelnok/beszedek-publikaciok-interjuk/orban-viktor-orszagertekelo-beszede-2011-februar-7.

Orbán, V. 2012. 'Ne Kapjon Segélyt, Aki Munkaképes', 26 July. Speech at the meeting of the National Association of Entrepreneurs and Employers. Last accessed 18 July 2023. Retrieved from: http://2010-2015.miniszterelnok.hu/beszed/ne_kapjon_segelyt_aki_munkakepes.

Orbán, V. 2014. 'The era of welfare states is over', 8 August. Speech at the Bálványos Summer Free University and Student Camp. Last accessed 20 July 2023. Retrieved from: https://www.youtube.com/watch?v=VAX-AaNMlG8.

Orbán, V. 2017. 'Orbán Viktor 19. évértékelő beszéde' (Annual State of the Nation Speech), 10 February. Last accessed 18 July 2023. Retrieved from: https://miniszterelnok.hu/orban-viktor-19-evertekelo-beszede/.

Orbán, V. 2022. 'Orbán Viktor évértékelő beszéde' (Annual State of the Nation Speech), 12 February. Last accessed 18 July 2023. Retrieved from: https://miniszterelnok.hu/orban-viktor-evertekelo-beszede-5/.

Orenstein, M. A. and B. Bugaric. 2022. 'Work, Family, Fatherland: The Political Economy of Populism in Central and Eastern Europe'. *Journal of European Public Policy* 29(2): pp. 176–195.

Orloff, A. S. 1993. 'Gender and the Social Rights of Citizenship: The Comparative Analysis of Gender Relations and Welfare States'. *American Sociological Review* 58(3): pp. 303–328.

Országgyűlési Napló. 2010. 'A 2010–2014-es országgyűlési ciklus Országgyűlési Napló—2010. évi nyári rendkívüli ülésszak, július 6 (22. szám)' [Parliamentary Protocol of the 2010–2014 parliamentary cycle—2010 summer extraordinary session, July 6 (No. 22)]. Last accessed 18 July 2023. Retrieved from: https://library.hungaricana.hu/en/view/ON1990_2010-2014_088/?pg=694&layout=s.

Palier, B. 2021. 'Continental Western Europe'. In *The Oxford Handbook of the Welfare State* (2nd edn), edited by Daniel Béland, Stephan Leibfried, Kimberly J. Morgan, Herbert Obinger, and Christopher Pierson, pp. 826–843. Oxford: Oxford University Press.

Palier, B., J. L. Garritzmann, and S. Häusermann. 2022. 'Toward a Worldwide View on the Politics of Social Investment'. In *The World Politics of Social Investment* (Volume I), edited by Julian L. Garritzmann, Silja Häusermann, and Bruno Palier, pp. 1–58. Oxford: Oxford University Press.

Palier, B. and K. Thelen. 2010. 'Institutionalizing Dualism: Complementarities and Change in France and Germany'. *Politics & Society* 38(1): pp. 119–148.

Pappas, T. 2019. *Populism and Liberal Democracy: A Comparative and Theoretical Analysis.* Oxford: Oxford University Press.

Parker, C. S. and C. C. Towler. 2019. 'Race and Authoritarianism in American Politics'. *Annual Review of Political Science* 22: pp. 503–519.

Payne, S. G. 1995. *A History of Fascism, 1914–1945.* London: UCL Press.

Pellizari, M. 2013. 'The Use of Welfare by Migrants in Italy'. *International Journal of Manpower* 34(2): pp. 155–166.

Petersen, J. H. and K. Petersen. 2009. 'The Coalition of the Willing and the Breakthrough of the Welfare State: The Political History of the Danish People's Pension'. In *The Politics of Age: Basic Pension Systems in a Comparative and Historical Perspective*, edited by Jörn Henrik Petersen and Klaus Petersen, pp. 19–40. Frankfurt am Main: Peter Lang.

Petersen, K. 2020. 'Welfare State Policies from the Beginning Towards an End?' In *The Oxford handbook of Danish politics*, edited by Peter Munk Christiansen, Jørgen Elklit, and Peter Nedergaar, pp. 540–558. Oxford: Oxford University Press.

Petrova, T. and T. Inglot. 2020. 'Introduction: Politics and Current Challenges of Demography in Central and Eastern Europe'. *East European Politics and Societies and Cultures* 34(4): pp. 879–892.

Pew Research Center. 2019. 'Many Across the Globe Are Dissatisfied With How Democracy Is Working'. April 2019. Last accessed 31 October 2023. Retrieved from: https://www.pewresearch.org/global/wp-content/uploads/sites/2/2019/04/Pew-Research-Center_Global-Views-of-Democracy-Report_2019-04-29_Updated-2019-04-30.pdf.

Pierce, J. R. and P. K. Schott. 2020. 'Trade Liberalization and Mortality: Evidence from US Counties'. *American Economic Review: Insights* 2(1): pp. 47–64.

Pierson, P. 1996. 'The New Politics of the Welfare State'. *World Politics* 48(2): pp. 143–179.

Pierson, P. 1998. 'Irresistible forces, immovable objects: post-industrial welfare states confront permanent austerity'. *Journal of European Public Policy* 5(4): pp. 539–560.

Plasser, F. and F. Sommer. 2018. *Wahlen im Schatten der Flüchtlingskrise. Parteien, Wähler und Koalitionen im Umbruch.* Vienna: Facultas-Verlag.

Polanyi, K. 1944 [2001]. *The Great Transformation*. Second Paperback edition. Boston: Beacon Press.

Pongracz, M. 2005. 'Opinions on Gender Roles: Findings of an International Comparative Study'. In *Changing Gender Roles. Report on the Situation of Women and Men in Hungary*, edited by Ildikó Nagy, Marietta Pongracz, and István György Toth, pp. 176–197. Budapest: Tárki Social Research Institute.

Pontusson, J. and D. Weisstanner. 2018. 'Macroeconomic Conditions, Inequality Shocks and the Politics of Redistribution, 1990–2013'. *Journal of European Public Policy* 25(1): pp. 31–58.

Profil. 2013. 'Die Volksempfänger: Heinz-Christian Strache und sein Mentor Jörg Haider', 7 October. Last accessed 18 July 2023. Retrieved from: https://www.profil.at/home/heinz-christian-strache-mentor-joerg-haider-10341391.

Przeworski, A. 2019. 'From Revolution to Reformism'. *Boston Review*, 28 January. Last accessed 18 July 2023. Retrieved from: https://www.bostonreview.net/articles/adam-przeworski-revolution-reformism-and-resignation/.

Rat, C. and D. Szikra. 2018. 'Family Policies and Social Inequalities in Central and Eastern Europe: A Comparative Analysis of Hungary, Poland and Romania between 2005 and 2015'. In *Handbook of Family Policy*, edited by Gudný, B. Eydal and Tine Rostgaard, pp. 223–235. Cheltenham: Edward Elgar Publishing Limited.

Rathgeb, P. 2018. *Strong Governments, Precarious Workers: Labor Market Policy in the Era of Liberalization*. Ithaca, NY: Cornell University Press.

Rathgeb, P. 2019. 'No Flexicurity without Trade Unions: The Danish Experience'. *Comparative European Politics* 17(1): pp. 1–21.

Rathgeb, P. 2021a. 'Makers against Takers: The Socio-Economic Ideology and Policy of the Austrian Freedom Party'. *West European Politics* 44(3): pp. 635–660.

Rathgeb, P. 2021b. 'Why trade unions should no longer rely on social democratic parties'. *LSE EUROPP Blog*, 4 November. Last accessed 18 July 2023. Retrieved from: https://blogs.lse.ac.uk/europpblog/2021/11/04/why-trade-unions-should-no-longer-rely-on-social-democratic-parties/.

Rathgeb, P. and M. Busemeyer. 2022. 'How to Study the Populist Radical Right and the Welfare State?' *West European Politics* 45(1): pp. 1–23.

Rathgeb, P. and J. Hopkin. 2023. 'How the Eurozone shapes populism: a comparative political economy approach. *Journal of European Public Policy*, online first.

Rathgeb, P. and M. B. Klitgaard. 2022. 'Protagonists or Consenters: Radical Right Parties and Attacks on Trade Unions'. *Journal of European Public Policy* 29(7): pp. 1049–1071.

Rathgeb, P. and A. Tassinari. 2022. 'How the Eurozone Disempowers Trade Unions: The Political Economy of Competitive Internal Devaluation'. *Socio-Economic Review* 20(1): pp. 323–335.

Rathgeb, P. and T. Wiss. 2020. 'Österreichische Familienpolitik verstärkt Geschlechterungleichheit'. Policy Brief. Vienna: Momentum Institut. Last accessed 18 July 2023. Retrieved from: https://www.momentum-institut.at/system/files/2020-03/pb_200304_kinderbetreuung.pdf.

Rathgeb, P. and F. Wolkenstein. 2016. 'A long goodbye to the grand coalition: Austria's presidential election'. *LSE European Politics and Policy (EUROPP) Blog*, 3 May. Last accessed 18 July 2023. Retrieved from: https://blogs.lse.ac.uk/europpblog/2016/05/03/a-long-goodbye-to-the-grand-coalition-austrias-presidential-election/.

Rathgeb, P. and M. Gruber-Risak. 2021. 'Deserving Austrians First: The Impact of the Radical Right on the Austrian Welfare State'. *Comparative Labor Law and Policy Journal* 42 (1): pp. 43–60.

Rathgeb, P. and F. Wolkenstein. 2022. 'When Do Social Democratic Parties Unite over Tough Immigration Policy?' *West European Politics* 45(5): pp. 979–1002.

Regeringen. 2011. 'Et Danmark der står sammen', 1 October. Government programme. Last accessed 18 July 2023. Retrieved from: https://www.regeringen.dk/aktuelt/tidligere-publikationer/et-danmark-der-staar-sammen-regeringsgrundlag/.

Regeringen. 2016. 'Værdig ældrepleje', 18 November. Press statement. Last accessed 18 July 2023. Retrieved from: https://www.regeringen.dk/nyheder/2016/finanslov 2017/finanslov-2017-vaerdig-aeldrepleje/.

Reisenbichler, A. and A. Wiedemann. 2022. 'Credit-Driven and Consumption-Led Growth Models in the United States and United Kingdom'. In *Diminishing Returns. The New Politics of Growth and Stagnation*, edited by Lucio Baccaro, Mark Blyth, and Jonas Pontusson, pp. 213–237. Oxford/New York: Oxford University Press.

Reiter, M. 2019. *Die Ehemaligen: Der Nationalsozialismus und die Anfänge der FPÖ*. Göttingen: Wallstein Verlag.

Rennwald, L. and G. Evans. 2014. 'When Supply Creates Demand: Social Democratic Party Strategies and the Evolution of Class Voting'. *West European Politics* 37(5): pp. 1108–1135.

Rennwald, L. and J. Pontusson. 2021. 'Paper Stones Revisited: Class Voting, Unionization and the Electoral Decline of the Mainstream Left'. *Perspectives on Politics* 19(1): pp. 36–54.

Reuters. 2011. 'Hungary's unorthodox mix makes new IMF deal tough', 18 November. Last accessed 18 July 2023. Retrieved from: https://www.reuters.com/article/us-hungary-imf-idUKTRE7AH0VG20111118.

Rieger, E. and S. Leibfried. 2003. *Limits to Globalization. Welfare States and the World Economy*. Cambridge: Polity Press.

Rodrik, D. 2011. *The Globalization Paradox: Democracy and the Future of the World Economy*. New York: W. W. Norton & Co.

Rodrik, D. 2018. 'Populism and the Political Economy of Globalization'. *Journal of International Business Policy* 1(1): pp. 12–33.

Rovny, J. 2013. 'Where Do Radical Right Parties Stand? Position Blurring in Multidimensional Competition'. *European Political Science Review* 5(1): pp. 1–26.

Rovny, J. and J. Polk. 2020. 'Still Blurry? Economic Salience, Position and Voting for Radical Right Parties in Western Europe'. *European Journal of Political Research* 59(2): pp. 248–268.

Rueda, D. 2007. *Social Democracy Inside Out. Partisanship and Labor Market Policy in Advanced Industrialized Democracies*. Oxford: Oxford University Press.

Ruggie, J. G. 1982. 'International Regimes, Transactions, and Change: Embedded Liberalism in the Postwar Economic Order'. *International Organization* 36(2): pp. 379–415.

Rydgren, J. 2004. 'Explaining the Emergence of Radical Right-wing Populism: The Case of Denmark'. *West European Politics* 27(3): pp. 474–502.

Rydgren, J. 2008. 'Immigration Sceptics, Xenophobes, or Racists? Radical Right-Wing Voting in Six West European Countries'. *European Journal of Political Research* 47(6): pp. 737–765.

Rydgren, J. and S. Van der Meiden. 2019. 'The Radical Right and the End of Swedish Exceptionalism'. *European Political Science* 18(3): pp. 439–455.

Salzburger Nachrichten. 2021. '70 Prozent der Familienbonus-Bezieher sind Männer', 20 October. Last accessed 18 July 2023. Retrieved from: https://www.sn.at/politik/innenpolitik/70-prozent-der-familienbonus-bezieher-sind-maenner-111144247.

Scheiring, G. 2020. *The Retreat of Liberal Democracy: Authoritarian Capitalism and the Accumulative State in Hungary*. Cham: Palgrave Macmillan.

Scheiring, G. 2022. 'The National-Populist Mutation of Neoliberalism in Dependent Economies: The Case of Viktor Orbán's Hungary'. *Socio-Economic Review* 20(4): pp. 1597–1623

Schmitt, C. 1932. 'Gesunde Wirtschaft im starken Staat'. *Mitteilungen des Vereins zur Wahrung der gemeinsamen wirtschaftichen Interessen in Rheinland und Westfalen* (Langnamverein) 21: pp. 13–32.

Schreurs, S. 2020. 'Those Were the Days: Welfare Nostalgia and the Populist Radical Right in the Netherlands, Austria and Sweden'. *Journal of International and Comparative Social Policy* 37(2): pp. 128–141.

Schwander, H. and S. Häusermann. 2013. 'Who Is in and Who Is Out? A Risk-Based Conceptualization of Insiders and Outsiders'. *Journal of European Social Policy* 23(3): pp. 248–269.

Sebök, M. and J. Simons. 2022. 'How Orban Won? Neoliberal Disenchantment and the Grand Strategy of Financial Nationalism to Reconstruct Capitalism and Regain Autonomy'. *Socio-Economic Review* 20(4): pp. 1625–1651.

Seelkopf, L. and P. Starke. 2019. 'Social Policy by Other Means: Theorizing Unconventional Forms of Welfare Production'. *Journal of Comparative Policy Analysis: Research and Practice* 21(3): pp. 219–234.

Skocpol, T. 2020. 'The Elite and Popular Roots of Contemporary Republican Extremism'. In *Upending American Politics: Polarizing Parties, Ideological Elites, and Citizen Activists from the Tea Party to the Anti-Trump Resistance*, edited by Theda Skocpol and Caroline Tervo, pp. 3–28. Oxford/New York: Oxford University Press.

Skocpol, T. and V. Williamson. 2011. *The Tea Party and the Remaking of Republican Conservatism*. New York: Oxford University Press.

Slobodian, Q. 2018. *Globalists: The End of Empire and the Birth of Neoliberalism*. Cambridge, MA: Harvard University Press.

Slobodian, Q. 2021. 'Hayek's Bastards: The Populist Right's Neoliberal Roots'. *Tribune Magazine*, 15 June.

Smith, J, S. 2022. 'The Rhetoric and Reality of Infrastructure during the Trump Presidency'. In *The Presidency of Donald J. Trump*, edited by Julian E. Zelizer, pp. 162–180. Princeton/Oxford: Princeton University Press.

Spierings, N. 2021. 'Homonationalism and Voting for the Populist Radical Right: Addressing Unanswered Questions by Zooming in on the Dutch Case'. *International Journal of Public Opinion Research* 33(1): pp. 171–182.

Spies, D. 2018. *Immigration and Welfare State Retrenchment: Why the US Experience is not Reflected in Western Europe*. Oxford: Oxford University Press.

Spies, D. and S. Franzmann. 2011. 'A Two-Dimensional Approach to the Political Opportunity Structure of Extreme Right Parties in Western Europe'. *West European Politics* 34(5): pp. 1044–1069.

Steen, J. R. 2015. 'Norway: Reaction to new Working Environment Act'. *Eurofound*, 22 December. Last accessed 18 July 2023. Retrieved from: https://www.eurofound.europa.eu/publications/article/2015/norway-reaction-to-new-working-environment-act.

Steffek, J. and Y. Lasshoff. 2022. 'Steve Bannon on "Productive Capitalism": Investigating the Economic Ideology of the American Populist Right'. Journal of Political Ideologies, online first.

Steiner, N. D., M. Mader, and H. Schoen. 2023. 'Subjective Losers of Globalization'. European Journal of Political Research, online first.

Stenographisches Protokoll des österreichischen Nationalrates, XXI. Gesetzgebungsperiode, 15. Sitzung, pp. 29–30.

Strache, H. C. 2018. Posting in *Facebook* (personal account), 18 November. Last accessed 19 September 2019; no longer publicly available.

Streeck, W. 2009. *Re-Forming Capitalism. Institutional Change in the German Political Economy*. Oxford: Oxford University Press.

Streeck, W. 2011. 'The Crises of Democratic Capitalism'. *New Left Review* 71(September/October): pp. 5–29.

Szelewa, D. and M. Polakowski. 2022. 'Explaining the Weakness of Social Investment Policies in the Visegrád Countries. The Cases of Childcare and Active Labor Market Policies'. In *The World Politics of Social Investment* (Volume II), edited by Julian L. Garritzmann, Silja Häusermann, and Bruno Palier, pp. 185–208. Oxford/New York: Oxford University Press

Szikra, D. 2014. 'Democracy and Welfare in Hard Times: The Social Policy of the Orbán Government in Hungary between 2010 and 2014'. *Journal of European Social Policy* 24(5): pp. 486–500.

Szikra, D. 2018. *Welfare for the Wealthy. The Social Policy of the Orbán-Regime, 2010–2017*. Budapest: Friedrich Ebert Stiftung.

Szikra, D. 2019. 'Ideology or Pragmatism? Interpreting Social Policy Change under the "System of National Cooperation"'. In *Brave New Hungary: Mapping the 'System of National Cooperation'*, edited by János Mátyás Kovács and Balázs Trencsényi, pp. 225–242. Lanham, Maryland: Lexington Books.

Tavits, M. and N. Letki. 2009. 'When Left Is Right: Party Ideology and Policy in Post-Communist Europe'. *American Political Science Review* 103(4): pp. 555–569.

Tax Policy Center. 2017. 'Distributional Analysis of the Conference Agreement for the Tax Cuts and Jobs Act', 18 December. Last accessed 18 July 2023. Retrieved from: https://www.taxpolicycenter.org/publications/distributional-analysis-conference-agreement-tax-cuts-and-jobs-act/full.

The Local Sweden. 2016. 'Sweden Democrats try to woo pensioners', 28 August. Last accessed 18 July 2023. Retrieved from: https://www.thelocal.se/20160828/sweden-democrats-try-to-woo-elderly-with-pensions/.

Thelen, K. 2014. *Varieties of Liberalization. The New Politics of Social Solidarity*. New York: Cambridge University Press.

Thelen, K. and A. Wiedemann. 2021. 'The Anxiety of Precarity. The United States in Comparative Perspective'. In *Who Gets What? The New Politics of Insecurity*, edited by Frances McCall Rosenbluth and Margaret Weir, pp. 281–306. Cambridge: Cambridge University Press.

Thulesen Dahl, K. 2012. 'Kristian Thulesen Dahls tale ved Dansk Folkepartis årsmøde 2012'. Speech. Last accessed 18 July 2023. Retrieved from: https://dansketaler.dk/tale/mit-danmark/.

Thulesen Dahl, K. 2014. 'Kristian Thulesen Dahls tale ved Dansk Folkepartis årsmøde 2014'. Speech. Last accessed 18 July 2023. Retrieved from: https://dansketaler.dk/tale/en-dansk-fremtid-med-tryghed-og-tillid/.

Thulesen, Dahl, K. 2019. 'Kristian Thulesen Dahls tale til Folkemødet 2019'. Speech. Last accessed 18 July 2023. Retrieved from: https://dansketaler.dk/tale/kristian-thulesen-dahls-tale-ved-folkemoedet-2019/.

Thulesen Dahl, K. 2020. 'Kristian Thulesen Dahls tale ved Dansk Folkepartis årsmøde 2020'. Speech. Last accessed 18 July 2023. Retrieved from: https://dansketaler.dk/tale/kristian-thulesen-dahls-tale-ved-dansk-folkepartis-aarsmoede-2020/.

Thurston, C. 2018. *At the Boundaries of Homeownership. Credit, Discrimination, and the American State*. Cambridge: Cambridge University Press.

Toplišek, A. 2020. 'The Political Economy of Populist Rule in Post-Crisis Europe: Hungary and Poland'. *New Political Economy* 25(3): pp 388–403.

Treib, O. 2012. 'Party Patronage in Austria: From Reward to Control'. In *Party Patronage and Party Government in European Democracies*, edited by Peter Kopecký, Peter Mair, and Maria Spirova, pp. 31–51. Oxford: Oxford University Press.

Trump, D. 2015. 'Donald Trump's Presidential Announcement Speech'. Last accessed 4 October 2022. Retrieved from: https://time.com/3923128/donald-trump-announcement-speech/.

Trump, D. 2017a. 'I Can Be More Presidential than Any President. Read Trump's Ohio Rally Speech'. Last accessed 4 October 2022. Retrieved from: https://time.com/4874161/donald-trump-transcript-youngstown-ohio/.

Trump, D. 2017b. 'January 20, 2017: Inaugural Address'. The White House. Last accessed 4 October 2022. Retrieved from: https://millercenter.org/the-presidency/presidential-speeches/january-20-2017-inaugural-address.

Trump, D. 2018. 'January 30, 2018: State of the Union Address'. The White House. Last accessed 4 October 2022. Retrieved from: https://millercenter.org/the-presidency/presidential-speeches/january-30-2018-state-union-address.

Trump, D. 2019. 'February 5, 2019: State of the Union Address'. The White House. Last accessed the 4 October 2022. Last accessed 18 July 2023. Retrieved from: https://millercenter.org/the-presidency/presidential-speeches/february-5-2019-state-union-address.

Valarino, I., A. Duvander, L. Haas, and G. Neyer. 2018. 'Exploring Leave Policy Preferences: A Comparison of Austria, Sweden, Switzerland, and the United States'. *Social Politics* 25(1): pp. 118–147.

Van Beyme, K. 1988. 'Right-Wing Extremism in Post-war Europe'. *West European Politics* 11(2): pp. 1–18.

VanGrasstek, C. 2019. *Trade and American Leadership. The Paradoxes of Power and Wealth from Alexander Hamilton to Donald Trump*. Cambridge: Cambridge University Press.

Vanhuysse, P. 2006. *Divide and Pacify: Strategic Social Policies and Political Protests in Post-Communist Democracies*. Budapest: Central European University Press.

Van Oorschot, W. 2006. 'Making the Difference in Social Europe: Deservingness Perceptions among Citizens of European Welfare States'. *Journal of European Social Policy* 16(1): pp. 23–42.

Verovsek, P. 2021. 'Caught between 1945 and 1989: Collective Memory and the Rise of Illiberal Democracy in Postcommunist Europe'. *Journal of European Public Policy* 28(6): pp. 840–857.

Vittori, D. 'Italy's Election wasn't just a Populist Takeover – It was also about the Demise of the Left'. *LSE European Politics and Policy (EUROPP) Blog*, 6th March of 2018.

Vlandas, T. and D. Halikiopoulou. 2019. 'Does Unemployment Matter? Economic Insecurity, Labour Market Policies and the Far-Right Vote in Europe'. *European Political Science* 18; pp. 421–438.

Vlandas, T. and D. Halikiopoulou. 2022. 'Welfare State Policies and Far Right Party Support: Moderating "Insecurity Effects" among Different Social Groups'. *West European Politics* 45(1): pp. 24–49.

Volkens, A., T. Burst, W. Krause, P. Lehmann, T. Matthieß, S. Regel, B. Weßels, and L. Zehnter. 2021. 'The Manifesto Data Collection'. *Manifesto Project* (MRG/CMP/MARPOR). Version 2021a. Berlin: Wissenschaftszentrum Berlin für Sozialforschung (WZB).

Waddan, A. 2014. 'The U.S. Welfare State since 1970'. In *Oxford Handbook of U.S. Social Policy*, edited by Daniel Béland, Christopher Howard, and Kimberly J. Morgan, pp. 95–111. New York: Oxford University Press.

Waddan, A. 2019. 'Trumpism, Conservatism and Social Policy'. In *The Trump Presidency. From Campaign Trail to World Stage*, edited by Mara Oliva and Mark Shanahan, pp. 179–201. London: Palgrave Macmillan.

Waldner, D. and E. Lust. 2018. 'Unwelcome Change: Coming to Terms with Democratic Backsliding'. *Annual Review of Political Science* 21(May): pp. 93–113.

Waslin, M. 2020. 'The Use of Executive Orders and Proclamations to Create Immigration Policy: Trump in Historical Perspective'. *Journal on Migration and Human Security* 8(1): pp. 54–67.

Wiggen, M. 2012. 'Rethinking Anti-immigration Rhetoric after the Oslo and Utøya Terror Attacks'. *New Political Science* 34(4): pp. 585–604.

Wiggen, M. 2021. 'As Norway's far Right declines in popularity, a new populist force rises'. Open Democracy. Last accessed 18 July 2023. Retrieved from: https://www. opendemocracy.net/en/countering-radical-right/as-norways-far-right-declines-in-popularity-a-new-populist-force-rises/.

Williams, J. C. 2017. *White Working Class: Overcoming Class Cluelessness in America*. Cambridge, MA: Harvard Business Review Press.

Wondreys, J. and C. Mudde. 2022. 'Victims of the Pandemic? European Far-Right Parties and COVID-19'. *Nationalities Papers* 50(1): pp 86–103.

World Bank. 2023a. 'Current account balance (% of GDP)'. World Development Indicators. The World Bank Group. Last accessed 19 July 2023. Retrieved from: https://data. worldbank.org/indicator/BN.CAB.XOKA.GD.ZS.

World Bank. 2023b. 'Trade (% of GDP)'. World Development Indicators. The World Bank Group. Last accessed 19 July 2023. Retrieved from: https://data.worldbank.org/indicator/ NE.TRD.GNFS.ZS.

World Bank. 2023c. 'Exports of goods and services (% of GDP)—United States'. World Development Indicators. The World Bank Group. Last accessed 19 July 2023. Retrieved from: https://data.worldbank.org/indicator/NE.EXP.GNFS.ZS?locations=US.

World Bank. 2023d. 'Imports of goods and services (% of GDP)—United States'. World Development Indicators. The World Bank Group. Last accessed 19 July 2023. Retrieved from: https://data.worldbank.org/indicator/NE.IMP.GNFS.ZS?locations=US.

Index